New Jersey In History
Fighting To Be Heard

Thomas P. Farner

Much of the material in this book previously appeared, in somewhat different form, in *The SandPaper* as a series of columns published between 1976 and 1995.

A CORMORANT BOOK

DOWN THE SHORE
PUBLISHING

S*The*ANDPAPER

For information, address:
Down The Shore Publishing, Box 3100, Harvey Cedars, NJ 08008
The words "Down The Shore" and "The SandPaper" and their respective logos are registered U.S. Trademarks.
Manufactured in the United States of America. First printing, 1996.
This book is printed on recycled paper — *10% post-consumer content.*
10 9 8 7 6 5 4 3 2 1

Library of Congress Cataloging-in-Publication Data

Farner, Thomas P. (Thomas Patrick), 1947-
    New Jersey in history : fighting to be heard / by Thomas P. Farner.
        p.   cm.
    Includes bibliographical references (p.   ) and index.
    ISBN 0-945582-38-2
    1. New Jersey--History.   I. Title
F134.5.F37   1996
974.9--dc20   96-19221
                                                          CIP

To my wife, Carol, without whose
support and help this book
never would have been written.

TABLE OF CONTENTS

For more than twenty years I have been writing a history column known as *200 Plus*, a column which focuses on the lesser known, sometimes overlooked or intentionally forgotten events of American history. Over the years, an ever-lengthening thread began to emerge in these columns as I recognized how often the role of the little state of New Jersey has been very much underestimated. Trapped between New York and Philadelphia, the state's place in history has always been underrated or, as James Madison once lamented, "Poor New Jersey, she is like a keg tapped at both ends."

The purpose of this book is to assemble a cross-section of my writings which fills in many of the holes in the fabric of American history. All of these selections deal with events or people that have a relationship not only to the state but also to the nation.

The basis for much of *New Jersey In History* is primary sources, that is, the letters, diaries and newspapers of the day. The reason for this is because I discovered that as events were interpreted and reinterpreted by historians, the role played by New Jersey diminished: In my opinion, in order to make their manuscripts more marketable, historians too often emphasized events and people from the publishing centers of New York, Philadelphia and Boston.

New Jersey In History: Fighting To Be Heard can be read in different ways. It is written chronologically for the true history buff, but the casual reader will find that individual stories offer in-depth looks at specific events and people.

There are still gaps in the historical tapestry, but I believe that readers will have new and interesting answers when someone asks, "Did anything ever happen in New Jersey?"

Thomas P. Farner
Manahawkin, N.J.

ACKNOWLEDGMENTS

To write acknowledgments for a project that has been more than ten years in its development is frustrating indeed, because for every one person I remember and mention I am certain there is one, or more, who is equally deserving and is missed, and for this I apologize.

Let me begin with the person who is the key to the project, my wife, Carol. Whether correcting my interpretations of the way words are spelled or spending a vacation rooting out historical facts in a library, Carol has always given me unflagging support and encouragement as well as critical guidance. Without her, this book would not exist.

Next, from *The SandPaper,* is publisher Curt Travers who had the wisdom and foresight to support the idea that a local newspaper could run weekly articles on history which moved beyond the actual geography of his paper's distribution. More recently and of utmost importance is Marion Figley who edited this book and helped me to transform a newspaper column into what I believe are enjoyable stories of history in New Jersey.

Thanks also to librarians, from the Library of Congress to those in local high schools, such as Kay Kline and Ruth Rosenberg, resourceful people who can locate old books and cross-reference from memory, in most cases faster than a computer. They can always be counted on to suggest a different and, in most cases, successful way to find information on a subject.

To my mother, a special lady who has every one of my columns in her scrapbook and thus made some of the work on putting this book together that much easier;

To my colleagues, particularly Kevin Dugan in the history department of Pemberton Township High School, who have challenged many of my theories and, as a result, have been instrumental in my reliance on primary sources as the basis for much of this book;

To my readers and my students who over the years have asked countless questions which I could not answer, leading me to more research and new articles;

And finally, to those who always look at facts with a different perspective: Your revolutionary hero may be my terrorist!

It is because of all these people and many others that digging into New Jersey's history has been made easier for me and resulted in a trip not into the past but into the fascinating unknown.

Thank you.

New Jersey In History
Fighting To Be Heard

CHAPTER 1

New Jersey:

In the Beginning

I f you enter any history class in New Jersey and ask some questions, you might be surprised by the answers. If you ask what was the first colony in America, you will probably be told Jamestown, Virginia. Who started Plymouth? The Pilgrims. You can ask about John Smith, Pocohontas, Miles Standish and William Penn and get reasonable answers. But if you want to bring the room to total silence, ask who founded New Jersey or the location of the first settlement between the Hudson and Delaware rivers. Most high school history books don't even mention the area until 1664, when it was taken over by the English: New Jersey's official founding date is when it was invaded, not when it was founded.

The story of the state's early years begins in the 1600s, although explorers like Giovanni da Verrazano, working for the French, had visited the coastline many years before. In 1609, Henry Hudson, working for the Dutch on the ship *Half Moon*, was the first to map and explore the Jersey coast line while looking for a water route to China. Hudson followed the coast from Delaware to the river which bears his name. As a result, shore towns like Egg Harbor and Barnegat have Dutch-sounding names.

When Hudson returned, the investors took over, looking for ways to make money. The Dutch West India Company was founded, and eventually a trading post was opened at the mouth of the Hudson River and named New Amsterdam. By 1624 another Dutch explorer, Captain Cornelius Mey — he named the Cape — brought thirty families to the New World to set up a trading post on the Hudson River. Two of the families were taken up the Delaware and dropped off on an island, today's Burlington Island. But four years later when a Dutch ship returned, it found the island abandoned.

By this time the Dutch had purchased Manhattan Island from the Manhattan Indians for twenty-four dollars. A land grant on the west side of the Hudson had been given to a Dutch official by the name of Michael Pauw. Pauw named the land "Pavonia," Land of the Peacock. To run it, he hired Cornelius VanVorst, who became the area's first permanent resident. Over the next few years other settlements dotted the west side of the Hudson, and by 1642 there were enough residents to construct America's first brewery in present-day Hoboken. But this brewery would lead to problems with the Indians.

The Indians far outnumbered the Dutch and had helped with the fur trade, but the exchange of alcohol for furs caused friction. Eventually, Dutch officials warned against "admitting them to the table, laying napkins before them, presenting wine to them and more of that kind of thing." But this was not enough. The Dutch governor chose February 25, 1643, to launch a surprise attack. Captain David DeVries was to take eighty soldiers to Pavonia, where Indians had camped on a peaceful trading mission. There, in the governor's words, DeVries was to "wipe their chops."

His orders were: "Drive away and destroy the savages.... Spare as much as it is possible their wives and children. Governor Kieft concluded by asking God to bless the expedition."

The captain disagreed on the plan's merits, saying, "You will go to break the Indians, but it is our nation you are going to murder."

That night DeVries wrote of what happened on the Jersey side of the Hudson.

"About midnight I heard a great shrieking and went to the ramparts of the fort and looked over to Pavonia, saw nothing but firing and heard the shrieks of the savages murdered in their sleep."

The Dutch ran wild in the night, striking viciously at the Indians, disregarding orders, and killing women and children alike. Papooses (babies) were "slain while fastened to their little boards ... youngsters being thrown into the river to drown. When parents waded in to save them, Dutch guns felled young and old."

For the next two years the west side of the Hudson was aflame with an Indian war. But while the Dutch were preoccupied with events there, another nation was moving to the south.

Peter Minuet, who had purchased Manhattan for the Dutch, sailed up the Delaware in 1638 at the head of six ships to start a new colony. Only this time Minuet was working for Sweden. A fort was constructed near present-day Wilmington, Delaware, and eventually another was built on the river's east bank in Salem County. Minuet disappeared on the return voyage, and the colony of New Sweden remained small.

In 1647 the Dutch colony received a new governor, Peter Stuyvesant. The peg-legged Stuyvesant ruled the colony with an iron fist, ordering families on the west side of the Hudson to form villages to protect themselves from Indian attacks. In 1651 he decided that the Swedes along the Delaware were a threat.

That spring, Stuyvesant marched at the head of 120 men from New Amsterdam across New Jersey to the Delaware. (This course would be followed by a more famous general in the American Revolution.) At the same time, eleven ships were to sail around Cape Mey to join them. The Dutch force was unable to dislodge the Swedes and built a fort downriver to cut them off from the sea. Eventually, in 1655, the last of the Swedes surrendered. Stuyvesant gave the residents a choice: leave for Sweden or stay and colonize under the Dutch. The majority stayed.

With the Swedes gone, the Dutch prospered, opening their colony to all religions and to immigrants from other countries. It was this prosperity which spelled their doom. The English, who held colonies to the north and south, became jealous. On March 12, 1664, the king of England, Charles II, rewarded his brother James, Duke of York, for his support in the recent civil war. The king granted all land between the Connecticut and Delaware rivers to James, urging his brother to govern "as he shall think to be fittest for the good of the adventurers and inhabitants there."

No matter that the Dutch already had a colony here.

In May, Colonel Richard Nicolls left England with four ships and 450 troops to attack the Dutch and take possession of New Netherland. By August, the fleet had arrived off Sandy Hook where Nicolls demanded that Stuyvesant surrender the fort and all of New Netherland.

Stuyvesant was ready for a fight, but the people were not. Years of living far away from Holland had made them independent. They felt that going from Dutch to English rule meant little more to their daily lives than changing the flag over the fort.

Ninety-three leading citizens signed a petition urging Stuyvesant to surrender. On August 27, Stuyvesant and his troops marched out without firing a shot. Nicolls, acting as deputy governor of all land he captured, issued a proclamation inviting the Dutch to stay if they would swear allegiance to England. Most did and renamed the colony New York, in honor of the duke.

Nicolls' next step was to order Sir Robert Carr to sweep the Dutch from the Delaware. With the main settlement gone, the Delaware forts surrendered as easily as New York. Now all of the land from the Connecticut River to the Delaware was under the king of England.

CHAPTER 2

A Tale of Two Jerseys

Did you know that Tuckerton and Manahawkin are in different Jerseys? That Perth
Amboy and Burlington are still under the jurisdiction of different capitals? That
when George Washington wrote, "My army has crossed the Delaware and is firmly in
the Jerseys," he knew what he was talking about?

Yes, there were and are two New Jerseys, not north and south, but east and west. Manahawkin is in East New Jersey and Tuckerton, just nine miles away, is in West New Jersey.

Any attempt to understand this must go back to June 24, 1664, when the Duke of York gave
two of his friends, Sir John Berkeley and Sir George Carteret, sole deed to the land between the
Hudson and Delaware rivers. York's only stipulation was that the land be named New Jersey for
the English Channel island where Carteret had been born. Thus, June 24 is New Jersey's own
Independence Day.

Ironically, Berkeley and Carteret never set foot on their new land. Carteret was expelled
from the House of Commons for embezzling funds, and Berkeley went to Ireland as governor.
They saw New Jersey as a moneymaking opportunity. They granted a charter allowing freedom
of religion and began to sell land to any person or religious group with hard cash. Business
remained slow, and by 1674 Berkeley was ready to sell out. This meant that there would have
to be a settlement, and Berkeley and Carteret decided to divide the land equally.

A line was drawn northwest from the coast to the Delaware River. Berkeley got one side and
Carteret the other. By 1683, the west side of the line, Berkeley's half, was bought by a group of

investors with a charter from the king to run the colony of West New Jersey. Meanwhile, Carteret died, leaving his land to his two heirs. In 1680, they sold it to a group of twelve investors who also received a charter to run the colony of East New Jersey.

Under the charter granted to both halves of Jersey, the so-named proprietors were given ownership to all of the land under their control, and only they could sell it. Thus, the proprietors made their profits by land sales.

This also meant the land in New Jersey became quite valuable to the two sets of proprietors. Where the dividing line was placed meant money, and the controversy began. The first line was drawn in 1687 by George Keith, a theologian and surveyor. The starting point for this line and all others is located south of Manahawkin in the little shore town of West Creek on Route 9. From there it travels northwest.

Keith never completed the line north of the Raritan River, and so the controversy of ownership continued. After years of bickering, the line was completed to a point just south of Dingman's Ferry on the Delaware River.

In the early years, each half of Jersey was operated by its proprietors as totally independent of the other. Two capitals were set up: Perth Amboy for the east and Burlington for the west. The rivalry between the two groups of proprietors and the dispute over the boundary were so intense that in 1702 Queen Anne took control of both East and West Jersey, establishing one government. However, several vestiges of the split still remained.

First of all, so as not to offend either half of the colony, New Jersey was left with the two capitals. For the next seventy-four years, the royal governor and his cabinet would have residences in both locations. Secondly, so as not to offend the investors, the new Royal Government Charter recognized the position that all unclaimed land in the colony still belonged to the proprietors of either East or West New Jersey.

With the coming of the Revolution and the independence of the state of New Jersey, some changes were made. The problem of dual capitals was finally solved by selecting Trenton as the state capital, also being considered for the nation's capital.

But in the new state constitution and in every one that followed, the state of New Jersey has recognized the rights of the first proprietors. Since the original shares had been sold or passed down to heirs and divided into fractions, a great number of influential families became members of the Board of Proprietors of either East or West Jersey. Today, the rule that any unclaimed land in New Jersey is the property of the appropriate proprietors remains in effect. The proprietors still meet, making the boards the oldest corporations in America.

And still land turns up. Every time property is sold in New Jersey, a deed search takes place and the proprietors have a slim chance of being named the true owners.

CHAPTER 3

Puritans Find Refuge In New Ark

Most people know the Puritans originally settled in Massachusetts, but few realize that this group also founded Newark. The story begins in Massachusetts with a Puritan minister named Abraham Pierson. Born and educated in England, he arrived in Lynn in 1639. For the next twenty years Pierson and his family roamed New England, looking for a true religious haven for his strict interpretation of the Scriptures. Feeling that other Massachusetts Puritans had become too worldly, he began to look outside New England.

Meanwhile, the lord proprietor of East Jersey, George Carteret, advertised throughout New England to entice settlers to move south with a system of self-government, promising "not to impose, nor suffer to be imposed, any tax, custom, subsidy or any other duty whatsoever upon any colour or pretense upon the said province and inhabitants thereof, other than what shall be imposed by the authority and consent of the general assembly."

By the spring of 1666 Pierson had gathered thirty families, all good members of his Congregational Church, for the trip south. On May 18 they sailed up the river that the Indians called Passaic. Once ashore they named "our town on the Passaic" New Ark for Pierson's boyhood home, also founded as a religious refuge.

The Puritans set to work building a town along the lines of Massachusetts settlements. A main road running north and south and 132 feet wide was cut and named Broad Street. Public land was set aside for militia training grounds, the grazing common and a marketplace. A six-acre lot in the center of town was selected for the site of a meeting house and cemetery. The meeting house would serve as church, town hall and fort, and it would be constructed by all members of the colony.

Once public lands were taken care of, a lottery was held to draw individual lots. Then, just six days after landing, the settlers held a meeting to set up a government for the colony. Organizers of the meeting declared it would be a godly place run in a godly way, saying, "God's blessing with one hand they may endeavor the carrying on of spiritual concernments, as also civil and town affairs, according to God and a Godly government; there to be settled by them and their associates."

The men who ran the church would also run the government. By June 1667 there were sixty-four families, totaling about 350 people. In the fall, a meeting was held to secure New Ark as a Puritan base.

To be elected to office, "none shall be admitted freemen or free burgesses within our town upon Passaic River in the province of New Jersey, but such planters as are members of some or other of the Congregational Churches, nor shall any but such be chosen to magistracy or to carry on any part of civil judicature ... nor shall any but such church members have any vote in any such election."

New Ark was to be run by the Puritans or, as they put it, "we shall, with care and diligence, provide for the maintenance of the purity of religion professed in the Congregational Church-es." These New Ark Puritans had set up the perfect godly town as they saw it. Next they would try to keep it that way: Only the pure could move in.

"It is fully agreed upon that every man that comes to be admitted an inhabitant with us shall first produce a certificate from the chief of the place from whence he comes ... about the good carriage and behavior of them otherwise," read the settlement's charter.

Prospective residents had to pledge to support the church. A new citizen "shall first sub-scribe his name and declare ... that they will, from time to time, pay or cause to be paid yearly in their full proportions equally to the maintenance and allowance agreed upon for the uphold-ing of the settled ministry and preaching of the word in our town."

And finally, what if a newcomer disagreed with the good people of the colony of New Ark?

"It is agreed upon that in case any shall come into us or arise up amongst us that shall willingly or willfully disturb us in our peace and settlements, and especially that would subvert us from the true religion and worship of God, and cannot or will not keep their opinions to themselves ... as a fundamental agreement and order, that all and persons so ill-disposed and affected shall, after notice given them from the town, quietly depart the place."

New Ark in the 1660s would try to cut itself off from the rest of the world. However, history shows us this: No colony or island can remove itself from the changing ideas of the world.

You can't be left alone forever.

CHAPTER 4

"Dressing" For Success:

The Governor Who Would Be Queen

Whenever a gubernatorial election rolls around, news articles compare candidates to the state's best governors. While others worry about the best, I'll take a shot at naming the worst.

On a Sunday morning in 1706, a small crowd gathered outside Hopewell Church, today the location of the Trenton Psychiatric Hospital. They were hoping to get a look at New Jersey's first royal governor, Edward, Lord Cornbury. Some in the crowd talked about the governor, and those stories were extremely unsettling.

The man Queen Anne had named as the colony's governor was already known to the citizens: Edward Hyde, Viscount Cornbury, a first cousin of the queen. Born in 1661, he had already served sixteen years in Parliament and had been the governor of New York for several years. It was his actions as New York's governor which caused the Hopewell crowd to gossip.

Cornbury had arrived on Manhattan Island May 3, 1702, with the official title of captain general, governor-in-chief, vice admiral. Cornbury also gave himself the title of "His High Mightiness."

In his first address to the New York Assembly, Cornbury requested a special allowance for himself of £2,000. This was the first indication that the new governor had financial problems. Later, at a banquet arranged to present the money to him, another of Cornbury's quirks came to light.

When he rose to speak he delivered a long, flowery tribute to his wife's ears which he described as "the most beautiful in Christendom." Then, to the astonishment of the guests, the gentlemen were invited to line up to have a close look and feel the lady's ears for themselves.

Not long afterward, the governor hosted a royal ball, but as New York's elite tried to enter the mansion, they were told they had to pay admission. Angered, some went home, only to receive a bill from Cornbury for the party. As the days passed the governor's behavior raised more eyebrows. He rode his horse into the King's Arms Tavern on Broadway just above Wall Street, and up to the bar, where he ordered a drink for himself and water for his horse.

The governor's financial escapades extended to Lady Cornbury, whose visits were feared by New York's upper class. One member of society wrote of Lady Cornbury, "As hers was the only carriage

Collection of the New York Historical Society

New Jersey's Royal Governor, Edward Lord Cornbury, whose private life caused almost as much scandal as his public actions.

in the city, the rolling of the wheels was easily distinguished, and then the cry in the house was, 'There comes my lady; hide this, hide that, take that away.' Whatever she admired in her visit she was sure to send for the next day."

As for dealing with the citizens of the United New Jersey, Queen Anne's instructions to Cornbury were specific: "You are to take care that no man's life, member, freehold, or goods be taken away or harmed in our said province otherwise than by established and known laws.... You are to permit a liberty of conscience to all persons, except papists, so they may be contented with a quiet and peaceable enjoyment of the same, not giving offense or scandal to the government."

And finally, the queen ordered Cornbury, "You are to take care drunkenness and debauchery, swearing and blasphemy, be discountenanced and punished. And for the further discountenance of vice and encouragement of virtue and good living, that by such example the infidels may be invited and desire to partake of the Christian religion, you are not to admit any person to public trusts and employments ... whose ill-fame and conversation may occasion scandal."

It would be these instructions which would lead to the new governor's downfall, because the crowds outside Hopewell Church were scandalized as they talked about another of the new governor's habits.

Anger over taxes had raised questions about Cornbury. It was said that while making the rounds of New York streets, the night watch had reported "spying what he took to be a drunken prostitute tottering about the ramparts of the fort, he discovered on approaching nearer, that 'she' was none other than His High Mightiness — who rushed at him, giggling, and pulled his ears. Before long, other male citizens underwent the same painful experience at the strong hands of the governor, who delighted in lurking behind trees to pounce, shrieking with laughter on his victims."

Subsequently, it became more and more common to see the High Mighty Governor of New York and New Jersey in drag. The citizens did not understand transvestite behavior and came up with several bizarre explanations, such as that the attire emphasized his facial resemblance to his cousin Queen Anne, or that he was taking quite literally his instruction to represent the queen in the Colony. Whatever, it soon became a popular guessing game to predict the governor's attire.

But Cornbury's downfall came not because of his dishonesty or his sexual habits, but because of his attempt to trample on the rights of New Jersey citizens. Cornbury detested members of the Society of Friends, known as Quakers, because of their refusal to bear arms in the war with France. When voters from Burlington County elected three Quakers to the Provincial Assembly, he refused to allow them to take their seats, claiming they would not swear allegiance to the Crown.

Fearing a general attack on all Quakers, one of them, Lewis Morris, wrote to the queen's secretary of state to inform officials in London of Lord Cornbury's habit of "dressing publicly in women's cloaths every day, and putting a stop to all publique business while he is pleasing himself with that peculiar and detestable magot." (A magot is, according to the *Oxford English Dictionary,* a whimsical or perverse fancy; a crotchet.)

The New Jersey Provincial Assembly publicly censured Cornbury, and its speaker read the document aloud to the governor in open session. Following Jersey's lead, the New York Legislature passed a similar censure in September 1708.

As the scandal spread to London, Queen Anne announced that Cornbury's "near relation to her ... should not Protect him in Oppressing her Subjects" and removed him from the governorships. When his replacement arrived, Cornbury attempted to sneak quietly back to London but was arrested in New York City and thrown into debtors prison, where he stayed for more than a year until his father died, leaving him enough money to pay off his American creditors. Once back in England, he was appointed to the Queen's Privy Council.

A historian described Cornbury as "a mean liar, a vulgar profligate, a frivolous spendthrift, an impudent cheat, a fraudulent bankrupt, and a detestable bigot.... We never had a governor so universally detested."

New Jersey citizens put up with all his faults until he attacked freedom of religion — considered a sacred right more than eighty years before it would become part of the Bill of Rights.

CHAPTER 5

The Mount Holly Witch Trials

W hen you think of witch trials, of course your mind turns to Massachusetts. But what about New Jersey? Were the colonists above belief in the supernatural, or did they also suspect that some of their neighbors were agents of Satan?

There were several isolated cases of witch trials in pre-Revolutionary New Jersey. The most notable supposedly took place in Mount Holly in Burlington County. It was reported in the *Pennsylvania Gazette* by none other than Benjamin Franklin, who used the purported incident to poke fun at ignorance and intolerance.

"Saturday last, at Mount-Holly, about eight miles from this Place, near 300 people were gathered together to see an Experiment or two tried on some Persons accused of Witchcraft."

What had the accused witches done to make people suspicious?

"It seems the accused had been charged with making their neighbours' Sheep dance in an uncommon Manner, and with Causing hogs to speak and sing Psalms, etc., to the great Terror and Amazement of the King's good and peaceable Subjects in this Province."

How do you prove someone is a witch?

Explained Franklin, "The Accusers (were) very positive that if the Accused were weightd in Scales against a Bible, the Bible would prove too heavy for them; or that, if they were bound and put into the River they would swim."

The accused, of course, wanted to clear their good names. They agreed to the experiment if two of the people who testified against them would undergo the same ordeal. Once this was settled, it was announced throughout Burlington County; on the day of the trial, according to Franklin, crowds gathered near the center of the village.

Franklin continued, "The Accusers were 1 Man and 1 Woman; and the Accused the same. The Parties being met and the People got together, a grand Consultation was held, before they proceeded to Trial; in which it was agreed to use the Scales first; and a Committee of Men were appointed to search the Men, and a Committee of Women to search the Women, to see if they had any Thing of Weight about them, particularly Pins."

Once the search was over, "A huge great Bible belonging to the Justice of the Peace was provided, and a lane through the Populace was made from the Justice's House to the Scales, which were fixed on a Gallows erected for that Purpose opposite to the House."

First to sit in the scale was the male accused of witchcraft.

"The Wizard was first put in the Scale, and over him was read a Chapter out of the Books of Moses, and then the Bible was put in the other Scale, (which being kept down before) was immediately let go; but, to the great Surprize of the Spectators, Flesh and Bones came down plump, and outweighed that great good Book byt abundance. After the same manner the others were served, and their Lumps of Mortality severally were too heavy for Moses and all the Prophets and Apostles."

All four had passed the test of the scales. Now came the trial by water, which would take place a short distance away on the banks of the Rancocas Creek. Franklin continued, "Accordingly a most solemn Procession was made to the Millpond, where both Accused and Accusers being stripped (saving only to Women their Shifts) were bound Hand and Foot and severally placed in the Water, lengthways, from the Side of a Barge or Flat, having for Security only a Rope about the Middle of each, which was held by some in Flat." The theory was that a witch would float, so a rope would be used to rescue a drowning, honest person. What happened?

"The accused man being thin and spare with some Difficulty began to sink at last; but the rest, every one of them, swam very light upon the Water."

Watching their case fall apart, a friend of one of the accusers "jump'd out upon the Back of the Man ... thinking to drive him down to the Bottom; but the Person bound, without any Help, came up some time before the other."

The woman accuser thought quickly: "Being told that she did not sink, (she) would be duck'd a second time; when she swam again as light as before. Upon which she declared, That she believed the Accused had bewitched her to make her so light, and that she would be duck'd again a Hundred Times but she would duck the Devil out of her."

Upon the inconclusive results of the trial, the crowd began to break up, but a satiric Franklin wrote, "The more thinking part of the spectators were of Opinion that any Person so bound and plac'd in the Water (unless they were mere Skin and bones) would swim, till their Breath was gone, and their lungs fill'd with Water. But it being the general Belief of the Populace that the Women's shifts and the Garters with which they were bound help'd to support them, it is said they are to be tried again the next warm Weather, naked."

CHAPTER 6

The Stamp of Revolution

Long before the Boston Tea Party, the first major resistance to British rule came over what was known as the Stamp Act. This tax was to go into effect in 1765 to help England pay for the French and Indian War.

The tax required special stamps on newspapers, legal documents and other printed materials: Anything more than five pages in length required a stamp. This definition stretched to playing cards with fifty-two "pages" and to a pair of dice, each face a "page." Across the Colonies, American voices protested Parliament's right to impose any tax.

There arose leaders like Patrick Henry of Virginia and James Otis of Massachusetts who led the call for a Stamp Act Congress to meet in New York City to protest the tax. In New Jersey, however, there was little interest at high levels. The colony's leaders turned down the invitation.

But New Jerseyans were more interested in rights than were their leaders. Letters to newspapers urged the newly appointed tax collectors to resign. The events forced a younger breed of Jerseyans to become interested in politics.

Richard Stockton, thirty-five years old, a graduate of the College of New Jersey at Princeton, lawyer and teacher, wrote to Robert Ogden, speaker of the New Jersey Assembly, of the popular feeling.

"I confess that I am much concerned about the present State of our Public Affairs. You see the spirit that the Stamp Act has raised throughout the Colonies. The People certainly ought to complain when they are oppressed ... wherefore I am humbly of Opinion that the Representatives of the People ought not to be silent."

Stockton, who would sign the Declaration of Independence twelve years later, was one of the first in New Jersey to attack Parliament's right to rule over the Colonies. He said, "They (New Jersey) should complain to the King; not to the Parliament whose Authority they do not and ought not to acknowledge. Upon mature Deliberation therefore I think that our Assembly ought to send Deputies at the Congress to be held this Fall at New York. If your House does not do it, we shall not only look like a speckled Bird among our Sister Colonies, but we shall say implicitly that we think it no Oppression."

Realizing that standing up to the government was dangerous, Stockton closed his plea to Ogden with, "I suggest, Burn my Letter after reading it over twice and considering It maturely."

But some wanted immediate action, like Elias Boudinot, a young lawyer who had studied under Stockton and who would become the first president of the United States. The lawyers of Essex County decided to boycott the tax; it was recorded that "We then proceeded to a free discussion of every Point worthy of Observation, and (torn) on the whole the following Question was Stated & put to Vote: 'Whether, if the Stamps should arrive in the Province, the Gentlemen present (as Lawyers) would make Use of them for any Purpose or under any Circumstances whatever?' It gives me Pleasure to say (as it must every lover of his Country) that it was carried in the Negative, without a dissenting Voice."

The feelings of the people were beginning to be obvious. Ogden called a special meeting of the Assembly at a tavern in Perth Amboy and reversed his decision not to attend the Stamp Act Congress. In October, four representatives went to New York City and met with those from eight other colonies to decide how best to resist the tax. Meanwhile, the people of New Jersey took matters into their own hands at local meetings.

"At a general Meeting of the Freemen, Inhabitants of the County of Essex, in New-Jersey, at the free Borough of Elizabeth, on the 25th day of October ... the said Freemen unanimously, and with one Voice declared,

"First, That they have at all Times heretofore, and ever would bear true Allegiance to his majesty King George the Third....

"Secondly, That the Stamp Act, prepared for the British Colonies in America, in their Opinion, is unconstitutional;

"Thirdly, That they will, by all lawful Ways and Means, endeavour to preserve and transmit to Posterity, their Liberty and Property....

"Fourthly, That they will discountenance and discourage by all lawful Measures, the Execution and Effect of the Stamp-Act.

"Fifthly, That they will detest, abhor, and hold in the utmost Contempt, all and every Person or Persons, who shall meanly accept Employment or Office, relating to the Stamp Act ... and all and every Stamp Pimp, Informer, Favourer and Encourager of the Execution of said Act; and that they will have no Communication with any such Person, nor speak to them on any occasion, unless it be to inform them of the Vileness."

While on one hand the people of New Jersey claimed loyalty to the king, on the other they declared that anyone who obeyed the king's law was their enemy. And that's exactly what Ogden became when he refused to sign the petition to the king. In New Brunswick on October 29, an enraged group of citizens hung Ogden in effigy.

The newspapers reported, "This morning, on an eminence in this city, was hung the effigy of a wretch, who on a late solemn occasion, subtilly procured himself an employment, and at once shewed the wickedness and dirtiness of his head, and the vileness and rancour of his heart, by basely betraying that important trust."

Once the effigy was hung, "Papers denoting his horrid crime were affixed to his breast, and from his mouth hung labels expressing such words and sentiments, as may well be supposed to come from the lips of such an abandoned miscreant in his last moments...."

"May such be the fate of every vile traitor, in whatever sphere they move! May they live despised! Die unpitied! and if they are remembered, let that remembrance only increase the detestation of posterity."

On November 26, the Colonial Assembly met to discuss the resolves of the Stamp Act Congress. That same day, Ogden resigned his powerful seat in the Legislature. After four days of debate, New Jersey passed its own resolves, which included an official blessing for resistance to a royal law.

As the resistance gained in strength, England faced massive drops in exports to the Colonies and repealed the hated Stamp Act on March 17, 1766. But to save face, Parliament passed the Declaratory Act which stated that the king and Parliament had "full authority" to legislate for the Colonies "in all cases what so ever."

As the colonists celebrated their victory and toasted good King George, some recognized the power to be tapped in the hands of common people like you and me. We the people could make kings back down and politicians resign.

The idea of where ultimate power resides had begun to take shape.

CHAPTER 7

Gloucester County Tea Party

New Jersey history is not emphasized in high schools or colleges. When someone brings up a fact, it usually begins with "Did you ever hear?" And so it is with the story of the New Jersey tea party. Most have heard of the one in Boston, but New Jersey's seems to be a different story.

In the years prior to the American Revolution, several towns in southern New Jersey prospered as seaports: Tuckerton and Chestnut Neck on the ocean coast and the town of Greenwich, located about five miles up the Cohansey Creek from the Delaware Bay, not far from Bridgeton. By 1750, Greenwich was a major shipping center.

It was during this time that relations between England and her Colonies began to deteriorate. Boycotts were organized and cries of taxation without representation could be heard in Boston, Philadelphia and New Jersey. The situation reached a head in 1772 when Lord North, Britain's prime minister, tried to deceive the colonists into paying a tax on tea.

For years there had been a colonial boycott of English tea, and a brisk trade for smuggled Dutch tea had grown up. North's plan was to help the British East India Company avoid bankruptcy and prove a point. By altering the regulation under which the company operated, the tea could be sold with the tax for about one-half the price of the illegal Dutch tea.

North's plan was simple. He believed the colonists would choose dollars and cents over principles. But he was wrong. On December 16, 1773, the Sons of Liberty had their famous tea party in Boston Harbor. The die was cast. In New York and Charleston, tea ships were turned away. The captain of a ship bound for Philadelphia turned back when he heard a reception was planned to "heave him keel cut, and see that his bottom be well fired, scrubbed … and his upper works too (be given) an overhauling."

Over the next twelve months positions became fixed. The Crown demanded payment for the destroyed tea and continued looking for a spot to land new shipments, believing that once the tea was in the shops America's resolve would melt. By December 1774 the British government made one last desperate effort to get the tea ashore. The target was the largest city in colonial America, Philadelphia.

As the ship *Greyhound* sailed up Delaware Bay, Captain Allen, the ship's master, learned of the resistance to his arrival planned by the local Sons of Liberty. He decided on a new course. He would land the tea in Greenwich. Then, with the help of those loyal to the king, the tea could be smuggled into Philadelphia. It would be in the shops before the Sons of Liberty could stop him.

On December 12, the *Greyhound* tied up on the Cohansey dock and Allen went ashore. Here he found a Tory merchant by the name of Dan Bowen who agreed to help. That night the tea was secretly unloaded and placed in Bowen's cellar where it would remain until transportation could be arranged.

Allen calculated that a little backwater New Jersey village would not have enough political awareness to know the importance of what was going on. But Allen did not count on men like Parson Philip Vickers Fithian.

The parson traveled a great deal for a man in the eighteenth century and had recently returned from Virginia and Maryland where he had been in contact with others resisting British policy. On December 18 Fithian wrote in his journal, "Early last week a Quantity of Tea said to be shipped at Rotterdam was brought and privately stored at Dan Bowens in Greenwich, a pro Temporre Committee was chosen to secure it till the County Committee be duly elected."

Once the word was out, a countywide meeting was called on the twenty-second. Its participants decided, "That this Committee, being ignorant of the principles on which the said tea was imported, or whence it came, and not being able to get information thereof, by reason of the importer's absence, do think it best to have it privately stored."

But this was just a cover. That night the parson and twenty-two other men met at his house and, in the Boston tradition, dressed as Indians. By torchlight the group headed for Dan Bowen's cellar where the tea was removed and taken to the market square. Then to the delight of the onlookers, the tea was set afire.

To cover themselves, the tea burners disavowed any knowledge of the party. The next day in his journal Fithian wrote, "Last night the Tea was, by a number of persons in disguise, taken out of the House and consumed with fire. Violent and different are the words about this uncommon Manoeuvre, among the Inhabitants — Some rave, some curse and condemn, some try to reason; many are glad the tea is destroyed, but almost all disapprove the manner of the destruction."

Members of the county committee met and stated that they had "found to their surprise that the tea had been destroyed, by persons unknown, the night before, at the time the committee were sitting at Bridgetown." The committee voiced disapproval of the tea party and recorded, "That we will not conceal, nor protect from justice, any of the perpetrators of the above fact."

The backwoods yokels had taken on the Crown. Twice in the next several months the royal governor would call for grand juries to indict those involved, but both times the jury refused, saying there was not enough evidence to name the perpetrators.

Today a granite monument in Greenwich stands witness to the tea burners, each name proudly carved for all to see. Of the twenty-three men, most would fight in the American Revolution. In the war four would die, two would become chaplains and four, doctors. Two rose to become members of the New Jersey State Legislature and one, Richard Howell, the third elected governor of the state.

CHAPTER 8

Treachery at Basking Ridge

In November of 1776, there would be no Thanksgiving for General George Washington and the Continental Army. Things had not been going very well. July had seen the euphoria of the signing of the Declaration of Independence only to be followed by the realization that the war must be won on the battlefield. To achieve this goal, England's General William Howe had arrived off New York City with thirty-five thousand troops, including the much feared professional mercenaries from Germany known as Hessians.

To oppose this foe, Washington had only a poorly trained army about half that size.

Over the summer, Howe attacked Long Island, Brooklyn Heights and Harlem Heights. At least twice, the Continental Army was very nearly surrounded. By November Washington had been driven out of New York City except for a strong garrison located on the banks of the Hudson River. Known as Fort Washington, the garrison, along with Fort Lee across the river in New Jersey, prevented the British from sailing up the river.

The events of the summer had taken a heavy toll on Washington. The rank and file were beginning to doubt his ability to defeat the British regulars in a stand-up battle. To add to this, General Charles Lee of Virginia, the second ranking officer in the Continental Army, was letting it be known that only he could save the army and the cause. Worst of all, Washington was losing confidence in himself. He listened to his staff more frequently and his orders sounded like suggestions.

He wanted to abandon Fort Washington, but he relented to General Nathaniel Green's assurance that the fort could be held and quickly evacuated if needed. At the same time, not knowing which way Howe would march from New York City, Washington divided his army into four parts, giving the largest force to Lee to protect the upper Hudson Valley. He gave himself a smaller detachment to prevent the British from marching across New Jersey toward the nation's capital, Philadelphia.

The loss of confidence caused several repercussions. Fort Washington's second in command, Captain Frederick MacKenzie, decided the war was lost and deserted to the British, presenting Howe with details of the defenses. Acting quickly, Howe massed his army for a major attack, striking at the fort from three sides at once. As the battle began, Washington and Green, along with two other generals, were rowed across the Hudson to confer with the fort's commander, Robert Magaw.

Washington made no attempt to take personal command or assign one of his generals to take charge. After a brief meeting, the generals left and watched from the Jersey side as the defenses slowly crumbled and Magaw finally surrendered his garrison in one of the worst disasters of the war.

Washington ordered the supplies removed from the now-useless Fort Lee and rode to his headquarters at Hackensack to write letters explaining the disaster to the Continental Congress. Three days later, a messenger rode up to inform the general that Fort Lee was next in line for attack: Several thousand British troops under Lord Cornwallis had crossed the Hudson and were marching toward the fort.

Washington acted immediately. His plan was to get the troops out before Cornwallis arrived. At Fort Lee, what Washington found would dismay any general. The men, on learning of the British approach, had broken into the liquor supply and many were drunk. Washington ordered the remainder into line and at a double-quick march made a dash for the only bridge across the Hackensack River.

All but two of the fort's cannons, hundreds of tents and tons of flour were abandoned, along with nearly a hundred men too drunk to march. Most awoke later as prisoners of war. Washington won the race to the bridge, but the road was littered with equipment as the frightened men dropped packs and even muskets to get away.

Washington knew that now almost nothing stood between the British and Philadelphia. He wrote a dispatch to Lee begging for help.

As he handed the dispatch to the courier, Washington did not see one of his most trusted officers, Colonel Joseph Reed, also give the messenger a letter addressed to Lee.

"I do not mean to flatter or praise you at the expense of any other ... but I confess I think it is entirely owing to you that this army, and the liberties of America ... are not totally cut off," Reed's letter went. "You have decision, a quality often wanted in minds otherwise valuable, and I ascribe to this our escape from York Island, from Kingsbridge and the (White) Plains, and have no doubt had you been here the garrison of (Fort) Washington would now have composed part of this army.... Oh! General, an indecisive mind is one of the greatest misfortunes that can befall an army; how often have I lamented it in this campaign!... Every gentleman of the family, the officers and soldiers generally, have a confidence in you ... I must conclude with my clear and explicit opinion that your presence is of the last importance."

Even Washington's officers had turned on him.

Although Washington's force lay between Cornwallis and Philadelphia, he was in no position to make a stand. The main road, King's Highway, today U.S. Route 1, ran through open, rolling countryside with no real natural defensive positions. In addition, almost all of the army's shovels and axes had been lost at Fort Lee, which meant that building defensive works was out of the question.

As his men were described, "Many were without shoes or stockings and several were observed to have only linen drawers on, with a rifle or hunting shirt without any proper shirt or waistcoat. They are also in great want of blankets."

Washington and his men began the long retreat across New Jersey, across the Passaic River to Newark, Cornwallis at their heels. As Washington's rear guard left Newark on the south side of town, Cornwallis' scouts entered from the north. Next came the Raritan River and a short rest at New Brunswick.

Here Washington got some help from the regiment under New Jersey's William Alexander, Lord Sterling, but at about the same time the enlistments of two Maryland and New Jersey regiments expired, and the men left the army en masse. Washington briefly tried to hold the bridge at New Brunswick but withdrew, not wanting to bring on a major battle.

One of Cornwallis' officers described Washington's actions: "As we go forward into the country, the rebels fly before us, and when we come back, they always follow us; almost impossible to catch them. They will neither fight, nor totally run away. But they keep at such a distance that we are always above a day's march from them. We seem to be playing at Bo-Peep."

Washington now received more bad news from Monmouth County, of which Ocean was a part. Loyalists had risen up, and the county was embroiled in a civil war. The Loyalists had even been able to capture Richard Stockton, a signer of the Declaration of Independence, and sent him to General Howe in New York City. This news, along with word that the British were offering local citizens pardons if they would swear allegiance to the Crown, could take New Jersey out of the revolution altogether.

Washington sent a dispatch to the Monmouth militia that they must use any methods to put down the Loyalists' uprising. The entire war could be in the balance.

By the time Washington reached Princeton on December 2, he had sent scouts north and south along the Delaware to requisition all boats. He would ferry his men across the river, taking the boats with them to prevent British pursuit. Here Washington got his first break as Cornwallis paused to rest his men at New Brunswick. When Cornwallis finally marched, Lord

Sterling fought a delaying action with two brigades, giving Washington the time to get his army — what was left of it — across the river to a safe haven.

Things were just as bad as they could get. General Lee had not yet acted on Washington's orders to come to his aid. At its capital in Burlington, the state government had dissolved. The Continental Congress had adjourned and fled Philadelphia for Baltimore, hastily naming Washington dictator with "full power to order and direct all things relative to the department and to the operations of war."

In an attached letter granting Washington complete power, Congress stated, "Happy it is for this country that the general of their forces can safely be entrusted with the most unlimited power, and neither personal security, liberty, or property be in the least degree endangered thereby."

Washington unfortunately felt it was too little, too late. He wrote his relative Lund Washington, "I would look forward to unfavorable events, prepare accordingly in such manner, however, as to give no alarm or suspicion to anyone." At about the same time, another man was putting his thoughts to paper. He had been with the army during the retreat across New Jersey. He had seen the desertions and the men going home. But he had also seen something in those hungry, half-dressed American soldiers that not even Washington had seen.

Thomas Paine put on paper the spirit he had seen in the eyes of the men as they crossed New Jersey. He called it "The Crisis."

"These," wrote Paine, "are the times that try men's souls. The summer soldier and the sunshine patriot will, in this crisis, shrink from the service of their country; but he that stands it now deserves the love and thanks of man and woman. Tyranny, like hell is not easily conquered; yet we have this consolation with us, that the harder the conflict, the more glorious the triumph. What we obtain too cheap, we esteem too lightly; it is dearness only that gives every thing its value."

In the words of George Washington, "The game is pretty near up." It would take a miracle to save the Revolution.

The dark days of December 1776 saw what was left of his little army huddled on the west bank of the Delaware. The beleaguered soldiers had been driven across New Jersey in a humiliating defeat. Loyalists in Monmouth County had captured patriot Richard Stockton and sent him to New York in chains.

The Congress had abandoned the capital of Philadelphia and fled to Baltimore. Trenton, Mount Holly, and even Burlington fell one by one to Hessian mercenaries working for King George. The only effective fighting force left in the area was under General Lee, Washington's leading rival for command of the rebel army.

Lee had about five thousand men, most of whom were battle-tested Continentals. During the disastrous rout across New Jersey, Washington had repeatedly sent messages to Lee, urging him to march from his position in New York and join Washington's outnumbered force.

At the same time, Washington had sent orders to other troops instructing them to join him in Pennsylvania. As he waited, he received some unexpected dispatches from Charles Lee.

Lee reported that since Washington had already crossed the Delaware there would be little use for reinforcements from the north. Lee had diverted troops from marching to Washington's aid, commanding them to join him instead. Since his troops were to the rear of the British, Lee wrote, they should act independently of Washington. The British could not continue "with so formidable a body hanging on their flanks or rear."

Lee told Washington to inform his men he would fight on — "It may encourage them." While Lee was thus saving the cause, he asked that Washington "take out of the way of danger my favorite mare" at Princeton.

Washington's retreat was a bitter one for him: Not only was he in flight, but he now knew that Lee coveted his command.

On the other hand, if Lee could take some action against the British in New Jersey, Washington hoped it would take the pressure off his soldiers and stop the advance on Philadelphia, at least for the winter.

Despite Lee's insubordination, Washington chose the action which he felt would benefit the cause. He sent Lord Sterling to find Lee with instructions that the two come up with a battle plan. As he waited for word on his orders, Washington must have known that any good news from Lee would spell the end of his own command of the Continental Army: He was resigned to personal disgrace if only a miracle would save his men.

But history is filled with strange twists that turn beggars into heroes and generals into fools. On December 12, Lee spent the night away from his troops, visiting a widow known as "Mrs. White," a tavern owner in the town of Basking Ridge. The next morning, while still in his night clothes, he began his correspondence to General Horatio Gates, again attacking Washington and promoting his own cause. Lee closed his letter with, "Unless something which I do not expect turns up, we are lost."

Within moments, something unexpected turned up. Outside the tavern the sound of horses was heard. When Lee looked out the window, he saw British dragoons under Banestre Tarleton riding up the lane. Tarleton reported, "I went on at full speed when perceiving two Sentrys at a Door and a loaded Waggon; I push'd at them making all the noise I cou'd. The Sentrys were struck with a Panic, dropp'd their arms and fled. I order'd my Men to fire into the House thro' every Window and door, and cut up as many of the Guard as they cou'd ... I carried on my Attack with all possible spirit and surrounded the House, tho' fir'd upon, in front, flank, and rear."

When Mrs. White ran outside and told Tarleton the general was inside, Lee's fate was cast. Tarleton shouted that if Lee would surrender, he and his attendants should be safe. "But if my summons was not complied with immediately, the house should be burnt and every person without exception should be put to the sword."

Several of Lee's guards were shot as they attempted to escape through the back door. Then finally from inside, it was shouted, "The general is coming out." Lee, savior of the American cause, was a prisoner of war. Tarleton put Lee on a horse, and the group set off in the direction of Cornwallis' headquarters.

The sound of firing at the tavern was heard in the main camp of Lee's army, and General John Sullivan sent a force to investigate, but they were unable to rescue Lee. Two days later, Washington learned of Lee's capture from Sullivan. "It gives the most pungent pain to inform your Excellency of the sad stroke America must feel in the loss of General Lee who was this morning taken by the enemy."

Sullivan went on to say that he would bring the troops across the Delaware. In a few days, Sullivan arrived, and Washington's army doubled in size. George Washington knew that if someone was going to save the cause it would have to be him. It was time to try one desperate gamble to save the Revolution — cross the Delaware and attack Trenton.

But of course, everyone knows about that.

CHAPTER 9

Washington Shows His Daring

The day after Christmas 1776, Washington and the main body of the Continental Army were on the move again. They had won a great victory by a bold stroke. Washington and his troops had surprised a Hessian detachment of about a thousand men under Colonel Johann Rall. Now, after the victory, Washington with his prisoners and their captured supplies marched north to McKonkey's Ferry where he had left his boats. The American force would cross back into Pennsylvania taking the boats with them; Washington knew that once the British headquarters in New York City learned of his Christmas raid they would send out a large angry force looking for revenge.

As word of the victory spread throughout New Jersey and Pennsylvania, Washington could take only a short pause for rejoicing. Contrary to popular myths, the core of Washington's army was not militia but Continental troops. While local militia joined and left camp at a whim, Continentals were enlisted for a set time. They were trained in the basics of eighteenth century warfare, and although the tatterdemalion troops did not look like soldiers, they were expected to act and fight like them.

The problem was that the Continental Congress had been nearsighted when it came to the army. Not being able to foresee the length or importance of the fighting taking place, the Congress had signed soldiers of the Continental Army to one-year enlistments. The vast majority of these enlistments would expire on January 1: Washington — even after his stunning victory at Trenton — would lose well over half of his trained men that day and the cause would be left in the hands of some untried militia.

On December 27, on the Pennsylvania side of the Delaware, Washington had a meeting with his officers and devised a plan to save the army. Word had arrived that General John Cadwalader, the thirty-four-year-old head of the Pennsylvania militia, was in Burlington, New Jersey. Washington decided to cross back into New Jersey. Once on the soil of the army's recent victory, he would try to get the men to extend their stay. If they did, he would lead them in another attempt to drive away the redcoats. If not, then he would try to do it alone at the head of Cadwalader's militia. His mood was set. He had but one goal, "Driving the enemy entirely from, or at least to, the extremity of the province of Jersey."

On December 30, Washington began his second crossing of the Delaware. For the men who made both, this was by far the more difficult. Large ice floes stopped the boats and there was six inches of snow on the ground. Once on the Jersey side, Washington marched south through Trenton. On the south bank of the Little Assunpink Creek, they made camp. Here Washington, the man who hated public speaking, who led by example, who showed little emotion in public, would ask his soldiers the unthinkable: to stay on after their enlistments expired.

A sergeant who was looking forward to going home for the winter later wrote, "At this time our troops were in a destitute and deplorable condition. The horses attached to our cannon were without shoes, and when passing over the ice they would slide in every direction and could advance only by the assistance of the soldiers. Our men, too, were without shoes or other comfortable clothing; and as traces of our march towards Princeton, the ground was literally marked with the blood of the soldiers' feet.

"At this trying time General Washington, having now but a ... handful of men and many of them new recruits in which he could place but little confidence, ordered our regiment to be paraded, and personally addressed us, urging that we should stay a month longer.... The drums beat for volunteers, but not a man turned out. The solders, worn down with fatigue and privations, had their hearts fixed on home and the comforts of the domestic circle, and it was hard to forego the anticipated pleasures of the society of our dearest friends."

The Revolution was over just as surely as if the British had wiped out the army on the battlefield. Then, in a last effort, Washington rode down the line on his white horse and entreated his troops.

"My brave fellows, you have done all I asked you to do, and more than could be reasonably expected; but your country is at stake, your wives, your houses and all that you hold dear. You have worn yourselves out with fatigues and hardships, but we know not how to spare you. If you will consent to stay only one month longer, you will render that service to the cause of liberty and to your country which you probably never can do under any other circumstances."

Then there was silence. Finally, after what must have seemed a lifetime, someone stepped forward, then another and another. In all, about half of the Continentals chose to stay on for one more month of cold, hunger and death.

The next day Washington spoke to his men at their camp on the Assunpink Creek just south of Trenton, preparing to put his army to use. He had sent word to Cadwalader's forces near Mount Holly to march north to join him. He also ordered Colonel Joseph Reed with twelve dragoons to scout in the direction of Princeton to find signs of the British. As Reed's men got close to the college, they saw a redcoat leave a house and walk toward the barn. They dashed forward at a gallop and surrounded the farmhouse where they captured twelve British solders who had been in the kitchen, "conquering a parcel of mince pyes."

At their interrogation, the prisoners told Washington there were about six thousand British and Hessian solders in Princeton with more expected at any minute. Once the reinforcements arrived, they warned, the British would push on toward Trenton looking for revenge. Meanwhile, Cadwalader was receiving the same information from spies in Princeton. With the help of local farmers he drew a map showing the British defenses and the locations of the roads leading from Princeton and Trenton.

As Washington prepared for the attack, the location of his camp left several points to be desired. All his boats were on the Delaware River. If the British got a force across the creek, they could cut off his avenue of escape and trap Washington and the entire Continental Army between the river and a superior British army.

Washington posted his men very carefully. Henry Knox was to position several cannons to stop any passage over the one bridge, and earthworks were constructed at each of the fords. Finally, thirty-two-year-old Colonel Edward Hand's elite company of Pennsylvania riflemen was sent up the road toward Princeton with orders to slow down the British if they advanced.

By dark on New Year's Day, the British reinforcements rode into Princeton. Heading the column was the best combat general in the British army, and Lord Charles Cornwallis was livid. When word arrived in New York City of Washington's daring raid on Trenton, Cornwallis was about to board a ship to spend the winter with his young wife in England. Unfortunately for Cornwallis and his wife, General Howe canceled his leave and sent him after Washington.

In Princeton, Cornwallis made his headquarters in the home of Richard Stockton, a signer of the Declaration of Independence, whose house later became the official New Jersey governor's mansion. From Morven, as it was called, Cornwallis made his plans. On the morning of January 2, he would take the main body of troops and artillery, march the eleven miles to Trenton and crush the rebels once and for all.

He would leave a small force in Princeton to guard his supplies and the road to Perth Amboy. The next day, as Cornwallis began his march, the cursed New Jersey winter joined the rebels' side. Temperatures shot above freezing and a light rain began to fall. This was a disaster to an army traveling on a dirt road. The upper layer thawed and turned to mud as thousands of feet churned it up. The cannons, with their narrow iron rims, sank in a sea of goo.

As the British column cursed its luck, an officer dropped from his horse, dead. Over the noise of the march came the bloodcurdling sound of a *pop*, no smooth-bore Brown Bess musket, but a sound that only a Pennsylvania long rifle could make. The British column had encountered Hand's backwoodsmen. These riflemen could hit a man from a range the British muskets could not match.

For the next five hours Hand's riflemen would fire a deadly volley, forcing the British column to stop and form a line of battle. The redcoats would advance only to find Hand's men gone to their next ambush site. The riflemen tore up bridges and, with the aid of only two small cannons, made Cornwallis think he was up against the entire American army.

It was not until late afternoon with its long winter shadows that Hand's men entered Trenton and fired as they retreated from building to building. Finally driven out of the town, the riflemen dashed across the Assunpink Bridge to the main American line. There, sitting on his white horse, was Washington to congratulate the Pennsylvanians for a job well done.

As the redcoats tried to cross the bridge, Washington gave the order to fire. The effect of Knox's artillery was awesome.

A soldier wrote, "We let them come on some ways ... then by a signal given, we all fired together. The enemy retreated off the bridge and formed again, and we were ready for them ... and such destruction it made, you cannot conceive. The bridge looked red as blood, with their killed and wounded, and their red coats...."

After failing at the bridge and one of the fords, Cornwallis called for a counsel of war with his officers. One wanted to attack at once, fearing Washington would escape during the night. Another argued that Washington was already cut off from his boats and a night attack with tired men could be costly. Furthermore, if Washington did try to turn his back and run, they still could destroy him as he marched.

Finally Cornwallis made up his mind. "We've got the old fox now. We'll go over and bag him in the morning."

What was going through the old fox's mind on the other side of the Assunpink Creek at that moment can never be known, but he recognized he was in serious trouble: If he stayed to fight and the redcoats crossed the creek, he would be trapped. If he retreated to South Jersey, they could hunt him down. Was there a third choice?

Washington had gambled everything by crossing the Delaware and won. Now he was outnumbered, outgunned and trapped; what would be the last thing Cornwallis would expect him to do? He was beginning to act like a fox.

That evening, Washington met with his officers to discuss his options: stand and fight or retreat. But Washington toyed with a third possibility. He talked with Cadwalader about a map which showed a back road heading to the northeast. A local resident, Philemon Dickinson, commander of the New Jersey militia, confirmed the road existed and that most maps did not even show it.

Washington proposed that a small portion of the army be left behind to feed the campfires and to make loud noises. This would convince the British that the Americans were planning to stay and fight. With the main body of the army, Washington would march via the back road some thirteen miles and attack the unsuspecting British rear guard and supply base located in the college town of Princeton.

That night the army made ready to march. Everything possible was done to muffle the cannons so the British could not hear the army depart. Slowly the soldiers broke camp and moved away.

Colonel Silas Newcomb and the South Jersey militia started digging to cover the sounds of the guns. Newcomb's force would spend the night pretending to be an entire army, even firing a cannon ball from time to time in Cornwallis' direction. Their orders were to keep up the deception as long as possible, then to melt away into the wilds.

At first the Americans faced the same problems the British had the day before. The road was a sea of mud from the warm weather, but throughout the night the temperature dropped rapidly below freezing. The mud froze, and cannons could easily be rolled on top. Underfed men in rags for uniforms marched in the cold, pitch dark, tripping on stumps or bumping into the man in front when he stopped. No one could even curse his luck or complain to a buddy for the general had ordered the army to move in silence.

Just outside Princeton, there was a fork in the road. Washington sent the majority of the army straight to Princeton, but the brigade of General Hugh Mercer was pulled out of line. They would take the back road which intersected with the main Trenton-Princeton road, entering Princeton on the main road. Along the way Mercer would also destroy the bridges to prevent Cornwallis from returning to Princeton.

What Washington and Mercer did not know was that several hours before, Cornwallis had sent to Princeton for reinforcements. Colonel Charles Mawhood and his brigade had just marched out of Princeton and were set on a collision course with Mercer. As the sun rose on a frost-covered countryside, the two forces drew closer. According to a sergeant in Mercer's force, "About sunrise ... reaching the summit of a hill near Princeton, we observed a light-horseman looking towards us as we view an object when the sun shines directly in our faces.

"General Mercer, observing him, gave orders to the riflemen who were posted on the right to pick him off. Several made ready, but at that instant, he wheeled about and was out of their reach.

"Soon after this, as we were descending a hill through an orchard, a party of the enemy who were entrenched behind a bank and fence, rose and fired upon us....

"We formed, advanced, and fired upon the enemy. They retreated ... to their packs, which were laid in a line. I advanced to the fence on the opposite side of the ditch which the enemy had just left, fell on one knee, and loaded my musket with ball and buckshot. Our fire was most destructive. Their ranks grew thin and the victory seemed nearly complete, when the British reinforced. Many of our brave men had fallen, and we were unable to withstand such superior numbers of fresh troops. I soon heard General Mercer command in a tone of distress, 'Retreat!' He was mortally wounded and died shortly after."

Mercer had been bayoneted repeatedly and died several days later. With their leader wounded, the Americans were in flight. Then on his white horse, as if in a movie, Washington himself rode onto the field to stop the retreat.

"At this moment, Washington appeared in front of the American army, riding towards those of us who were retreating, and exclaimed, 'Parade with us, my brave fellows, there is but a handful of the enemy, and we will have them directly.' I immediately joined the main body and marched over the ground again...."

Washington rallied his men thirty yards from the British lines as the redcoats massed to fire a volley at him sitting on his horse. Soldiers in the American line hid their faces. They could not bear to watch him die, but when the smoke cleared away, there sat the general. Now Washington ordered a charge shouting, "It's a fine fox chase my boys."

"The British were unable to resist this attack and retreated into the College, where they thought themselves safe," continued the sergeant's account. "Our army was there in an instant, and cannon were planted before the door, and after two or three discharges, a white flag appeared at the window and the British surrendered. They were a haughty, crabbed set of men as they fully exhibited while prisoners on their march to the country."

A cannon ball fired by Captain Alexander Hamilton at Nassau Hall had neatly decapitated the painting of King George III, convincing the redcoats inside to surrender. The battle had been short but bloody.

Cornwallis never knew the Americans were gone until he heard firing to the rear. By the time he got back to Princeton the battle was over and Washington was gone with his supplies and prisoners. Cornwallis, embarrassed, had no choice but to return to New York City vowing revenge.

New Jersey was free of the invaders. Washington had fought three battles in ten days and reversed the course of the Revolution. His men had proven once and for all they were not sunshine patriots, and he had proven he was one of the most daring men ever to command the affection of American soldiers.

And finally, New Jersey had a name for one of its counties: Mercer.

CHAPTER 10

Blacks Fight for the Nation

W hen George Washington took command of the Continental Army in 1775, he attempted to keep "free blacks" out. However, the need for manpower and the fact that the British were enlisting slaves changed Washington's mind; in December 1776 he ordered the enlistment of "free negroes." In little Rhode Island, blacks made up a large percentage of the state's first regiment. The troops were integrated, and blacks fought side by side with whites.

This regiment, under the command of Colonel Christopher Greene, was ordered to Fort Mercer, New Jersey, in Gloucester County in October 1777. Mercer and its twin on the Pennsylvania side of the Delaware River, Fort Mifflin, anchored ends of a giant chain which prevented British ships from bringing supplies up the river to the recently captured city of Philadelphia.

That autumn was a low point in the Revolutionary War. The capital had fallen and holding these two river forts became a symbol of America's will to continue to fight.

Fort Mercer was an earthen defensive position with fourteen cannons and about four hundred men. On October 22, a force of more than two thousand Hessians, under the command of Count Karl von Donop, approached the fort and demanded its surrender. Greene refused, saying, "We ask no quarter nor will we give any." He then ordered his men to fall back to the inner defenses and hold their fire, since they were low on ammunition.

Von Donop ordered his confident, professional soldiers forward. When they were within point-blank range, the Americans opened a devastating fire. American cannon loaded with canister (hundreds of lead balls) blew holes in the Hessian line. Von Donop was mortally wounded, and his feared Hessians turned and ran. Greene and his Rhode Islanders, outnumbered 5-to-1, held the field. Almost six hundred Hessians were killed or wounded, while Greene's men had only eleven casualties.

The importance of Greene's feat was not lost on his commander, Brigadier General James Varnum. Impressed by the bravery of Greene's black troops, he proposed to Washington that a black regiment be recruited from Rhode Island, telling the Commander-in-Chief, "A battalion of Negroes can easily be raised there." He also recommended that Greene be placed in command of the new black regiment.

Washington agreed, and wrote to Rhode Island's governor. "Enclosed you will find a copy of the letter from General Varnum upon the means which might be adopted for completing the Rhode Island troops to their full proportion in the continental army." He urged the governor, "You will give the officers employed in this business [recruiting the regiment] all the assistance in your power."

But Rhode Island went further. It recruited not only free blacks, but slaves. In February 1778 the state Legislature observed, "The wisest, the freest, and bravest Nations [in times of emergency have] liberated their slaves and enlisted them as soldiers to fight in defense of their Country."

So that slave owners would not prevent their slaves from enlisting, a system was set up to reimburse them for their loss. A committee would "examine each slave after he had passed muster and ... put a price on him according to his value. The enlisting officer thereupon was to give to the owner of every enlisted slave a certificate which would forever discharge the Negro from his service. The note was to be payable on demand with interest at six percent a year." The only hitch was that the master would not be paid for his Negroes until the "Continental Congress first reimbursed Rhode Island for them."

This hitch led some slave owners to attempt to keep slaves from enlisting. One owner told his slaves that "the Negroes were to (be used as Breastworks) ... that they were always to be employed upon the most dangerous service and ... that they were to be put in the front of the Battle [used as shock troops] as the Hessians were in the British army. Furthermore, were they taken prisoners they would not be treated as prisoners of war, but would be sent to the West Indies and sold as slaves." The latter threat was sufficient to strike terror into most New England slaves, to whom the prospect of West Indian slavery was equivalent to, or worse than, the death penalty.

But slaves did join, and the black Rhode Island regiment served with distinction until June 1783, after which it was disbanded and forgotten. The men who had proven themselves on a New Jersey battlefield never got the glory they so rightly deserved.

CHAPTER 11

Monmouth:

Crucial Test of Steel

June has always been a time for tests, graduations, and new beginnings. In June 1778, George Washington ventured into New Jersey to take the ultimate test for an army.

That spring, British general Sir Henry Clinton had received orders to move his entire army of about fifteen thousand from the captured American capital of Philadelphia, where he had spent a comfortable winter, to New York City.

The move was to be carried out by a march through Camden, Haddonfield, Mount Holly, Englishtown, and on to Sandy Hook. On June 16, the first of the British troops began to cross the Delaware.

Washington received the news optimistically; his confidence in his troops was high. His men had just suffered through the terrible winter at Valley Forge, but Washington knew they were better for it. Those months had not been wasted shivering in the cold. From Prussia, Baron Friedrich von Steuben had arrived and volunteered his services. Washington at once decided the baron would become the army's drillmaster, and over the weeks the ragged, un-trained volunteers became an army. They could now march *en masse* and load their muskets faster, items of vital importance to an eighteenth century army.

Morale was high because word arrived that the French had signed a Treaty of Friendship, promising to bring supplies and assistance from the French army and navy to America. Also, General Charles Lee had returned as Washington's second in command. He had been captured and spent eighteen months as a prisoner under house arrest in Philadelphia. Now, through an exchange, he was back to give Washington advice gleaned from his experience in the British army.

As soon as word reached Washington that the British had evacuated Philadelphia, he called a council of war. His first impulse was to strike at Clinton's long line of supplies and men as they marched. Most of the other generals agreed, but Lee argued against the move. He reminded Washington that the rebels had never stood the test of cold steel and that a bayonet charge had always made the Americans run. He argued that the British were retreating anyway — why rush a battle?

Although Lee put a damper on the general's boldness, Washington decided to make the British pay for their trip through Jersey. He called out the New Jersey militia under Philemon Dickinson and sent the New Jersey Light Infantry under "Scotch" Willie Maxwell to harass the British and look for any signs of weakness.

Immediately the word went out to the militia to drive the British from the state. Men took up arms, and units from as far south as Manahawkin began the march to intercept Clinton. For the British the march was agonizingly slow, since Clinton had more than 1,500 wagons, thousands of Tory refugees who were fleeing Philadelphia, and soldiers lugging eighty pounds in their packs.

Conditions worsened in the "Jersey Desert," the pinelands which covered much of the state. The cannons either sank in the sand or, when a thunderstorm hit, disappeared in the mud. Worst of all were the mosquitoes that covered horses and men.

Dickinson and Maxwell fought in similar ways. They would lie in ambush on back roads and pick off an officer, then fly into the pines to safety. Washington crossed the Delaware and stayed close enough to the British to attack if the opportunity presented itself.

Finally, on June 27, Washington could wait no longer. He sent part of his army to attack the British rear guard near the town of Monmouth Courthouse, today's Freehold. If the British made themselves vulnerable, he would commit the rest of the army in a general engagement. Command of the attacking force was offered to Lee who turned it down as unimportant and rash. The command was then given to the Marquis de Lafayette, a Frenchman. This angered Lee, who then agreed to take the command.

Clinton sensed Washington might try something, and he ordered his army into action. Before dawn on the twenty-eighth, he sent all of his wagons and refugees down the road to Sandy Hook under a light guard. He held back the majority of his best troops, the Grenadiers, Queen's Rangers and some dragoons, as a rear guard.

Almost at once the New Jersey militia attacked. Dickinson reported to Washington and Lee that his farmers and shopkeepers had engaged the elite of the British army. Lee wanted to withdraw and let the militia fend for itself, saying an assault would only fail, but Washington ordered Lee to attack.

Over the next several hours, Lee sent orders to his various commanders to march, countermarch, move forward and withdraw; to some like Dan Morgan, he gave no orders at all. Lee's men were thoroughly confused, and Clinton seized the opportunity to drive both the militia and Lee's men back, thus ensuring the safety of the wagon train. As soon as Lee saw the British massing for the attack, he ordered a retreat. His men, beaten before they fought, started to the rear.

What they found there made them prefer fighting the redcoats. Washington rode to the front to discover why his orders had not been carried out. "On that memorable day he swore like an angel from Heaven," one soldier wrote later. When Washington found Lee he demanded an explanation but, dissatisfied, he did something which perhaps won the Revolution. He ordered Lee to leave the field, a great disgrace for a general. Lee would never lead American troops again.

As the battle developed around him, Washington assumed command. To "Mad" Anthony Wayne of Pennsylvania he gave the assignment to delay the British long enough so he could reorganize the army. He put Nathaniel Greene on his right and New Jersey's Lord Sterling on his left. Wayne's men valiantly bought him time before being driven back. Finally, the line was formed and as the temperature broke the hundred-degree mark, Washington and the Continental Army were ready for their test.

Collection of the Monmouth County Historical Association, Gift of the Descendants of David Leavitt, 1937

Washington "swore like an angel from heaven" as he relieved General Charles Lee from command during the Battle of Monmouth. Lee had attempted to undermine Washington's command since the fall of 1776.

Three times the pride of the British army, bayonets fixed, advanced across Jersey fields. For the first time, the American army under Washington broke them. On the final charge, Molly Pitcher replaced her husband at his cannon and won a place in history.

The British had thrown the best they could at Washington's troops and failed. Now he prepared to counterattack, but the heat played havoc with both armies as darkness fell. Washington ordered Sterling, who had already begun to attack, to wait for morning.

That night the British decided they had had enough. Their best troops marched down the road to Sandy Hook and the protection of the British fleet. While other battlefields are better remembered and other anniversaries celebrated, it was on the scorching fields of Monmouth that Washington's band of rebels passed its crucial test of steel and became a real army.

CHAPTER 12

The Pride of Forked River

The roar of a cannon echoes across the water. The smoke hangs low in the morning stillness like a fog. Men with cutlass and pistol line the rails of their ship, ready for the order to board.

If you think this is a scene from an old Errol Flynn movie about the Spanish Main, you are wrong. This was Barnegat Bay during the American Revolution.

For years historians and the general public have known that New Jersey's coastal waters were home to dozens of privateers. These privately owned ships were issued a license, or marque, by either the Continental Congress or the state Legislature. The marque granted the ship's owner permission to become a legal pirate. Any loot taken by the ship would be split between its owner and the government.

Fortunes could be made in privateering, and Jersey shoremen turned places like Toms River and Chestnut Neck, just south of Tuckerton, into armed naval bases. Although most of the activities of these "rebel pirates" have been lost to time, a document in the National Archives in Washington, D.C., fills in some of the blanks about the war in Ocean County.

In 1832, Congress passed a bill granting pensions to Revolutionary War veterans who could prove and document their service. Of the men applying was one Thomas Brown, who at the outbreak of fighting at Lexington and Concord lived in Forked River.

In New Jersey, the Revolution was also a civil war, with about a third of the people loyal to the king. This made life on land dangerous for Brown and other privateers since the vast Pine

Barrens became a home for Loyalists. In Brown's words, "An immense tract of uncultivated and uninhabited land covered with forests and swamps, in many parts almost impassable, were taken possession of by that portion of the inhabitants of the state who had abandoned the standard of their country and flown to the British for refuge from their justly incensed country-men, the forests and swamps furnishing fastnesses from which it was difficult to dislodge them. And from their retreats they made incursions into the cultivated parts of the state, committed every species of depredations, carried the plunder seized in these incursions into the woods...."

To protect themselves, local towns formed militia companies. At age sixteen, Brown joined the Forked River company of the Monmouth County militia. His father, Samuel, was the captain.

"A company of about thirty men was formed who chose the said Samuel Brown as their captain, Joseph Bell, lieutenant, and William Holmes, ensign," the younger Brown wrote. "This company were called minutemen, their duty being understood to be to hold themselves continually in readiness, to turn out at a moment's warning, to resist the depredations of the Tories and refugees in whatever place their services might be required...."

The company set up a base near the mouth of the Forked River, almost directly across the bay from Barnegat Inlet. The Forked River men then decided to build a privateer to prevent seaborne attacks and to raise money to compensate themselves for their time away from their farms and jobs.

While off duty, Brown and the other men constructed a large cedar-plank gunboat. Meanwhile, the war was not going well for the American rebels. Independence had been declared, but Washington and his men were defeated at Long Island; by the fall of 1776 the army was being chased across New Jersey toward the Delaware River. This encouraged the Loyalists, who marched from Shrewsbury to capture Toms River.

Work was stopped on the gunboat, and the company fortified the road (today's Route 9) from Toms River to Manahawkin. The precautions worked. "[John] Morris and his refugees, who having learnt the position of the company, and being aware of the advantages ... did not venture to approach them, but remained quietly at Toms River until the month of January following, when he returned with his force to Shrewsbury, having done nothing during his three month's stay at Toms River...." Brown wrote.

Work resumed on the gunboat until the spring of 1777, when a Toms River privateer under Captain Joshua Studson sailed into the Forked River. Studson, looking for British merchant ships, was short five crewmen for his double-ended whaleboat which carried a sail and several swivel cannons. Thomas Brown and four of the militiamen set out with Studson.

"Having entered on board the said boat ... about the first of April ... proceeded in the night to sea through Barnegat Inlet and reached Sandy Hook passed the *Roebuck* man-of-war then lying there, and in Ambou Bay boarded a British schooner, captured her, and took her into Middletown Creek in the county of Monmoyt, where we were shortly afterwards blockaded by British vessels, from which a force superior to ours was landed who attacked us in the night, retook the schooner, and after a short contest, burnt our boat ... and then returned to their vessels," Brown wrote.

By the end of April, young Brown and the four other men returned overland to Forked River and went back to work on the gunboat. By May it was finished. The rebels could take pride in their work. Armed with one six-pounder, four swivel guns, two whale pieces (large mounted muskets), and carrying a crew of forty, the new gunboat could sweep the British from Barnegat Bay.

The pride of Forked River, named the *Civil Usage,* was ready to fight and proved her worthiness early.

"Shortly after the said gunboat was so armed, equipped, and manned, and during the early part of the summer of the year 1777, while cruising in the said gunboat off Barnegat Inlet, we captured a British brig from the West Indies bound to New York loaded with rum, sugar, molasses, and limes, and carried her into Toms River," noted Brown.

The rest of the summer was quiet at the shore. As the stormy winter approached, "We run the said gunboat up Oyster Creek into a cedar swamp and placed her in the best situation we could select in the said creek to protect her through the winter...."

In the spring, the *Civil Usage* was brought back to the bay, but most of her crew, along with the rest of the local militia including the Manahawkin company, had been called out by Washington. The British were marching from Philadelphia to Sandy Hook, and the local men were assigned to General Daniel Morgan's rifle company in the Battle of Monmouth.

"After the Battle of Monmouth, Capt. Samuel Brown returned and again manned and took the command of the said gunboat, and during the same summer, whilst on a cruise, succeeded in capturing a boat of the enemy engaged in trading with Loyalist residents at a village then called Clam Town [now Tuckerton] in the township of Little Egg Harbor.... In the following spring, in the year 1779 Capt. Brown and his said company again manned and resumed cruising in the said gunboat, and to the southward of Barnegat descried, engaged, and captured a gunboat belonging to the refugees under the command ... of a Capt. Whiley, armed with four swivels and a whalepiece and with a crew of from 25 to 30 men. After the capture of the refugee gunboat, we continued to cruise for some time, when, in the latter part of June or the beginning of July of the same year, having discovered that our gunboat required repair, we run her into harbor at Toms River for that purpose."

While the *Civil Usage* was undergoing repair, Samuel and Thomas returned to Forked River, but by now the area was a constant battleground as bands of Loyalists terrorized patriots. In support of King George, some attacked and raided the houses of the Jersey shore. Others were more interested in the property they could steal or in settling prewar arguments. The leader of the Loyalists around Manahawkin was Captain John Bacon. North of his territory, the Loyalists were under the command of Captain Davenport.

By now this fighting had become very personal, with both sides taking revenge on each other. As Captain Brown and his son were at their home, Davenport paid a visit. "The next morning, as the sun was rising, we were alarmed by the dog barking fiercely, and, immediately running to the window, saw a large number of ... refugees engaged in fording a creek about 30 paces from the house."

Thomas woke his father, and the two made a run for it to avoid capture. Before they reached the safety of the trees, they had to "Pass through a cleared level field of 30 acres, and no obstructions intervened between this field and the position occupied by the refugees but a slight fence. Capt. Brown and this deponent left the house with no other garments than their shirts and, though fired at by the whole body of the refugees, were so fortunate as to reach their gunboat at Toms River unhurt."

Samuel Brown learned that Davenport and his 160 men would be passing through Barnegat Inlet, headed for New York. Brown got two other local boats, and the fleet headed out Cranberry Inlet (located where Seaside Heights stands today) to intercept them. Davenport heard of the fleet waiting outside Barnegat Inlet and instead "returned to Forked River and finding Capt. Brown's house without other guard than his wife and younger children, they robbed it of everything of value that it contained, forced his wife and children to leave it, and then burnt the house, barn, shop and other outbuildings to ashes. And at the same time, they burnt a valuable schooner belonging to Capt. Brown. The ship weighed 40 or 50 tons burthen and was then in Forked River."

Because the refugees had become a strong presence on Barnegat Bay, *Civil Usage* was taken to the Raritan River that winter. Captain Brown now needed time at home to put his personal business back in order. As a result, a new captain, Aaron Swain, was appointed with Thomas Brown promoted to the rank of lieutenant.

With the *Civil Usage* away, the Loyalists became bolder on Barnegat Bay. Their base at Clam Town was a major problem. Supplies were sent from Tuckerton to New York, the British army's headquarters. An attack on Tuckerton would strike a blow at the British in New York City.

Wrote Brown, "In the fall of the year 1780, a considerable body of refugees and Tories being located at Clam Town in the township of Little Egg Harbor ... parties of them were dispatched from thence to penetrate into and commit depredations in the cultivated parts of the counties of Burlington and of Monmouth. By these marauding parties, Clayton Newbold, John Black and Caleb Shreve of the county of Burlington and John Holmes of the county of Monmouth were robbed of large quantities of silver plate, money, clothing, and other articles ... the marauders took their booty to Clam Town and put the same on board a lumber sloop lying there under the control of the refugees, to be transported to New York as soon as the navigation should open in the spring."

Swain saw an opportunity for revenge on the Loyalists along with a chance for profit. He "conceived the idea of intercepting the booty in its passage to New York. He rejoined his crew and ordered his gunboat to Shrewsbury Inlet to watch the motions of the enemy."

But the schooner remained in Tuckerton for the winter. As 1781 began, *Civil Usage* returned to her home area to guard the waters of Barnegat Bay once more.

"Early in the spring ... we proceeded to Barnegat Inlet, and on our way we fell in with and captured the schooner containing the booty which had been taken by the refugees in the previous fall as before set forth and had the satisfaction of restoring the same to its owners."

From the captured crew it was learned that Davenport was at Tuckerton, the same Loyalist who had burned Samuel Brown's farm and ship. But the *Civil Usage* could not carry a large enough crew to attack the town.

"Immediately after the capture of the schooner, we fell in with Capt. [Robert] Gray from Rhode Island commanding an American privateer. With him we concerted the plan of dispersing the refugees established at Clam Town. It was agreed that he should approach Clam Town from the sea through Egg Harbor Inlet and decoy them out to sea in their boats, and that we should approach the same inlet through the bay, keeping ourselves concealed, and in case he should succeed in decoying them out, we were to follow and support him in the engagement, placing the enemy between two fires."

The ships split, Gray's privateer sailing south off the ocean beach of Long Beach Island. The *Civil Usage* sailed parallel down Barnegat Bay. As the gunboat waited, Gray rounded the southern tip of the island and headed for Tuckerton with her guns covered, looking like an innocent merchantman.

"When they were out at sea, Capt. Gray hove about and stood for them. The vessels engaged. Capt. Davenport and eight or nine of his men were killed by the first broadside from the privateer, when the galley of the refugees struck and was immediately taken possession of by Capt. Gray and sunk. The survivors of the galley's crew were received on board the privateer and from thence sent to the gaol of Burlington County. After this defeat, the refugees and Tories broke up their establishment at Clam Town...."

With the loss of their schooner and sinking of their galley, the refugees headed deeper into the pines. By now word reached the Jersey shore that the British general Cornwallis had surrendered at Yorktown. The *Civil Usage* returned to the Raritan River and, in the closing days of the war, even entered New York Harbor and captured a small British warship.

After the Revolution, Brown, now twenty-four, was discharged and settled in Manahawkin where he lived out his life as a Jersey shoreman. In 1832 the federal government accepted his request for a pension based on his sworn testimony of his wartime actions as part of the Forked River navy.

CHAPTER 13

The Last Royal Governer

W illiam Franklin was born early in 1731; the name of his mother is unknown. His father would admit only that she was one of the "low women" whom he had frequented when he was a newlywed. Benjamin Franklin brought William home to be raised by his wife, Debra. What effect being raised as the world's most famous bastard had on William can only be guessed, but Ben saw to it that his son received a good education in Philadelphia.

William served with distinction in Pennsylvania's militia, and in the 1750s when Ben traveled to London on colonial business, William accompanied him to attend Oxford University, where he passed the bar in 1758. Ben was the best known of all America's colonists, and his scientific experiments opened many a door for him and his son in London society. In fact, it was William who actually flew the famous kite.

In 1763 William was named Royal governor of the colonies of East and West Jersey, recently combined into New Jersey. He and his wife, Elizabeth, set sail for the Colonies, leaving behind William's own illegitimate child, Temple, to be raised by Ben.

Once in America, Franklin set out to deal with colonial problems. The original division of East and West Jersey was more than just a boundary line, stretching roughly from Tuckerton to High Point. It divided the colony in many other ways. East Jersey looked to New York as its port and center of culture, West looked to Philadelphia. Each had its own capital, Perth Amboy and Burlington respectively. Each distrusted and was jealous of the other. Each wanted the governor to make his residence in their section.

In February, Franklin arrived in Perth Amboy and showed himself a true politician. "I thank you for your kind congratulations," he told the city's residents. "The esteem which you so gratefully and justly express for my predecessors is no less agreeable to me. And wherever I may reside, which is as yet uncertain, I shall be glad of every opportunity of showing my regard for the City of Perth Amboy."

He then traveled south, was sworn in all over again and told the residents there the same thing about *their* town. For the next thirteen years, New Jersey had two capitals. The official governor's mansion was in Perth Amboy, but Franklin resided on a farm outside Burlington, and the Colonial Assembly alternated sites for its meetings.

This fence-sitting also was Franklin's position as the American Colonies grew restive. He had been born an American colonist and had sworn to uphold King George III. This placed Franklin in a powerful position in the years before the Revolution. While the Stamp Act and Boston Massacre brought violent reactions in other colonies, Franklin held New Jersey in line. When Jerseyans complained of Parliament's actions, he claimed to understand and, in some cases, agree. But always he argued moderation, to work within the system.

But while Jersey remained the quiet eye of the storm, events were moving quickly elsewhere. First, England answered the tea party in Boston with punishment, then closed the harbor and created other "intolerable acts." The colonists held an extralegal meeting in Philadelphia to plan a boycott and other actions.

Twelve years after William's arrival, the shots fired at Lexington and Concord were heard even in New Jersey. The Monmouth County militia, fearing British troops would enter the colony, was called out and paraded in front of Franklin's mansion as a show of force and support for the Minutemen of Massachusetts.

By 1776, rebellion had grown into revolution, and Franklin took up this challenge. He called for the Colonial Assembly to meet officially in Burlington on June 20. The rebels reacted quickly and, just days before, called a popularly elected Provincial Congress to meet in Burlington. They announced the Assembly should not meet, saying it was "in direct contempt and violation of the resolve of the Continental Congress." It was reported that "the governor had discovered himself to be an enemy to the liberties of this country, and they insisted that measures ought to be immediately taken for securing the person of the said William Franklin, Esquire."

Once the Provincial Congress made its decision, events began to move quickly. Its instructions to Colonel Nathaniel Herd read, "It is the desire of Congress that this necessary business be conducted with all the delicacy and tenderness which the nature of the business can possibly admit. For this end you will find among the papers the form of a written parole, in which there is left a blank space for you to fill up, at the choice of Mr. Franklin."

Franklin would be offered "house arrest" but "should he refuse to sign the parole, you are desired to put him under strong guard and keep him in close custody, until the further order of this congress.... We refer to your discretion what means to use for that purpose; and you have full power and authority to take to your aid whatever force you may require."

Herd arrived at the governor's mansion in Perth Amboy and showed the governor his instructions. Franklin then demanded to know "by what authority such an impertinent order had been issued."

Herd explained he was acting under orders of the Provincial Congress. Franklin argued, "To be represented as an Enemy to the liberties of my country [one of the worst characters] merely for doing my duty in calling a meeting of the legal Representatives of the People, was ... sufficient to rouse the indignation of any man not dead to human feeling."

Franklin was led to his coach and, under armed guard, escorted to Burlington, where he was to be interrogated by the Reverend John Witherspoon, president of the College of New Jersey in Princeton and a leading advocate for independence. Witherspoon questioned "Mister" Franklin who retorted that Witherspoon had no right to challenge a royal representative. Franklin also refused to be paroled on his honor, and the Congress decided he was "a virulent enemy to this country, and a person that may prove dangerous."

On June 25, Franklin was sent to Connecticut and wrote to Temple, who was living in Philadelphia with his grandfather. "I leave tomorrow morning.... I must go (I supposed) dead or alive.... If we Survive the present Storm, we may all meet and (enjoy) the Sweets of Peace with greater Relish."

Franklin would spend the next two years in various states of confinement. First, under house arrest, he was caught spying, so his quarters were changed to what he described as a "most noisome filthy Room ... the very worst gaol in America." It was reported, "The one-windowed room, situated above a tavern, was overrun with flies, lice, and rats who became the governor's sole companions during his protracted confinement."

Meanwhile, his wife had been driven from New Jersey and took refuge in New York City where she died. Franklin wrote the governor of Connecticut that she had died "of a broken heart," which he predicted would soon be his fate. Finally, in October 1778, Franklin was exchanged for the rebel governor of Delaware, John McKinly.

He then rode to New York City, which was still under British control. Here he put his affairs in order and pondered his future. As a Royal official he had remained loyal to the king. For this he had spent more than two years in prison. He could return to England and receive another post, or he could stay and live as a refugee under the protection of the British army like thousands of other loyal civilians crowded into New York.

Not being one to sit and wait, Franklin gambled on a third course: to fight. He would organize Loyalists to defeat the rebels and restore the legal government. Then he could return to his rightful place as governor of New Jersey. The risks would be great but so could the rewards from a grateful king.

And the battleground would be New Jersey.

CHAPTER 14

Atrocity at Sandy Hook

William Franklin was an ambitious man. Born Ben Franklin's bastard son, he had risen to be Royal governor of New Jersey. He had remained loyal to his king, and when New Jersey declared its independence, he was imprisoned for two years. Once released, he traveled to British-held New York City. From here he planned to mastermind the reinstatement of Royal authority.

The key to Franklin's plan was the thousands of Loyalists like himself. He was convinced that most Americans still wanted to live under the Crown, that they were simply misled by a few radicals, including his father. He was sure this silent majority, if given the chance, would rally to the king's colors and stamp out the rebellion.

Franklin proposed to British commander Sir Henry Clinton that an independent force of American Loyalists be formed. They would serve under American officers, and the organization would be totally independent of Clinton's control and under the command of an American — Franklin.

But Clinton was not the type of general to give away power. For more than a year he dragged his feet. Like most British officers, he looked down on all colonists and distrusted the Loyalists because the British could not understand how Americans could fight Americans.

Frustrated, Franklin used his political connections and went directly to King George who supported the plan and ordered Clinton to begin work with William. Slowly, there evolved what was called the Board of Associated Loyalists with Franklin at its head. Clinton, however, still held control over proposed targets and operations by limiting Franklin's access to ships.

A major disagreement between the two arose over treatment of rebel prisoners. Clinton wanted them turned over to the British army for "humane treatment," fearing that intentional mistreatment would be matched by the Americans holding British prisoners. Franklin, on the other hand, wanted prisoners captured by the Loyalists to be held by the Loyalists.

Franklin claimed that Loyalist prisoners in New Jersey were "treated with almost every Species of Cruelty ... they were malnourished, shut up in cells where the windows were opened wide, in the severity of winter, and nailed tightly shut in the summer so that there was scarcely light enough to pick off the vermin which swarm in abundance. They were beaten, tortured, and even wantonly executed without benefit of trial." Franklin wanted what he considered to be "just vengeance," a little retaliation to match atrocity for atrocity, but for most of the war, the British held the prisoners.

Clinton also severely limited the raids carried out by Franklin's men, and their effort had little effect on the war which by 1781 was going badly for the British and even worse for the Loyalists. When General Cornwallis was forced to surrender at Yorktown, some of Franklin's Loyalists were with him. In the document of surrender, Cornwallis asked that these men not be "punished for their part in the battle." George Washington summarily rejected the request, arguing that "the treatment of the loyalist forces was altogether of civil resort."

Fearing that if Britain made peace the Loyalists would be abandoned to the rebels, Franklin took matters into his own hands. He would attempt to escalate the war by forcing a major military action. Since talks had already begun between Washington and Clinton, Franklin acted quickly.

Franklin chose Toms River as his target. A small saltworks and privateer base, it was protected by a blockhouse under the command of Captain Joshua Huddy. Franklin ordered his Loyalists to attack and burn the town, which they did on March 20, 1782, capturing Huddy and two other men. The prisoners were taken to New York.

But this action didn't lead to the outcry Franklin had hoped for. Meanwhile, Loyalist Philip White was killed while trying to escape from the Freehold jail — or so the rebels said. In another attempt to escalate the war, Franklin had Huddy taken from his New York jail to Sandy Hook by Richard Lippencott, one of Franklin's men.

Huddy was told to write his will, which began, "In the name of God, amen ... I Joshua Huddy, of Middletown, in the county of Monmouth, being of sound mind and memory, but expecting shortly to depart this life, do declare this my last will and testament."

A rope was placed around his neck as he stood on a barrel, which was then kicked out from under him. As he slowly strangled, a sign approved by Franklin was pinned to Huddy's chest.

"We, the refugees, have with grief long beheld the cruel murders of our brethren, and finding nothing but such measures daily carrying into execution, we, therefore, determine not to suffer without taking vengeance for the numerous cruelties, and having made use of Captain Huddy as the first object to present to your view, and further determine to hang man for man, as long as a refugee is left existing. UP GOES HUDDY FOR PHILIP WHITE."

The people of Monmouth reacted as Franklin hoped. At a meeting in Freehold, a petition "approved by upwards of 400 respectable inhabitants of Monmouth County" was drawn up to be sent to Washington.

The petition stated, "The act of hanging any person, without any, even a pretended trial, is in itself not only disallowed by all civilized people, but it is considered as barbarous in the extreme....

"The law of nature and of Nations, points to retaliation as the only Measure which can in such cases give any degree of Security that the practice shall not become general." The citizens threatened that if Washington did not act, they "may, in vindicating themselves, open to view a scene at which humanity itself may shudder."

This was exactly what Franklin wanted: a bloodbath where the Loyalists would be forced into fighting to the last.

Washington's reaction to the petition was swift. He broke off negotiations with Clinton and demanded that he turn over for trial those guilty of the act, saying, "to save the innocent, I demand the guilty." Washington declared that if Clinton would not comply, he would choose a British officer of rank equal to Huddy's and hang him to appease Monmouth residents.

Clinton said he could never give in to all of Washington's demands, but wrote back, "When I heard of Captain Huddy's death, four days before I received your letter ... I instantly ordered a strict inquiry to be made into all its circumstances, and shall bring the perpetrators of it to an immediate trial."

Washington was not fully satisfied with the prospects of the British trying a Loyalist for hanging a rebel, so he decided to proceed with his threat to hang a British officer. He sent orders to the commander of the prisoner of war camp holding British officers captured at Yorktown to "designate, by Lot for the above purpose, a British Captain who is an unconditional Prisoner ... send him under a safe guard to Philadelphia, where the Minister of War will order a proper Guard to receive and conduct him to the Place of Destination."

As fate would have it, the unfortunate officer selected was Captain Charles Asgil, son of a former mayor of London; his mother was a friend to the royal family of France, America's major ally.

Meanwhile, the British had found their scapegoat: the man who actually hanged Huddy, Captain Richard Lippencott of the Associated Loyalists. As with most government cover-ups, Lippencott was supposed to support William Franklin's claim that he had not known anything about the execution of Huddy.

But the idea of going to the gallows for his superior did not appeal to Lippencott, who based his defense on the claim that he had been following orders. He said to the court, "I, as an Associated Loyalist, was subject to be ordered on such services as the Honorable Board of Directors should be pleased from time to time to enjoin, and to act implicitly in obedience to such orders; that I received Huddy from the Provost in virtue of an Order from that Board and disposed of him afterwards according to the meaning of my orders, as explained by several of the Members of the Board."

In his defense, Lippencott produced Samuel Blowers, a Massachusetts Loyalist and former law partner of John Adams. Blowers was secretary to Franklin and had been present when Lippencott showed Franklin the sign which ended up around Huddy's neck. Blowers testified Lippencott had handed it to Franklin, saying, " 'This is the paper we mean to take down with us' ... or words to that effect, and gave the paper to the Governor. Franklin just looked on the paper and William Stewart, discovered an inclination to look over his [Franklin's] shoulder to take it from him. William Cox hastily said, 'We have nothing to do with that paper, Captain Lippencott. Keep your papers to yourself. The Board does not wish to see them or hear them read.' or words to that purpose; the paper was then directly given back to Captain Lippencott."

Franklin then said, according to Blowers, "Will you execute [Huddy] when you take him out?" Lippencott answered, "Yes, or I couldn't have asked for him." To which Franklin replied, "Then you shall have him."

In Europe, peace talks ground to a halt as the British waited to see if Washington would hang a British officer. Not knowing his son was involved, Ben Franklin wrote to the British negotiators.

"It cannot be supposed that General Washington has the least desire of taking the life of that gentleman. His aim is to obtain the punishment, committed on a prisoner in cold blood by Captain Lippencott.... I doubt General Washington cannot well refuse what appears to them so just and necessary for their common security. I am persuaded nothing I could say to him on the occasion would have the least effect in changing his determination."

The new British commander, Sir Guy Carleton, wrote immediately to Washington. "To your excellency's cooler judgment, it is now referred to consider ... the [transcript of the] trial of Lippencott is now in your hands and you will find that he has been acquitted upon the oaths of men of rank and character, on all circumstances of the case. To show my thorough disapprobation of the execution of Huddy, I have given orders to the Judge Advocate to make further inquisition and to collect evidence for the prosecution of such other Persons as may appear to have been criminal in this Transaction."

Carleton would be forced to go after New Jersey's Royal governor or else Asgil would hang. Carleton also informed William Franklin that he would continue the investigation. Franklin knew exactly what this meant. Just as Lippencott had been the sacrifice for his superiors, Franklin was now supposed to sacrifice himself for the peace talks.

Franklin had no stomach for personal sacrifice; before he could be charged, he sailed out of New York City on a packet bound for England. Now the decision remained with Washington. Would he hang Asgil?

To make matters worse, Asgil's mother had written to the French royal family as one of nobility to another, saying, "My son (an only son) and dear as he is brave ... is now confined in America an object of retaliation! Shall an innocent suffer for the guilty?... Surrounded as I am by objects of distress; distracted with fear and grief; no words can express my feelings or paint the scene.

"Let me again supplicate your goodness, let me respectfully implore your high influence in behalf of innocence in the cause of justice."

The French government asked Congress to step in, and it finally did.

"Resolved, that the Commander-in-Chief be (notified) and he is hereby directed to set Captain Asgil at liberty."

Had Franklin gotten away with murder? Not completely. Back in England, this American colonist was never fully accepted, and the British government turned down most of his claims for financial loss.

Benjamin Franklin spoke with William only one more time. And the ever-witty Ben got the last laugh on New Jersey's ex-governor, his only living male heir, when William read the line in Ben's will which said, "The part he acted against me in the late War ... which is of public Notoriety, will account for my leaving him no more of an Estate (than) he endeavored to deprive me of."

CHAPTER 15

The Barnegat Light Massacre

Towns and cities across America proudly display and relive their histories, but in southern Ocean County the Revolutionary War has largely been forgotten. In October 1782, a chain of events started on the beach at present-day Barnegat Light and did not end until after the last battle of the American Revolution was fought in the pines of Barnegat.

For New Jersey and Ocean County (then a part of Monmouth County), the war was more than a revolution; it was also a civil war. The county was almost equally divided between the upstart American "rebels" and the Loyalists who remained true to the Crown. Many skirmishes took place between Jerseymen fighting on opposite sides. To aggravate the situation, a war brought with it opportunities for quick money. Many rebels in Ocean County turned to privateering. They would obtain a letter of marque from the Continental Congress granting them license to become legal pirates, to capture any British transport, and to keep or sell the cargo so long as Congress received a percentage of the profits.

The bays and inlets were perfect hiding places for these privateers as they preyed on transports heading for British-occupied New York or Philadelphia. Many a Jersey family's fortune began as booty of a legalized pirate.

For those who remained loyal to King George there was also a route to quick riches. While men from the rebel families were away fighting in the war or at sea on a privateer vessel, their farms were mostly unguarded. As the area was sparsely settled, it was easy to raid a farmhouse in the name of the Crown and steal everything of value. Since these pines were called the

"Jersey Desert" and were almost totally uninhabited, they became the hiding place for Loyalists known as Refugees or "pine robbers."

One of these pine robbers was Captain John Bacon, the leader of a group that ranged from Tuckerton in the southern part of the county to Toms River. Bacon was responsible for dozens of attacks on rebels in Barnegat and Forked River. It was Bacon who had shot and killed Lieutenant Joshua Studson, second-in-command of the Toms River militia when he tried to stop Bacon's boat in Barnegat Bay. That December, Bacon and his men also had attacked the Manahawkin militia at their headquarters in Reuben Randolph's tavern, chasing them all the way to West Creek.

Before the war Bacon had worked for Joseph Soper, a ship builder in Barnegat. Since Soper was an ardent rebel and member of the militia, Bacon and his men took pleasure in robbing or attacking the Soper homestead, then retreating to their headquarters, a cave in what is today Warren Grove. Many county residents, whether out of fear or a secret loyalty to the king, gave Bacon information on whose houses were unprotected and where the militia was stationed.

During a storm on the night of October 25, a cutter out of Belgium, bound for St. Thomas in the British-held Virgin Islands, was blown far off course and ran aground on the "Barnegat Shoals," about a mile south of present-day Barnegat Inlet. The next morning an American privateer out of Cape May, an armed row galley called the *Alligator,* spotted the cutter in the surf. The *Alligator,* under the command of Captain Andrew Steelman, possessed a marque that allowed her to operate from Little Egg Harbor to the mouth of the Delaware River.

Steelman's men landed on Long Beach and at once realized that the cutter was in danger of breaking up. If there was to be any prize money, Steelman and his crew had to unload the ship quickly. A messenger was sent over to the mainland and landed near Barnegat. He told the people that all able-bodied men were needed to unload the cutter, and soon several men, including Joseph Soper and his two sons, set sail for the island.

An Englishman living in Waretown by the name of Bill Wilson also heard the news of the cutter, but instead of joining the party to unload her, he got a horse and went to find Bacon.

All through the next day, Steelman and volunteers unloaded heavy barrels and boxes, struggling with them through the surf, then carrying them back across the beach to the dunes. But though the work was hard, there was a carnival-like atmosphere as these relatively poor people opened the boxes and discovered that the cargo included a quantity of Hyson tea (Chinese green tea), a commodity very rare in America since the Boston Tea Party in 1773. This would bring a good price at public auction, and the hard cash would be divided among Steelman, his crew and the local volunteers.

Even as the cutter was being unloaded, Wilson found Bacon who gathered his men. Together they boarded his boat, *Hero's Revenge*, and set sail for Long Beach.

That night, Steelman and his party slept on the beach, exhausted from the hard day's work and fortified by some of the ship's rum and their own "Jersey lightning." The party was unsuspecting. No guards had been posted because the British commander in New York City had promised to cease raids into Jersey. With no ships on the horizon, the men felt safe.

Hero's Revenge landed on the bay side of the island, and Bacon and his band quietly crossed over to the beach. In the darkness, they pounced on the unprotected rebels, hacking at the sleeping men with bayonets and swords. Muskets flashed as Bacon's men opened fire on the mostly unarmed local volunteers. Those who managed to escape the carnage ran down the beach as Steelman and his men, including one of the Soper boys, spilled their last drops of blood on the white sand of Long Beach Island. More Americans died that night on the beach than Washington lost at the famous Battle of Trenton.

The island was then such a remote area that the massacre was largely ignored. A Loyalist paper in New York reported, "A cutter from Ostend, bound to St. Thomas, ran aground on Barnegat Shoals, October 25, 1782. The American galley *Alligator,* Captain Steelman, from Cape May, with twenty-five men, plundered her on Saturday night last of a quantity of Hyson tea and other valuable articles, but was attacked on the same night by Captain John Bacon with nine men, in a small boat called the *Hero's Revenge,* who killed Steelman and wounded the first lieutenant, and all the party except four or five were either killed or wounded."

After the massacre, Bacon returned to his base at Warren Grove, but the story of John Bacon had just begun.

CHAPTER 16

Revolution Ends in The Pinelands

Historians of the American Revolution have long debated where the last skirmish of the war took place. In his two-volume pictorial field book, Benjamin J. Lossing claimed that the final engagement was fought on September 11, 1782, in Wheeling, West Virginia. Lossing was challenged by Mark M. Boatner III in his *Dictionary of the American Revolution,* which gives the honor to a skirmish on Johns Island, South Carolina, on November 4, 1782.

As with most facts dealing with the war in southern New Jersey, local history is all but forgotten. The last skirmish of the American Revolution did not take place in West Virginia or South Carolina, but in what is today Barnegat Township in Ocean County.

During the early part of the twentieth century, Route 72, running from New Lisbon to Manahawkin, was built. In most cases it followed the old road originally approved by the king of England in the 1700s. However, near its junction with Route 539, the new highway was moved about a mile farther north where the ground was drier, thus abandoning part of the original road.

On this section of dirt road there was a small settlement including a mill, a tavern and several houses known as Cedar Bridge or, sometimes, Cedar Creek for the nearby stream. Cut off from modern-day traffic and with two other locations in the county known by the same or similar names, Cedar Bridge was soon dropped from road maps and forgotten. But it was here in December 1782 that the last skirmish of the Revolution was fought.

Captain John Bacon was the leader of a group of Loyalists known as "pine robbers" or "Refugees" who made their headquarters in the pines around Cedar Bridge. From this base Bacon launched raids from Toms River to Clam Town (Tuckerton) against the families and troops of those who revolted against the king.

Following Bacon's most famous raid, the Barnegat Light Massacre in October 1782, and another raid into Burlington County, Governor William Livingston met with his advisors and offered a reward for Bacon, dead or alive. By late December, information concerning Bacon's hideout reached the Burlington County militia under the command of Colonel Israel Shreve of the Second New Jersey Regiment.

Israel decided to send his nephew, Captain Richard Shreve, with a force of six light horse and twenty infantry to deal with Bacon. They left Burlington County for the Jersey shore on Christmas Day. After several frustrating days searching for Bacon, Shreve decided to return home. As the men marched west from Manahawkin they came upon the Cedar Creek Tavern where Shreve and his men rested.

In the words of the official report, "While refreshing at a tavern near that place (Cedar Creek), Bacon and his party appeared at the Bridge." The Loyalists barricaded the bridge and prepared to fight.

Captain Shreve assembled his men and ordered his uncle, Benjamin Shreve, and the cavalry to charge the bridge. The heavy fire from the Loyalists killed one man and wounded several horses. The troops were driven back, except for Benjamin, who found himself surrounded and alone on the far side of the bridge.

In a hailstorm of musket balls, Benjamin turned his horse and escaped into the woods. In the meantime, Richard Shreve had formed his infantry and began a full-scale attack on the bridge. Bacon's men literally fought for their lives, as most would face the hangman if captured.

Just as Shreve was gaining the upper hand, the local citizens of the village grabbed their muskets and joined the battle — but on the side with Bacon and his Loyalists.

Shreve's surprised men had to halt their attack to beat back the local citizens. Seizing the opportunity, a wounded Bacon ordered his men to retreat into the pines. With the full attention of the militia now turned on the residents, the locals quickly surrendered. Angered by their action, Shreve took seven as prisoners of war and had his men search the town where they confiscated a large quantity of goods and burned several small buildings. On January 8, *The New Jersey Gazette* published the only public account of the battle:

"On Friday, the 27th, Capt. Richard Shreve, of the Burlington County Light Horse, and Captain Edward Thomas of the Mansfield Militia, having received information that John Bacon, with his banditti of robbers, was in the neighborhood of Cedar Creek ... collected a party of men and went immediately in pursuit of them. They met them at the Cedar Creek bridge. The Refugees ... had greatly the advantage of Capts. Shreve and Thomas' party ... but it was nevertheless determined to charge them.

"The onset on the part of the militia was furious, and opposed by the Refugees ... for a considerable time, several of them having been guilty of such enormous crimes as to have no expectation of mercy should they surrender. They were, nevertheless, on the point of giving way when the militia were unexpectedly fired upon from a party of the inhabitants ... who had suddenly come to Bacon's assistance. This put the militia into some confusion and gave the Refugees time to get off....

"The militia are still in pursuit of the Refugees and have taken seven of the inhabitants prisoners and are now in Burlington jail, some of whom have confessed the fact."

Bacon's escape and Cedar Bridge's spot in history would soon be forgotten as the village all but disappeared. But today, of the many historic sites of the American Revolution, Cedar Bridge remains unchanged. Time stands still as you walk the dirt road and cross the wooden bridge to stand in front of the old tavern, now a private home.

In the quiet of the pines, it is difficult to envision the battle which almost put Ocean County into every history book and tourist brochure.

CHAPTER 17

The Revolution's
Last Fatality

As spring arrived at the Jersey shore in April 1783, the people awaited another arrival. Stories and rumors about the peace negotiations in Paris ran rampant. There was a possibility that after eight long years the American Revolution would finally end. There had been no reports of fighting since the skirmish at Cedar Bridge Tavern in Barnegat in December, and it appeared that both Loyalists and rebels would quietly wait for the news of a treaty.

But some men were not quite ready for peace, among them Joel Cook of Burlington County. Cook had a personal score to settle, and if the war ended he would not be able to get revenge on his hated enemy, John Bacon.

By 1783 Bacon had become a legend at the Jersey shore, commanding a group of Loyalists known as "pine robbers." Bacon had raided and attacked the Americans from Tuckerton to Toms River. He had personally led the raid known as the Barnegat Light Massacre. He had defeated the local militia at Manahawkin and had escaped in what turned out to be the last battle of the war, in Barnegat. There, William Cook Jr. had died at Bacon's hands. Because of this, his brother, Joel, had sworn revenge.

Cook went to Captain John Stewart of Arneytown (Pemberton) to ask for his help. Cook reminded him that Governor William Livingston had declared Bacon an outlaw and was offering a reward of 50 pounds sterling for his capture. Stewart and four other men agreed to make one last attempt to take Bacon before word of the peace treaty arrived. On April 2, the party entered the Jersey pines.

The pine robber was rumored to have his headquarters in a cave near Warren Grove, but Stewart and Cook found nothing. They passed by the tavern at Cedar Creek Bridge where local citizens had chosen to fight on Bacon's side against the patriots. They entered Manahawkin and headed south, down what is today Route 9, hoping to find him in the Clam Town area (Tuckerton).

Between West Creek and Clam Town, the party came upon the house of William Rose, used occasionally as a tavern. Cook and Stewart crept up to the window. Inside, they saw Bacon sitting by himself, his musket between his knees.

Stewart entered the tavern first. Catching Bacon by surprise, Stewart pointed his musket at him and ordered him to surrender. Bacon jumped to his feet and, in the close quarters of the tavern, attempted to prime and cock his musket. Stewart, who could have fired and killed him instantly, chose instead to take him alive.

Stewart grabbed Bacon and the two men fell to the floor. Outfought, Bacon surrendered and asked for quarter. Still holding on to Bacon tightly, Stewart called Cook to join them. Cook entered the room from behind the two and ran Bacon through with his bayonet. Bacon groaned; his body grew limp and Stewart allowed it to collapse to the floor, thinking the prisoner had fainted.

Without saying a word to Stewart, Cook went outside to tell the others. Stewart was standing over Bacon when suddenly the Loyalist revived and jumped up. Stewart tried to block his escape by pushing a table in front of the door, but Bacon shoved it aside. As Stewart regained his feet, he picked up his gun and fired. The musket ball passed through Bacon, killing him instantly, then passed through the door and wounded Cook on the other side.

This account is Stewart and Cook's official explanation of why Bacon was bayoneted and shot from behind. What really happened the night of April 3 in that tavern will most likely never be known, but many witnessed what the men did with Bacon.

The body was loaded onto a flatbed wagon and placed on its back, the head hanging out over the end of the wagon. The victory party retraced its steps to Burlington County, stopping at each village to show off the prize: the infamous John Bacon. Back through the Pine Barrens which had hidden Bacon for years they traveled, finally arriving in Jacobstown. This was where the Cook family lived and was also not far from where Bacon's wife and brother resided.

During the long ride from the shore, Stewart and Cook decided on a fitting send-off for the hated Bacon. They would not lay him to rest in the holy ground of a church cemetery. Instead he would be buried under the main road of Jacobstown where the daily traffic of wagons and horses would prevent his soul from getting any peace.

As a crowd watched the road being dug up, Bacon's brother arrived. After many pleas he was able to convince the good citizens to turn the body over to him for private burial.

With this final act, the legend of John Bacon ended. Ironically, the incident probably gave him a lasting place in history. The American Revolution, which had started on the green at Lexington when the first Minutemen fell in April 1775, was quickly drawing to a close. The death of John Bacon came less than a week before news was announced of a peace treaty.

John Bacon was probably the last fatality of the war for independence.

CHAPTER 1

Princeton, New Jersey

Capital of the United States

Amerca's first official Independence Day 1783 was one of turmoil. Congress had been driven from Independence Hall by an angry mob of mutinous troops who hadn't been paid. Congress's president, Elias Boudinot, ordered that body's members to abandon Philadelphia and cross the Delaware to find a refuge in his home state, New Jersey.

The prestige of the U.S. Congress was at a new low point. Part of the army had mutinied because Congress was broke and did not have the power to tax. At the end of the war, troops had been paid with IOUs rather than money. When they mobbed Independence Hall, Pennsylvania refused Boudinot's plea for protection.

With Congress run out of town, John Dickinson, president of Pennsylvania, called out the state militia and promptly put down the revolt. The problems centered around a single overriding issue: Would America be thirteen independent countries or a single united one?

Many in Philadelphia rejoiced at Congress's flight. One local paper wrote, "The grand Sanhedrin [supreme council] of the nation, with all their solemnity and emptiness, have removed to Princeton and left a state where their wisdom has long been questioned, their virtue suspected, and their dignity a jest."

The *Philadelphia Gazetteer* ran the following: "The honorable Congress of the United States of America, having been for eight years past resolving and resolving, did, on Tuesday last, without their usual mature deliberation, hastily resolve to exchange their old sitting place for the more salubrious air of Princeton in the state of New Jersey.... Though the citizens of Philadelphia do not regret the loss of Congress, yet they are sorry better reasons were not assigned for their removal. The late Congressional proceedings exhibit neither dignity, fortitude, nor perseverance."

After the hasty adjournment, Congress planned to meet again in either Trenton or Princeton. How it was received once it entered New Jersey might hold the key for the future of a united government. On June 24, Trentonians met at the French Arms Tavern to decide what to do when Congress arrived. That night, the residents made their choice:

"Resolved unanimously, that we consider the support of Civil Government and the majesty of the Laws as among the first of Social duties, and riotous Citizens who disturb the public order and violated the dignity of the Union as the worst of Enemies.

"Resolved unanimously that we would deem ourselves highly honored by the presence of Congress, and by an opportunity of testifying our zeal in support of their Dignity and Priviledges, should they in their wisdom think proper to adjourn to or fix their Residence in this State."

But Trenton would not become the capital. Instead, a smaller village a few miles away would receive the honor. Princeton was a town familiar to many from Congress; no fewer than seven of its members had attended college there. Boudinot had lived there as a boy and had married Hannah Stockton, sister to Richard Stockton, whose house was called "Morven." This would become the presidential residence. Finally, Congress received several generous offers from Colonel George Morgan, whose two hundred-acre farm was a model for the times.

"Colonel Morgan presents his most respectful Compliments to his Excellency the President of Congress, and begs leave, through him, to offer to Congress the Use of several Buildings, on their own Terms, during their Stay at Princeton ... Any or every part of his Farm and meadows shall also be at their Command."

The second offer came from the town's college. "The governors and masters of the college, happy in an opportunity of paying to the Congress of the United States their profoundest and sincerest honours, beg leave to offer ... If the Hall, or the library room, can be made of any service to Congress as places in which to hold their Sessions, or for any other purpose, we pray that they would accept of them during their continuance in this place."

Finally, on June 26, the people of Princeton met and decided the future of the little village. "The inhabitants of Princeton and its Vicinity, being informed that gross Indignities have been offered to Congress by a number of People in Arms in Philadelphia, do resolve unanimously ... That we do with the utmost Cheerfullness pledge our Lives & Fortunes to the Government under which we live for the Protection of Congress in whatever way our Services may be required, whether in resisting Foreign Invasions or in quelling [internal] tumults. That we esteem ourselves highly honor'd by the Confidence of Congress in the Choice of the Town as the Place of their Residence, and we take the Earliest Opportunity to testify our Zeal to Support of their Dignity and Privileges, and that we will use our utmost exertions for their comfortable Accommodation ... Signed on behalf of the inhabitants of Princeton and its neighbourhood...."

For the next several weeks, Princeton was the United States capital, and General Washington moved his headquarters to nearby Rocky Hill.

The morning of August 26 dawned warm and humid but Washington awoke perspiring for another reason: That day he would fight a personal battle which would take more courage than crossing the Delaware. He would stand before Congress and give a speech.

Around eleven o'clock, Washington mounted his favorite horse, a roan gelding — reddish; he seldom rode a white horse — with its old saddle and distinctive saddlecloth, "buff and blue with a flowered pattern," and at the head of thirteen dragoons started down the dusty road toward the College of New Jersey (Princeton University).

The little village had a festive atmosphere. People had come from Philadelphia and New Brunswick to see the great event, and each stagecoach brought more visitors. Local farmers had brought their children to catch a glimpse of the great hero. Outside Nassau Hall where Congress met, the college students in their black gowns lined the walkway to see a living legend.

Inside, the gallery was filled with important visitors. The floor was reserved for

To replace the picture of King George III destroyed during the Battle of Princeton, the College ordered the portrait of George Washington painted and hung in Nassau Hall to commemorate the building's use as the Capitol of the United States.

Congress. In the front sat the president of the United States, Elias Boudinot, wearing his hat as a sign of the superiority of civilian government over military. To his right was an empty chair for the general. Over the chair was a massive, gilded, empty picture frame which had once held a full-length portrait of George III. The painting had been torn away by a cannon ball when Washington's men attacked the building in January 1777.

Congress could tell the general was approaching by the cheers of the crowd outside. As the clock struck noon, the general and two members of Congress entered and proceeded to the president's chair.

In the room were the signs of a changing America. Many of the older members had signed the Declaration of Independence; many of the younger would write and sign the Constitution. Two future presidents also sat in the room.

Boudinot, remaining seated in another sign of civilian superiority, read a message carefully worded and approved by Congress.

By His EXCELLENCY

Elias Boudinot, Efquire,

Prefident of the United States in Congrefs Affembled.

A PROCLAMATION.

WHEREAS a body of armed Soldiers in the fervice of the United States, and quartered in the Barracks of this City, having mutinoufly renounced their obedience to their Officers, did, on Saturday the Twenty-Firft Day of this inftant, proceed, under the direction of their Serjeants, in a hoftile and threatning manner, to the Place in which Congrefs were affembled, and did furround the fame with Guards: And whereas Congrefs in confequence thereof, did on the fame Day, refolve, " That the Prefident and Supreme Executive Council of this State " fhould be informed, that the authority of the United States having been, that Day, grofly infulted by the " diforderly and menacing appearance of a body of armed Soldiers, about the Place within which Congrefs were affem- " bled; and that the Peace of this City being endangered by the mutinous Difpofition of the faid Troops then in the " Barracks; it was, in the Opinion of Congrefs, neceffary, that effectual Meafures fhould be immediately taken for " fupporting the public Authority:" And alfo whereas Congrefs did at the fame Time appoint a Committee to con- fer with the faid Prefident and Supreme Executive Council on the practicability of carrying the faid Refolution in o due effect: And alfo whereas the faid Committee have reported to me, that they have not received fatisfactory Affurances for expecting adequate and prompt exertions of this State for fupporting the Dignity of the foederal Government: And alfo whereas the faid Soldiers ftill continue in a ftate of open Mutiny and Revolt, fo that the Dignity and Authority of the United States would be conftantly expofed to a repetition of Infult, while Congrefs fhall continue to fit in this City, I do therefore, by and with the Advice of the faid Committee, and according to the Powers and Authorities in me veft- ed for this Purpofe, hereby fummon the honourable the Delegates compofing the Congrefs of the United States, and every of them, to meet in Congrefs on Thurfday the Twenty Sixth Day of June inftant, at Princeton, in the ftate of New-Jerfey, in order that further and more effectual Meafures may be taken for fuppreffing the prefent Revolt, and maintaining the Dignity and Authority of the United States, of which all Officers of the United States, civil and military, and all others whom it may concern, are defired to take Notice and govern themfelves accordingly.

GIVEN under my Hand and Seal at Philadelphia, in the ftate of Pennfylvania, this Twenty-Fourth Day of June, in the Year of Our Lord One Thoufand Seven Hundred and Eighty-Three, and of the Sovereignty and Inde-pendence, the feventh.

ELIAS BOUDINOT.

Atteft.

SAMUEL STERETT, Private Secretary.

National Archives

The proclamation, signed by the president of the Continental Congress, saved the U.S. government by moving it from Philadelphia to the safety of Princeton, New Jersey.

"It has been the singular happiness of the United States that during a war so long, so dangerous and so important Providence has been graciously pleased to preserve the life of a general who has merited and possessed the uninterrupted confidence and affection of his fellow citizens.

"Hostilities have now ceased, but your Country still needs your services. She wishes to avail herself of your talents in forming the arrangement which will be necessary for her in time of peace."

George Washington, the general who showed little fear in battle, hated large groups of people. He had trouble speaking in public because he had no teeth and was embarrassed about being tall, but he carefully read:

63

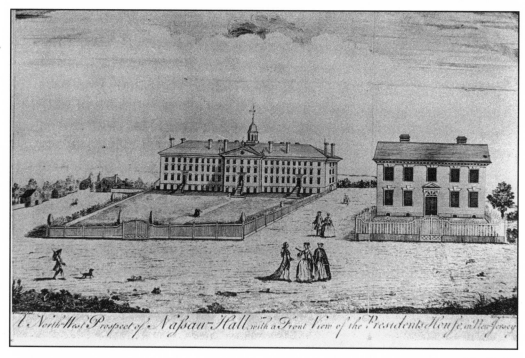

Nassau Hall, seedbed of the Reverend John Witherspoon's revolutionary ideas, was the last refuge of the British troops in January 1777.

"Notwithstanding Congress appears to estimate the value of my life beyond any services I have been able to render the United States.... I cannot hesitate to contribute my best endeavors towards the establishment of the national security in whatever manner the Sovereign power may think proper to direct, until the ratification of the definitive treaty of peace, or the final evacuation of our country by the British forces; after either of which events, I shall ask permission to retire to the peaceful shade of private life.

"Perhaps, sir, no occasion may offer more suitable than the present to express my humble thanks to God and my grateful acknowledgments to my country for the great and uniform support I have received in every vicissitude of fortune and for the many distinguished honors which Congress have been pleased to confer upon me in the course of the war."

Washington did not mention the problems Congress had caused him over the years, nothing about men starving for want of supplies, nothing about attempts by members of Congress to have him relieved of his command. He would not mention any of these things because all he wanted to do was to retire to Mount Vernon and live out his days watching the Potomac and farming. Never again did he want to have to deal with politicians or give a speech.

The people of Princeton celebrated long into the night, but the spotlight of history, which since 1776 had shown so brightly on New Jersey, was soon to be turned off. The curtain was about to be drawn and the main characters ready to go home.

After weeks of excitement caused by visits from important people and the gossip created by the debates inside Nassau Hall, all was now replaced with goodbyes. Boudinot, having completed his term, said farewell to his sister and left Morven for Elizabeth. James Madison packed his papers and prepared to move to Annapolis, the new seat of government. In those papers were the planned changes for the government suggested by Alexander Hamilton, changes which eventually became the United States Constitution.

Thomas Jefferson, the newest member of Congress, had just arrived from Virginia and hadn't even unpacked. On November 10, he complained to a friend, "I arrived at this place, not hearing till I had almost reached it that Congress had determined to remove for a time to Annapolis. Being engaged in some necessary business and knowing that the first day of the new Congress at Princetown would be emploied in chusing their president and other formalities of no public consequence, I did not join them there till the second day, and that evening they adjourned from that place; so that I have had and shall have the trouble of travelling near 400 miles more than would have been necessary...."

Even Charles Thompson, the secretary of Congress, was packing. All the records of the Princeton session were loaded onto wagons for the rough journey over dirt roads to Maryland. Among the papers was a document that had been in Princeton since July, the Declaration of Independence. But the College of New Jersey would have a reminder of its days of importance.

The board of trustees, in thanking General Washington for his attendance at commencement and his role in winning the Revolution, voted to honor him by having his portrait painted. The trustees "ordered that his portrait, when finished be placed in the hall of the college in the room of the picture of the late king of Great Britain, which was torn away by a ball from the American artillery in the battle of Princeton."

Four miles outside of Princeton, George Washington was also packing, but he was going north. He had one last job to do before laying down his sword and becoming a gentleman farmer. He would ride to West Point to monitor the activities of the last British troops in America. They still held New York City proper and Paulus Hook in New Jersey.

Washington was negotiating with British Commander Sir Guy Carlton about the evacuation and planned to enter the city with the remainder of the Continental Army as soon as the last redcoat set foot aboard ship.

Meanwhile, Washington sent his important papers south to Virginia with his wife, Martha. Then the general said goodbye to his "Patsy" and promised to try to be home by Christmas. He mounted and, with his escort of dragoons, rode to the final act of the drama.

Everywhere he passed, people turned out to wave, and each night brought dinners with comrades, followed by thank yous and farewells. As he rode through New Jersey, his attention turned to the citizen soldiers of the state who had served him time and time again.

"Gentlemen: I thank you for polite attention you pay to me in your address and for the affectionate anxiety you express for my happiness," he said as he addressed militiamen in Somerset County.

"With a heart deeply impressed by the happy issue of a long and painful contest I most cordially participate with you in the general Joy and earnestly join my wishes with yours for the future prosperity and happiness of our Country. The repeated proofs of unabated valour and perseverance which I have been witness to in the officers and Militia of the County of Somerset demanded from me the acknowledgements which, for the last time, I have now the honor of making you, and as your Zeal in the field and in the services of your Country cannot fail to endear you to your fellow Citizens. It is with much pleasure that in taking my final leave of you I can with the purest sincerity add this last testimony in your favor."

Congress was in Maryland, and New Jersey returned to its sleepy prewar quiet.

By mid-November Washington was encamped at West Point with only two objectives left in his military career: to get the last redcoat out of New York and New Jersey and to be home by Christmas.

CHAPTER 2

Washington Lingers in New Jersey

As Washington crossed the Hudson River on December 4, 1783, after saying an emotional goodbye to his officers at the tavern of Samuel Fraunce, he must have looked forward to his future retirement with pleasure and satisfaction. In addition, he must have thought of his promise to his wife, Martha, to spend their first Christmas together in eight years at Mount Vernon.

Considering the roads of eighteenth century America and the unpredictable December weather, Washington's travel plan was an ambitious one. He would stop in Philadelphia to present his expense accounts to United States Secretary of Finance Robert Morris. (Washington had served for eight years without pay, but he expected the government to reimburse him for his expenses.) From Philadelphia, he would ride to Annapolis, Maryland, where Congress was meeting, to hand in his resignation and then, finally, home to Mount Vernon.

As the general rode across New Jersey for what he thought was the last time, he was cheered by citizens in each town. When he reached Trenton on the sixth, he found waiting for him an address from Governor William Livingston and the General Assembly thanking him for his service to the state.

New Jersey had become a second home for Washington. He had fought more battles on its soil than anywhere else over the past eight years. He had spent more time in New Jersey than in any other state. Washington could not just accept the thanks of the people of New Jersey and ride off. He would stop long enough to say farewell to his adopted home.

In Trenton, the site of what many historians call the most important battle of American history, Washington told the Assembly, "Gentlemen: I want for Words to express the heart-felt pleasure I experience on receiving the congratulations and plaudit of so respectable a Body, as the Legislature of the State of New Jersey. I cannot however suppress the effusions of my gratitude for their faltering allusion to an event which hath signalized the name of Trenton; for the delicate manner of their recalling to mind none but grateful ideas; as well as for all their former assistance at the period of our deepest distress.

"I am heartily disposed to join with you, Gentlemen, in adoration to that all wise and most gracious Providence which hath so conspicuously interposed in the direction of our publick affairs and the establishment of our national Independence."

He spoke of the people of the state who had been overrun by the enemy only to rally and drive the invader from their home. "The faithful page of History, will I doubt not, record all the patriotic sufferings and meritorious Services of the gallant little Army I have had the honor to command; nor, (if my testimony and the voice of truth can avail anything), shall the efficacious exertions of the State of New Jersey, or the almost unrivalled bravery of its Militia ever be forgotten...."

"For me, it is enough to have seen the divine Arm visibly outstretched for our deliverance ... but for my gallant Associates in the Field, who have so essentially contributed to the establishment of our Independence and national glory, no rewards can be too great.

"I am now to bid you a long farewell, and to recommend, you Gentlemen, and the State whose welfare you are appointed to superintend, to the indulgent care of Heaven. May unanimity and wisdom ever prevail in your public councils! May Justice and liberality distinguish the Administration of your Government! and may the Citizens of New Jersey be completely happy in the practice of Industry, economy and every private Virtue."

After this formal farewell, Washington still did not hasten to leave. He remained to say personal goodbyes to many people he had come to know during the war. Finally, at noon on the eighth, he boarded the ferry to cross the Delaware to Philadelphia. On the river once again, his mind must have echoed with the words of Lord Cornwallis, who, after Washington captured him at the Battle of Yorktown in Virginia, had been asked if Yorktown was Washington's greatest victory. Cornwallis turned to Washington and said, "When the part that your Excellency has borne in the long and laborious contest becomes a matter of history, fame will gather your brightest laurels rather from the banks of the Delaware than those of the Chesapeake."

For Washington, New Jersey would always remain a special place, whether it was to recommend Princeton to a stepson or to write Jack Laird for the recipe to make "Jersey lightning." The general would never forget the "Jerseys" nor would the Jersey people forget him.

CHAPTER 3

Slavery Hangs on the Vote Of One Man

O ne favorite discussion question among historians is "Could the Civil War have been prevented?" For those who say yes, it becomes a search to find out who failed: Whose mistake sentenced a nation to be torn apart? Just after the American Revolution, there seems to have been one brief moment when the abolition of slavery was possible. The people at that particular time, it appears, were open to reform and experimentation.

It was during this period that most of the Northern states passed laws ending slavery outright or favoring a gradual emancipation over a period of years. In the South, it was before the rise of King Cotton when plantation owners were more willing to listen to moral arguments against slavery if their financial losses were small.

It was during this time that the national government attempted to limit slavery. The first government for the United States was established under the Articles of Confederation. The government was run by the thirteen states in Congress, each receiving a single vote. To pass a law took nine votes.

From the nation's beginnings, one of the biggest obstacles to unity was the land west of the Appalachian Mountains. The former colonies had many land claims which overlapped and threatened to divide the newly united states. Finally, a compromise was worked out. All western land would be ceded to the national government. The 1780 agreement stated that all land ceded "by any particular states ... shall be disposed of for the common benefit of the United

States, and be settled and formed into distinct republican States ... with the same rights of sovereignty, freedom and independence, as the other States."

During the winter of 1784, a congressional committee headed by Thomas Jefferson met in the nation's capital at Annapolis, Maryland, to draw up a resolution to deal with this new land. It would be divided into territories with names like Michigania and Illinoia as well as Saratoga, Polypotamia and Pelisipia. When the territories had a certain number of voting males, they could form a temporary government and finally petition Congress to become a state and a voting member. In an age of empires and colonies, the idea of creating equal states was unique.

The report continued: "Provided that both the temporary and permanent Governments be established on these principles as their basis, 1. That they shall forever remain a part of the United States of America. 2. That in their persons, property and territory they shall be subject to the Government of the United States in Congress assembled and to the articles of confederation in all those cases in which the original states shall be so subject."

Jefferson was a Virginia slave owner who had written repeatedly that the institution was wrong in an age of reason. Now would be the chance for the new country to take a stand to right a wrong. The resolution also read, "That after the year 1800 of the Christian era, there shall be neither slavery nor involuntary servitude in any of the said states, otherwise than in punishment of crimes, whereof the party shall have been duly convicted to have been personally guilty."

This would mean that slavery would never move west of the coastal states, and what would become Tennessee, Kentucky, Alabama and Mississippi would never know slavery. Now all Jefferson had to do was win the support of nine states, no easy matter since only eleven states had sent representatives to Annapolis.

For several days there was heated debate, but one by one the members were brought around, all but South Carolina and Maryland.

One of the votes Jefferson counted on was that of New Jersey's representative, John Beatty, a thirty-four-year-old doctor from Princeton. Beatty had graduated from the College of New Jersey in 1769 and served in the Revolution. He had been captured by the British, released in a prisoner exchange and eventually commissioned as a colonel. The day of the key vote on the slave issue, Beatty was ill and could not reach the Capitol. The vote was called. Eight to abolish slavery in the western lands, two nays and Beatty absent.

"The voice of a single individual ... would have prevented this abominable crime from spreading itself over the new country," wrote Jefferson. "Thus we see the fate of millions unborn hanging on the tongue of one man, and Heaven was silent in that awful moment."

Jefferson knew the chance to end the curse might never come again.

"What a stupendous, what an incomprehensible machine is man! Who can endure toil, famine, imprisonment or death itself in vindication of his own liberty, and the next moment be deaf to all those motives whose power supported him thro' his trial, and inflict on his fellow men a bondage, one hour of which is fraught with more misery than ages of that which he rose in rebellion to oppose."

The failure to act frightened Jefferson who speculated on the future of slavery.

"When the measure of their tears shall be full, when their groans shall have involved heaven itself in darkness, doubtless a god of justice will awaken to their distress, and by diffusing light and liberality among their oppressors, or at length by his exterminating thunder, manifest his attention to the things of this world."

If Beatty hadn't gotten sick, could the nation have avoided the thunder of the Civil War? One man, one vote. If only...

CHAPTER 4

Fighting to Be Heard:

David vs. Goliath

As June 1787 began, hopes were high for the men of the larger states, especially James Wilson of Pennsylvania and James Madison of Virginia. Early victories during the Constitutional Convention had given them a sense of destiny. The big states, they believed, were an unstoppable force that would roll on to create a government which would suit them best. In an early vote, they had won a victory when the convention voted to virtually scrap the Articles of Confederation which defined the powers of the United States government and to consider instead a proposal known as the "Virginia Plan."

Under this plan, the government would have legislative, executive and judicial branches, but all powers would rest with the legislative branch which would elect members of the executive branch and appoint judges. The legislative branch was the key, and it would consist of two houses. Members of the upper house would be elected by members of the lower, while membership in the lower would be based on population. Thus, the large states would have the most power in the lower house, which would be responsible for everything. The lower house would even be able to veto state laws and make war on a state!

Tiny Rhode Island refused to attend the convention. For New Jersey and Delaware, the threat of the Virginia Plan also was real. If the plan was put into effect, their role in national politics would be nil, and they would not even be able to run their own states without permission from the big states.

William Paterson, attorney general of New Jersey, and David Brearley, chief justice of the state supreme court, bided their time, waiting to make a stand. They would have to pick the issue carefully. It would be a gamble, with the fate of New Jersey hanging in the balance.

Silence from New Jersey's delegates led men like Wilson and Madison to become overconfident. During debates on the individual points of the Virginia Plan, the vote always went in their favor. On the question of the executive branch, Wilson favored a vigorous election of one man. Finally, it was agreed that there would be a single president who would be paid for his seven-year term.

Starting on the fifth, there was a ray of hope that the onslaught could be stopped. On that day one of the few men recognized as a national leader, Governor William Livingston of New Jersey, took his seat in the convention. He had attended the First and Second Continental congresses. He had been New Jersey's wartime governor and had led the state since the Revolution. He at once began to meet with Paterson, Brearley and William Churchill Houston, who was dying of tuberculosis but who came to the convention so New Jersey could have a quorum. Now the preparations for a counterattack began.

On the seventh the first challenge came. John Dickinson of Delaware proposed that the upper house of the legislature be chosen by the state legislatures. The big states attacked the plan as "unjust to the people" but finally gave in, reasoning that if Delaware got one vote, Virginia and Pennsylvania would each have thirty.

To the Jersey delegation, this was a clear and present danger. On the ninth, Judge Brearley rose to speak to find out if the larger states wanted to join the Union or ruin it. Brearley argued that while representation based on population seemed just, in reality it was a plot of subjugation. "The large states — Massachusetts, Pennsylvania and Virginia — will carry everything before them. Virginia with her sixteen votes will be a solid column indeed, a formidable phalanx, while Georgia with her solitary vote and the other little states will be obliged to throw themselves constantly into the scale of some large one in order to have any weight at all."

The large states argued for the will of the people and fairness to the majority. Brearley countered that if the large states were so interested in fairness to the people, then there was a solution. "One only, that a map of the United States be spread out, that all the existing boundaries be erased and that a new partition of the whole be made in thirteen equal parts."

Powerful men from Virginia and Pennsylvania were not ready for a proposal that fair. Jersey's Paterson then drew the line the convention must not cross. "I therefore declare," Paterson stated, "that I will never consent to the present system, and I shall make all the interest against it in the state which I represent that I can. Myself or my state will never submit to tyranny or despotism!"

Wilson retorted, "Shall New Jersey have the same right or council in the nation with Pennsylvania? I say no! It is unjust — I never will confederate on this plan. The gentleman from New Jersey is candid in declaring his opinion. I commend him for it. I am equally so. I say again I never will confederate on his principles. If no state will part with any of its sovereignty, it is in vain to talk of a national government."

By the fourteenth, the Virginia Plan had rolled over the opposition and, virtually unchanged, was posted for a final vote. Paterson rose, seizing the floor first, and stated "that it was the wish of several deputations, particularly that of New Jersey, that further time might be allowed them to contemplate the plan reported from the Committee of the Whole, and to digest one purely federal, and contradistinguished from the reported plan." He said they hoped to have "such a one ready by tomorrow to be laid before the Convention; and the Convention adjourned that leisure might be given for the purpose."

As the Jerseymen met that night, they knew that they could never get their proposals through the convention. But if they presented a counterplan to Virginia's which contained their principal point of protecting New Jersey's place in the family of states, then maybe a compromise could be worked out.

The next day, Paterson read his plan to the convention. It began, "Resolved, that the Articles of Confederation ought to be so revised, corrected and enlarged, as to render the federal Constitution adequate to the exigencies of Government, and the preservation of the Union."

In effect, Paterson's New Jersey Plan would strengthen the Articles of Confederation but would make some major changes. A three-branch government would be made up of the legislative, executive and judicial sectors. The latter two would be represented by members chosen by Congress. The key provision was that representation in Congress would be equal — one vote for each state. Finally, the Constitution would be the supreme law of the land dealing with national matters, but the states themselves would be responsible for enacting laws dealing with matters strictly local in nature.

In fact, the New Jersey Plan was a hodgepodge of ideas from many delegates. To win their support, Paterson had added any proposal. His plan was to use them all as trading chips — with one exception. In the national legislature, New Jersey must stand equal with any other state. On this point he would not budge.

The next day the debate began in earnest. John Lansing of New York struck at the heart of the issue after both plans were heard, the Virginia Plan being read by Edmund Randolph.

"Mr. Paterson's plan," Lansing said fervently, "sustains the sovereignty of the respective states, that of Mr. Randolph destroys it." Not only had the convention no power to propose or discuss Randolph's plan, but it was improbable the states would ratify it, Lansing said. "The scheme is itself totally novel. There is no parallel to it to be found. The one plan was federal, the other national. The states will never sacrifice their essential right to a national government. Had New York suspected a consolidation of the states and the formation of a national government, she would never have sent delegates to this Convention."

Paterson attacked representation by population. "If the Confederacy was radically wrong," he began, "let us return to our states and obtain larger powers, not assume them of ourselves....

We have no power to vary the ideal of equal sovereignty. The only expedient that will cure the difficulty is that of throwing the states into hotchpot. Let it be tried and we shall see whether the citizens of Massachusetts, Pennsylvania and Virginia accede to it."

The debate became heated as Wilson of Pennsylvania shot back, "Why should a national government be unpopular? Has it less dignity? Will each citizen enjoy under it less liberty or protection? Will a citizen of Delaware be degraded by becoming a citizen of the United States?"

Randolph ended the meeting saying that the Virginia Plan was the last chance to form a national government. It would be now or never!

On June 18, a delegate from New York rose to speak for the first time. He was thirty-two years old and already nationally known. To John Adams, he was "that bastard brat of a Scotch peddler." He was either loved or hated; there was no middle ground with Alexander Hamilton. The speech Hamilton delivered that hot Monday would last five hours. For Paterson and the other small states men, the speech showed just how far some delegates were willing to go to form a "strong" national government.

Hamilton proposed having a single executive, chosen for life by electors and given the power of absolute veto. "And why should we fear an elective monarch for life more than one for seven years?" he asked. "Were not the governors of the states elective monarchs? The monarch must have proportional strength.... He ought to be hereditary and to have so much power that it will not be his interest to risk much to acquire more. The advantage of a monarch is this — he is above corruption. He must always intend, in respect to foreign nations, the true interest and glory of the people."

He finished with: "But the people ... begin to be tired of an excess of democracy. And what even is the Virginia Plan but democracy, or pork still with a little change of the sauce?"

The next day, the New Jersey Plan came to the floor for a vote. As the debate raged, James Madison pointed out the heart of the issue.

"The great difficulty lies in the affair of Representation; and if this could be adjusted, all others would be surmountable. It was admitted by both the gentlemen from New Jersey [Brearley and Paterson] that it would not be just to allow Virginia, which was 16 times as large as Delaware, an equal vote only. Their language was that it would not be safe for Delaware to allow Virginia 16 times as many votes."

But Madison was not ready for a compromise, not even when John Dickinson told him, "You see the consequence of pushing things too far. Some of the members from the small States wish for two branches in the General Legislature, and are friends to a good National Government; but we would sooner submit to a foreign power, than submit to be deprived of an equality of suffrage, in both branches of the legislature, and thereby be thrown under the domination of the large States."

Finally, the New Jersey Plan was put to the test with the motion to drop it and keep the Virginia Plan. Massachusetts, "Aye." Connecticut, "Aye." New York, "Nay." New Jersey, "Nay." Pennsylvania, "Aye." The final vote: seven ayes, three nays. Maryland was divided, and New Hampshire and Rhode Island were not present. The Virginia Plan had won. The big states could rejoice. The vote had been decisive. Now Paterson and the Jersey delegation were supposed to take their subservient positions at the feet of the big states. But only a few could see that Paterson was down but not out, or as one delegate from Massachusetts grudgingly wrote, "New Jersey was almost as real a political entity to Jerseyites as was Virginia to Virginians."

The small state delegates now tried to propose a compromise. They suggested that membership in the lower house be based on population, and the states be given equal representation in the upper house. But the larger states would not hear of a compromise. They had won and believed everything should go their way.

Nathaniel Gorham of Massachusetts even suggested that Delaware be annexed to Pennsylvania and New Jersey split between New York and Pennsylvania. Once again, for New Jersey, it would either be submit and lose its identity to its giant neighbors, or fight. The Jersey delegation of Paterson, Livingston, Brearley, and the youngest member at the convention, twenty-six-year-old Jonathan Dayton, decided to fight the giants. It would be David versus Goliath.

For the next several days New Jersey waited to take up the issue. Meanwhile, progress was made in other areas, and the new government began to take shape. There would be a two-house legislature. Members of the lower house would be elected by the people, and members of the upper house would be elected by the state legislatures. (United States senators were not elected by the people until 1913.) This would keep the "common people" from having too much influence. Terms of office were set at two and six years, respectively. Underneath all this was the ticking bomb, and on June 27 it exploded when John Rutledge of South Carolina rose and called for representation of the upper house to be based on population. "Resolved that the right of suffrage in the first branch of the national Legislature ought not to be according to the rule established in the Articles of Confederation."

The battle erupted. Luther Martin of Maryland, who had been born in New Jersey and graduated from Princeton in 1766, seized the floor. He was known as a hard drinker and an energetic speaker, and here he proved it with a violent three-hour attack on the big states.

Paterson summed up the speech in a few lines: Under the present government, New Jersey had one-thirteenth of the vote in Congress. *She was a force.* If the Virginia Plan passed, the state would "sink to nothing." Dayton sparked more heated debate when he proposed to strike the word "not" from the resolution so that each state would have an equal vote.

Now from the floor, men spoke angrily. Threats were made. The convention was on the verge of collapse. Finally, Benjamin Franklin suggested asking for spiritual guidance. "Mr. President ... we have not hitherto once thought of humbly applying to the Father of Lights to illuminate our understandings? In the beginning of the contest with Great Britain, when we were sensible of danger, we had daily prayer in this room for the divine protection. Our prayers, Sir, were heard, and they were graciously answered.... God governs in the affairs of men. And if a sparrow cannot fall to the ground without his notice, is it probable that an empire can rise without his aid?"

Franklin's motion was seconded but defeated. The convention had no money to pay a minister, and delegates feared that people outside might discover how badly things were going inside. Dayton's proposal was postponed until the next session.

On the twenty-ninth, more debates. Dayton's motion was defeated, 6-4. Then, by the same vote, the motion to base representation on population in the lower house passed. The small states men had only one shot left, the upper house. Now was the time to try anything.

The following day, Brearley rose and proposed that Washington write to New Hampshire, a small state whose delegation had not arrived, urging them to hurry up. Paterson seconded, but the larger states defeated the motion. According to Madison, "It was well understood that the object was to add New Hampshire to the number of states opposed to the doctrine of proportional representation, which it was presumed from her relative size she must be adverse to."

Defeated again, Connecticut's Oliver Ellsworth, Princeton 1766, now proposed equal representation in the upper house. The debate raged all over again. Benjamin Franklin tried to compromise. "When a broad table is to be made, and the edges (of planks do not fit), the artist takes a little from both, and makes a good joint. In like manner, here both sides must part with some of their demands, in order that they may join in some accommodating proposition."

The large states refused. By July 2, Ellsworth's motion for equal representation ended in a tie 5-5 vote. Madison and the large states seemed to have won, but the tide was turning. From South Carolina came a proposal to appoint a committee to look into the matter and propose a compromise.

Finally, the constant battling started to have its effect. Some delegates, like Abraham Baldwin of Georgia, began to sympathize with the small states and decided they did deserve some representation.

The small states' supporters saw a chance when they noticed that Daniel Jenifer of Maryland was late for the session. Oliver Ellsworth called an immediate vote, starting with the Northern states.

They voted. Rhode Island and New Hampshire were not present: Pennsylvania, nay; New Jersey, aye; Virginia, nay; Maryland, aye. When it got to Georgia, the vote was 5-5. Baldwin now switched, splitting the Georgia vote and making the tally five ayes, five nays and one divided.

Because of this, a committee was formed to work out a compromise while the convention adjourned for Independence Day. The committee included Paterson, Ellsworth and Baldwin along with Franklin and others.

On July 5 the convention reconvened and the committee issued the following: "On condition that both shall be generally adopted, the substance of these proposals: 1. That in the first branch each state should have one representative for every 40,000 inhabitants, counting three-fifths of the slaves, and that money bills should originate in the first branch and should not be amended by the second branch. 2. That in the second branch each state should have an equal vote."

The three-fifths fraction was already being used by the Congress and caused little debate. It was the second part which again opened the wounds. Over the next days the debate grew hotter, and with the temperature, tempers rose. Gouverneur Morris of Pennsylvania addressed the Jersey delegation.

"Let us suppose that the larger States shall agree; and that the small refuse; and let us trace the consequences," he said. "The opponents of the system in the smaller states will no doubt make a party, and a noise for a time, but the ties of interest, of kindred and of common habits which connect them with the other States will be too strong to be easily broken." In New Jersey particularly he was sure a great many would follow the sentiments of Pennsylvania and New York. "This country must be united. If persuasion does not unite it, sword will.... The scenes of horror attending civil commotion cannot be described, and the conclusion of them will be worse than the term of their continuance. The stronger party will then make traytors of the weaker; and the Gallows and halter will finish the work of the Sword."

Earlier, Gunning Bedford had gone to the extreme in the other direction when the Delaware delegate, another Princeton graduate, said to the large states, "I do not, gentlemen, trust you.... Will you crush the smaller states, or must they be left unmolested? Sooner than be ruined, there are foreign powers who will take us by the hand. I say not this to threaten or intimidate, but that we should reflect seriously before we act."

It now became a battle of wills between Madison and Paterson. Each looked for weaknesses in the other's argument, then attacked like a shark. On July 9, Paterson went after Virginia. If Virginia wanted things based on population, fine, but the state's slaves should not count.

By the tenth the entire New York delegation went home. Luther Martin wrote, "We were on the verge of dissolution ... scarce held together by the strength of an hair...."

A friend wrote of George Washington, "The look on his face ... reminded me of its expression during the terrible months we were in Valley Forge Camp."

The crisis was real. Anything could happen.

On Monday morning, July 16, each side filed into the State House in Philadelphia. Seven weeks of arguing had brought them to this point. Only one side would walk out victorious. Threats had been hurled by both sides. They had been acting in secret because they were going far beyond their instructions. Because of this the New York delegation had walked out. Rhode Island refused even to send a delegation, and New Hampshire had not arrived.

So right or wrong, only ten states would vote on the compromise. From north to south they voted. Massachusetts first, could not vote. Its delegation was evenly split. Connecticut, AYE. New Jersey, a unanimous AYE. Pennsylvania, NAY. Delaware, AYE. Maryland, AYE. Virginia, NAY. North Carolina with its two Princeton graduates carried the day. AYE. South Carolina, NAY. Georgia, NAY.

The count: five AYES, four NAYS, one divided.

The small states had won. Paterson and his Jerseyites had prevailed, but the large states counterattacked.

Randolph of Virginia rose and spoke, "The vote of this morning ... had embarrassed the business extremely. All the powers given in the Report from the (Committee) of the Whole, were founded on the supposition that a proportional representation was to prevail in both branches of the Legislature. When he came here this morning his purpose was to have offered some propositions that might if possible have united a great majority of votes, and particularly might provide (against) the danger suspected on the part of the smaller States, by enumerating the cases in which it might lie, and allowing an equality of votes in such cases. But finding from the preceding vote that they persist in demanding an equal vote in all cases, that they have succeeded in obtaining it, and N. York if present would probably be on same side.... It will probably be in vain to come to any final decision with a bare majority on either side...."

Randolph and Madison were now trying some fancy footwork since they had lost in a close vote. This vote should not count? He went on.

"For these reasons, the convention might adjourn, that the large States might consider the steps proper to be taken in the present solemn crisis of the business and that the small States might also deliberate on the means of conciliation...."

He was asking the winner to reconsider and give in to the loser. Three weeks before when the New Jersey Plan had been defeated, the Jersey delegation had stayed, showing its commitment to the convention. Now Randolph was wavering.

Paterson jumped to his feet. Now was the time and here was the place. The large states would have to put up or shut up. Paterson looked at the Virginian and said "that it was high time for the Convention to adjourn, that the rule of secrecy ought to be rescinded, and that our constituents should be consulted. No conciliation could be admissible on the part of the smaller states on any other ground than that of an equality of votes in the second branch. If Mr. Randolph would reduce to form his motion for an adjournment *sine die,* he would second it with all his heart."

To adjourn *sine die* would mean the convention was over. Paterson now turned his eyes to the large states. Would they risk everything? Their bluff was called.

After long moments Charles Pinckney of South Carolina asked Randolph if that was what he wanted. Randolph answered that he "had never entertained an idea of an adjournment *sine die;* and was sorry that his meaning had been so readily and strangely misinterpreted. He had in view merely an adjournment till tomorrow in order that some conciliatory experiment might if possible be devised, and that in case the smaller states should continue to hold back, the larger might then take such measures, he would not say what, as might be necessary...."

Paterson and all the other small states knew now that they could stand by their hard-earned victory. The large states would stay even if they lost. He seconded Randolph's motion but could not help but get in a last shot, saying he "seconded the adjournment till tomorrow, as an opportunity seemed to be wished by the *larger* states to deliberate further on conciliatory expedients."

Paterson, New Jersey and the United States had won, and the United States Senate had been born. The next morning the large state delegates met but now could not agree on anything. They were beaten, and they still could not believe how David had killed Goliath.

CHAPTER 5

New Jersey Joins the Union

rticle 7 in the proposed United States Constitution stated that the new form of government would go into effect upon "ratification of the conventions of nine states." Delaware
had been the first to ratify. Next, using some highly questionable methods, came
Pennsylvania. Now it was New Jersey's time in the sun.

The ratifying conventions in some states were subject to local politics. In New Jersey, the
real issue had little to do with the Constitution.

Word of the signing of the Constitution first reached the state in late September, and a copy
of the text appeared in *The Trenton Mercury* on the twenty-fifth. By early October, copies of a
petition signed by wealthy merchants calling for a ratifying convention were delivered to the
state Legislature.

"We are convinced, after the most serious and unprejudiced examination of the different
articles and sections of articles of the Constitution, that nothing but the immediate adoption of it can
save the United States in general, and this state in particular, from absolute ruin," the petition stated.

On October 25, the petition was read to the state Legislature meeting in Trenton. It was
followed by the reading of a letter from Governor William Livingston, who had attended the
convention in Philadelphia, and the letter from the Continental Congress forwarding the Constitution and calling for a ratifying convention. The next day a report signed by three of the four
delegates from New Jersey who had attended the Philadelphia convention was presented. By
the twenty-ninth the state voted.

"Resolved unanimously, that it be recommended to such of the Inhabitants of this State as are entitled to vote for Representatives in General Assembly, to meet in their respective counties on the fourth Tuesday in November next, at the several places fixed by Law for holding the annual Elections, to choose three suitable persons to serve as Delegates from each county in a State Convention...."

The state then instructed "the persons so elected to serve in State Convention, to assemble and meet together on the second Tuesday in December next, at Trenton in the county of Hunterdon, then and there to take into consideration the afd. Constitution, and if approved of by them, finally, to ratify the same in behalf and on the part of this State."

Several days later, someone pointed out that this was illegal, that under the state constitution the Legislature had never been given this kind of power. On November 1 a red-faced Legislature approved "an Act to authorize the People of this State to meet in convention, deliberate upon, agree to, and ratify the Constitution of the United States proposed by the late general Convention ... that it shall and may be lawful for the people thereof, by their Delegates to meet in convention, to deliberate upon, &, if approved of by them, to ratify the Constitution for the United States, proposed by the general Convention, held at Philadelphia...."

The second revolution was in full swing in New Jersey, and with a stroke of a pen an illegal act became legal *ex post facto,* after the fact.

At the end of November the people spoke, and each county chose three delegates. The most notable members of the ratifying convention were Judge David Brearley, a delegate in Philadelphia and chairman of the committee that had devised the Electoral College, and the intellectual giant of New Jersey, the Reverend John Witherspoon, president of the College of New Jersey (Princeton University) and a signer of the Declaration of Independence. Witherspoon had taught James Madison and had a strong influence on many of the delegates who had gone to Philadelphia.

Most of the delegates chosen to go to Trenton strongly favored the new Constitution. The document would protect little New Jersey from her giant and ambitious neighbors.

But there was also an ulterior motive.

The delegates convened at the Blazing Star Tavern located at King and Second streets (today Warren and State). Then most of the three days was spent writing rules for the convention, choosing a presiding officer and going over instructions. Finally, there was one reading of the Constitution and almost no debate:

"Now be it known that we the Delegates of the State of New Jersey, chosen by the people thereof for the purposes aforesaid, having maturely deliberated on, and considered the aforesaid proposed Constitution, do hereby for and on the behalf of the People of the said State of New Jersey agree to, ratify and confirm the same and every part thereof.

"Done in Convention by the unanimous consent of the members present, this eighteenth day of December in the year of our Lord one thousand seven hundred & eighty-seven, and of the Independence of the United States of America, the twelfth. In witness whereof we have hereunto subscribed our names."

A public reading and musket salutes to the thirteen states followed, and then one volley each for Delaware, Pennsylvania and New Jersey, the states that had now ratified the Constitution. The delegates next went to Mr. Vandergrift's tavern, where they celebrated long into the night, drinking toasts to "the Constitution; the United States in Congress; the perpetuity of the Union's independence; princes and states in alliance with the United States; the state; those who had fallen; religion, learning, the arts, manufacturers, and commerce, in harmony and in mutual subserviency to each other; the daughters of America; and America, the asylum of invaded liberty."

The delegates dragged themselves back to the Blazing Star for one last meeting in which they divulged New Jersey's real motive for quick ratification.

In a resolution attached to the document ratifying the Constitution, New Jersey reminded the Congress that the Falls of the Delaware had been the site selected for the new federal capital. The state of New Jersey expected that the new government would fully accept the site and that Trenton would be the capital of the brand-new "United States of America."

CHAPTER 6

A Scandalous First Election

Our Constitution does not share the same birth date as our country. Written in Philadelphia during the summer of 1787, it was forwarded to the states to debate and ratify. The document technically took effect in June 1788 when New Hampshire became the ninth state to ratify.

By the fall, the outgoing Congress of the Articles of Confederation authorized its own demise and declared that new elections for Congress and president, under the Constitution, would take place. At once preparations began to select a president, two senators from each state and a number of representatives to Congress based on each state's population.

The first federal election held in New Jersey gives some insight as to what the founding fathers meant when they penned "We the People." First, a look at the presidential election: There wasn't any. There were no candidates or speeches. Almost everyone expected the winner to be General George Washington, but there was no election as we know it.

The Constitution had established a republican system known as the Electoral College. The plan was to have respected citizens from each of the states meet and, as representatives of the people, select a president to govern for the good of the country. Unfortunately, the Constitution wasn't clear on how these electors would be chosen.

In some states, such as Virginia, the people went to the polls to choose representatives, but not in New Jersey. Under the state's system, agreed to in October 1788, the selection of presidential electors was left to the governor, William Livingston, and his cabinet, called the Privy Council.

So in New Jersey, it was assumed that the governor knew what was best for "We the People." Even so, the chosen electors were an impressive lot worth the governor's confidence. David Brearley, a judge and delegate to the Constitutional Convention, and Mathais Ogden, a Revolutionary War hero, were joined by James Kinsey, John Neilson, David Moore and John Rutherford.

According to the Constitution, the two United States senators would be chosen by the state Legislature and not by the people. The New Jersey Legislature chose forty-four-year-old Dr. Jonathan Elmer of Burlington, the president of the State Medical Society and former congressman under the Articles of Confederation, and William Paterson. The latter was known as the "Father of the United States Senate" since it was his arguments which had created that upper house of Congress.

Where was the role of "We the People" in the new government? That was left to the House of Representatives, the common person's voice in the national government. From the start, it seemed as if the House was supposed to be the rough-and-tumble world of a largely uneducated electorate. In setting up the election rules, the New Jersey Legislature did everything it could to make this come true.

First, based on the state's population, New Jersey was entitled to four representatives, but instead of dividing the state into four districts as is done now, the Legislature elected the four at large.

Next, the system for nominating the candidates was simply too democratic. Any qualified voter could nominate four candidates to Congress simply by delivering the list to his county court of common pleas. The county clerk then forwarded all nominations to the governor's office, where a master list was compiled for the voters.

The state Legislature decided that the election should take place beginning on the second Wednesday in February 1789. The problem was that there was no specified date to end the election. The county government or the governor could extend or end voting at a whim. Also, polling places could be created or moved after the election had begun.

With so many candidates, the election broke into factions according to geographic lines. Since New Jersey had once been divided into east and west parts, that's the way alliances fell. East Jersey was the section most populated and closest to New York City. West Jersey was more rural and nearer to Philadelphia.

The election that followed has to be the most corrupt and complicated in the state's history. There were the usual charges of financial improprieties that accompany most elections, as well as charges of candidates being openly hostile to General Washington. But it was the operation of the election which makes it stand out. There were no secret ballots, and local polling officials could reject votes they didn't like. Votes cast in unofficial polling places were counted. Some towns held more than one election.

The seven northern counties closed their polls in late February with their candidates showing a substantial lead. Rural counties like Burlington and Cumberland promptly extended their voting into March. Essex County countered by extending *its* voting until April.

Governor Livingston and his council met to count the votes on March 3 but felt that not enough returns were in to name a winner. The final tally took place on the eighteenth despite the fact that the votes from one county were missing. Livingston, however, declared the four winners. Elias Boudinot of Burlington, Lambert Cadwalader of Trenton, James Schureman of New Brunswick and Thomas Sinnickson of Salem were elected to Congress.

The losers were enraged and wrote letters to the new government demanding an investigation. When the first Congress met in New York City, the temporary capital, it was decided that the new nation could not withstand the scandal of throwing out an entire state's congressional delegation for election fraud.

Congress stonewalled the issue, letting the crisis die down. In September, eight months after the election, Congress voted to accept the Jersey delegation. Suspect as the state's election had been, "We the People" of New Jersey finally had their representation in the government.

CHAPTER 7

Jersey Case Sets Precedent

Many times in the history of America, a decision of the United States Supreme Court has overridden the legislative or executive branches of government. This power, known as judicial review, is not mentioned in the Constitution. From where, then, is this awesome power derived?

Most students of history will answer that it was Supreme Court Chief Justice John Marshall's decision in the Marbury vs. Madison case in 1803. Some say Marshall's decision was based on an even earlier ruling involving New Jersey's William Paterson, a member of the Marshall Supreme Court. That case dealt with a 1778 law written only two years after the Declaration of Independence and nine years before the United States Constitution.

Following the Battle of Monmouth in June 1778, the British army retreated to Sandy Hook, then to New York City where the redcoats would maintain a base for the remainder of the war. This led to the inevitable black market trade between the opposing territories of rebel-held New Jersey and Loyalist New York. To stop this trade with the enemy, the New Jersey Legislature passed an act that made it "unlawful for any person or persons whomsoever to seize and secure provisions, goods, wares and merchandise attempted to be carried or conveyed into or brought from within the lines or encampments or any place in the possession of the subjects or troops of the King of Great Britain."

For those who violated the act, a trial would be held in county court and "in every cause where a jury of six men give a verdict as aforesaid there shall be no appeal allowed." The goods would then be divided between the government and the officials who had seized them.

Under the act, Elisha Walton, a major in the local militia, seized goods belonging to John Holmes and Solomon Ketcham, both of Monmouth County. The goods were of considerable value: "between seven hundred and eight hundred yards of silk, between four hundred and five hundred yards of silk gauze ... and many other articles, such a quantity and such a quality as could not be purchased in all the stores of New Jersey."

The case was tried before Judge John Anderson at Monmouth Courthouse, today's Freehold, on May 24, 1779. The jury of six men ruled in favor of Walton.

Even before the verdict was in, Holmes' attorney appealed to the New Jersey Supreme Court, and the case was brought before New Jersey Chief Justice David Brearley. On November 11, the case was heard as Holmes vs. Walton when William Paterson was state attorney general. Before the court, Walton's attorney argued the ruling should be overturned on the grounds "that the jury who tried the said plaint before the said justice consisted of six men contrary to the constitution of New Jersey."

Brearley took the case under advisement. A decision was twice delayed, and it wasn't until the following year that the state Supreme Court gave its verdict.

In their ruling the justices wrote that New Jersey's state constitution guaranteed a trial by a very specific jury. "The common law of England, as well as so much of the statute law as have been heretofore practiced in this colony, shall still remain in force, until they shall be altered by a future law of the legislature; such parts only excepted as are repugnant to the rights and privileges contained in this Charter; and that the inestimable right of trial by jury shall remain confirmed as part of the law of this colony without repeal forever."

Just what was trial by jury? According to the Concessions and Agreement of 1676, "The trial of all cases, civil and criminal, shall be heard and decided by the verdict or judgment of twelve honest men of the neighborhood." Later, in 1699, the New Jersey Legislature stated, "All trials shall be by the verdict of twelve men." And so the state Supreme Court ruled that the act passed by the Legislature was unconstitutional.

Even outside the state, notice was taken. Gouverneur Morris, in an address to the Pennsylvania State Legislature, wrote in 1785: "A law was once passed in New Jersey, which the judges pronounced unconstitutional, and therefore void. Surely, no good citizen can wish to see this point decided in the tribunals of Pennsylvania. Such power in judges is dangerous."

This precedent, although not written into the Constitution, was well known by at least three Jersey signers: Governor William Livingston, David Brearley and William Paterson. With the Constitution described as "the Supreme Law of the Land" in the document, they would have known who would make the final decision. So when Chief Justice John Marshall was given credit for "inventing" judicial review, it didn't come as a surprise to Associate Justice William Paterson. Credit and glory are sometimes misplaced.

CHAPTER 8

Trenton — A Capital Idea

Even innocuous deals and decisions change history and the future. One notable example of this is the decision that made the District of Columbia, rather than Trenton, the capital of the United States.

In the summer of 1783 the capital of the United States was Philadelphia. When unpaid troops marched on Congress to demand their money, the Commonwealth of Pennsylvania refused to protect Congress, and its members fled. The only state to offer protection was New Jersey, so Princeton became the new U.S. capital. During its stay, Congress began to debate the site for a permanent capital. New Jersey offered a section of land located at the Falls of the Delaware River, today part of Trenton. A second proposed site was located on the Potomac River in Virginia.

A debate on the sites arose between Northern and Southern states, and a compromise was reached to establish dual capitals. Trenton would be the capital for six months each year and Annapolis, Maryland, for the other six months. This arrangement, of course, was a grand failure, so the debate reopened, and this time the New Jersey site won.

New York was chosen to serve as the temporary capital until Trenton was ready. Meanwhile, the course of events was overtaking Trenton's bid. The Constitutional Convention met in Philadelphia in 1787, and a new government was born. When the Jersey delegates met to ratify the Constitution, they attached a letter reminding the new government that they fully expected the capital to be in their state.

Everything went well until 1790. The new government was organized. George Washington was president, and Alexander Hamilton of New York was the secretary of the treasury. Hamilton, a close friend of New Jersey Governor William Livingston, had promised support for Jersey's capital plans.

Then in January, Hamilton presented to the Congress his plans for organizing the finances of the new nation, entitled a "Report Relative to a Provision for the Support of Public Credit." The Revolutionary War had been fought with borrowed money, and the time had come to pay it back. The problem was that during the lean years most people had sold their government bonds at one-tenth their value. Now the speculators would benefit from their insider tradings.

What Hamilton proposed next would open a hornet's nest. Hamilton was a Nationalist. He wanted "We the People" to think of themselves as Americans.

"The Secretary, after mature reflection on this point, entertains a full conviction, that an assumption of the debts of the particular states by the union ... will be a measure of sound policy and substantial justice.

"It would, in the opinion of the Secretary, contribute, in an eminent degree, to an orderly, stable and satisfactory arrangement of the national finances."

The problem was that most of the Southern states had already paid off their debts. Now, as Americans, they would be forced to pay off the debts of the Northern states. James Madison, longtime friend of Hamilton — they had served in the Congress at Princeton and coauthored "The Federalist Papers" — became his political adversary.

Wrote Madison, "The subject at present before a Committee of the whole, is the proposed assumption of the State debts. On this, opinions seem to be pretty equally divided.... A simple unequalified assumption of the existing debts, would bear peculiarly hard on Virginia. She has paid I believe a greater part of her quotas since the peace than [Massachusetts]."

As the debate in the House raged over the debts, in the Senate the Southerners revived the Potomac site proposal for the national capital. The argument threatened to split North and South. To calm the waters, Thomas Jefferson of Virginia, the new secretary of state, intervened.

He later recalled, "On considering the situation of things I thought the first step towards some conciliation of views would be to bring Mr. Madison and Colo. Hamilton to a friendly discussion of the subject. I immediately wrote to each to come and dine with me the next day, mentioning that we should be alone, that the object was to find some temperament for the present fever and that I was persuaded that men of sound heads and honest views needed nothing more than explanation and mutual understanding to enable them to unite in some measures."

The meeting of the two Virginians and one New Yorker would spell doom for New Jersey's capital hopes, just as France, England and Germany met before World War I to decide the fate of an unrepresented Czechoslovakia. To get Southern support, Jefferson remembered, "It was observed, I forget by which of them, that as the pill would be a bitter one to the Southern states, something should be done to soothe them, that the removal of the seat of government to the Patowmac was a just measure and would probably be a popular one with them, and would be a proper one to follow the assumption."

To guarantee the deal and the sellout of New Jersey, Pennsylvania was brought into the plot. Jefferson continued, "But the removal to Patowmac could not be carried unless Pennsylvania could be engaged in it. This Hamilton took on himself, and chiefly, as I understood, through the agency of Robert Morris, obtained the vote of that state, on agreeing to an intermediate residence at Philadelphia."

And so the dirty work was done. Philadelphia would become the temporary capital until the new federal city could be constructed on the banks of the Potomac.

What did New Jersey get?

Her people got to work hard to earn little pieces of paper with Alexander Hamilton's picture, to send to Washington, D.C. — the compromise capital.

CHAPTER 9

Leaks, Lies and the Press

Getting the Dirt on Hamilton

Today they are called dirty tricks. Terms like "leak" and "informed source" hide from the populace how the media find out information about one political party or the other. Some newspapers are called tabloids for printing enraging and unfounded stories, but none of this is new to American politics.

But where and when did such activity start? The answer involves some of the founding fathers and a man from the Jersey shore. The founding fathers may have pulled the dirty tricks, but Philip Freneau of Monmouth County took the blame.

The story begins in early 1791, when President George Washington had his secretary of the treasury issue several reports. Alexander Hamilton put together a series of plans designed to rebuild the finances of the new nation. A national bank would be set up. Former debts would be repaid and government revenues increased through taxes. Hamilton's view of America's future was an industrialized country run by bankers and the well-educated.

This view was not shared by two other prominent Americans, James Madison, a congress-man from Virginia, and Thomas Jefferson, Washington's secretary of state. Their vision of Amer-ica was a country of yeoman farmers, independent and running a country by the ballot — the rule of the common man, as it would eventually be known.

As Congress voted, one by one Hamilton's proposals scored victories. First, assume pre-Revolution state debts. Next, set up a national bank, then put a tariff into effect to protect domestic manufacturers. Madison and Jefferson feared the nation was heading down the road of control by the monied interests, a ruling class which eventually would result in the creation of a royal family and monarchy, as Jefferson put it.

"I hold it to be one of the distinguishing excellences of elective over hereditary successions, that talents which nature has provided in sufficient proportion, should be selected by the society for the government of their affairs, rather than that this should be transmitted through the loins of knaves and fools, passing from the debauches of the table to those of the bed," he wrote.

Jefferson and Madison had already begun calling their views "Republican" and those of Hamilton and his supporters "Royalist," but to criticize Hamilton meant to criticize Washington and Congress. They needed someone to carry the attack. Thomas Paine came to mind, but he was in France. Madison suggested his college roommate from Princeton, Philip Freneau of Freehold.

Madison remembered Freneau's wit and satire. When they graduated from Princeton in 1771 and the Colonies were still fiercely loyal to the King, Freneau had shocked the school at commencement exercises by lauding the Boston Massacre, saying,

> *I see a train, a glorious train appear,*
> *Of Patriots plac'd in equal fame with those*
> *Who nobly fell in Athens or for Rome.*
> *The sons of Boston, resolute and brave,*
> *The firm supporters of our injur'd rights,*
> *Shall lose their splendours in the brighter beams*
> *Of patriots fam'd and heroes yet unborn.*

Freneau was known as the "Poet of the Revolution" and used satire to attack the British. Later in the war he was captured and held by the British. Madison was certain that Freneau would embrace "Republican ideas." At the time he was working on a newspaper in New York City, but the capital was Philadelphia. Some way would have to be found to bring Freneau to the capital.

In the spring of 1791, Jefferson offered Freneau a job as translator for the State Department with an annual pay of $250, explaining in a strange statement "that the work was so slight that it would not interfere with other occupations at the seat of government." What Madison and Jefferson wanted was to have Freneau set up a newspaper in the capital to criticize the government. Jefferson later explained his offer.

"I should have given him the perusal of all my letters of foreign intelligence and all foreign newspapers; the publication of all proclamations and other public notices within my department, and the printing of the laws, which added to his salary would have been a considerable aid."

Eventually Madison traveled to New York City where he succeeded in talking Freneau into taking Jefferson's job offer and on the side starting a truly "Republican" paper, the *National*

Gazette. Madison and Jefferson would give him the inside story and even at times write under aliases for the paper. The first issue was printed, fittingly, on October 31.

Freneau wrote of his newspaper,

> *"Thus launch'd as we are on the Ocean of News,*
> *In hopes that your pleasure our pains will repay,*
> *All honest endeavors the author will use*
> *To furnish a feast for the grave and the gay;*
> *At least he'll essay such a track to pursue*
> *That the world shall approve...and his news shall be true."*

What's true depends on what newspaper you read — if you can believe anything you read in the papers.

Of course, newspapers took Hamilton's side, too. John Fenno of New York started the *U.S. Gazette* in 1789 and always mirrored the national government's position. When the nation's capital moved to Philadelphia, so did the *Gazette*.

Now the two papers squared off in support of their mentors. Hamilton fired the first salvo when he wrote of Jefferson and Madison as "a sect of political doctors; a kind of Popes in government; standards of political orthodoxy, who brand with heresy all opinions but their own; men of sublimated imaginations and weak judgments; pretenders to profound knowledge, yet ignorant of the most useful of all sciences — the science of human nature; men who dignify themselves with the appellation of philosophers, yet are destitute of the first elements of true philosophy; lovers of paradoxes; men who maintain expressly that religion is not necessary to society, and very nearly that government itself is a nuisance; that priests and clergymen of all descriptions are worse than useless."

While no names were mentioned, everyone knew to whom the writer referred, and while the letter was signed with a pseudonym, everyone knew who had written it. Freneau fired back in the *National Gazette* with "rules for changing a limited republican government into an unlimited hereditary one." This headline was followed by an outline of Hamilton's plans for improving the nation's financial situation. Then came a direct shot at Hamilton's handling of government funds, claiming "corrupt speculation and avaricious jobbing."

Hamilton responded by giving the information that Freneau was on Jefferson's payroll at the State Department. Fenno ran the story on the front page. "The Editor of the *National Gazette* receives a salary from the government. Query — Whether the salary is paid him for translations; or for publications, the design of which is to vilify those to whom the voice of the people has committed the administration of our public affairs — to oppose the measures of government, and by false insinuations, to disturb the public peace? In common life it is thought ungrateful for a man to bite the hand that puts food in his mouth; but if the man is hired to do it, the case is altered."

These were serious charges. The president at once began to investigate: George Washington wrote to Jefferson demanding an explanation. Jefferson's smooth reply could serve as a model for all future politicians when asked the tough questions.

"I cannot recollect ... whether it was at the same time or afterwards, that I was told he had thought of setting up a newspaper there. But whether then, or afterwards, I considered it as a circumstance of some value, as it might enable me to do, what I had long wished to have done, that is, to have the material parts of the *Leyden Gazette* brought under your eye and that of the public, in order to possess yourself and them of a juster view of the affairs of Europe.... But as to any other direction or indication of my wish how his press should be conducted, what sort of intelligence he should give, what essays encourage, I can protest in the presence of heaven, that I never did by myself or any other, directly or indirectly say a syllable, nor attempt any kind of influence."

The only thing missing from the eighteenth century version of leaks, lies and the press is sex.

Would the newspapers of the nation's founders sink to those prurient depths?

You bet!

Alexander Hamilton and Thomas Jefferson aimed to destroy each other. By the end of 1791, charges began appearing in the *National Gazette* that Hamilton was using his office as treasury secretary for personal gain, most notably by buying up certificates from Revolutionary War veterans. These certificates had been issued as promises of payment for service in the army, but a bankrupt Congress had never paid them and their value had dropped to ten cents on the dollar.

Hamilton was accused of buying up the certificates shortly before he announced that the government would pay them at full value. Congressional investigations were getting nowhere when Jefferson's supporters got a break. A James Reynolds of New York was arrested for trying to defraud a Revolutionary War veteran out of his certificates. From jail, Reynolds hinted that in return for his release he "had it in his power very materially to injure the Secretary of Treasury."

One of the congressional committees investigating Hamilton included James Monroe of Virginia. The committee visited Reynolds in prison where his wife produced signed checks from Hamilton to her husband totaling $1,100. Reynolds claimed that he had been part of Hamilton's scheme.

On December 15, 1792, the committee walked into Hamilton's office in Philadelphia and told him of the charges and their proof. Stunned, Hamilton asked them not to go public until he told them his side of the story. They agreed, and the next day behind closed doors Hamilton appeared with Oliver Wolcott, Connecticut's lieutenant governor, as his witness.

Hamilton and his witness explained that during the summer of 1791 while Hamilton's wife was in New York with their children, a woman named Maria Reynolds had come to his office. According to Hamilton, she sobbed that her husband had deserted her and that she needed money to return to New York City. She asked if Hamilton could make her a loan. Hamilton told her he did not have the cash at his office but would bring the money to her apartment. That night he did and, in his words as he entered her rooms, he felt "that other than pecuniary consolation would be acceptable. After this I had frequent meetings with her, most of them at my own house."

Hamilton continued, "One day, I received a letter from her ... intimating a discovery by her husband. It was a matter of doubt with me whether there had been really a discovery by accident, or whether the time for the catastrophe of the plot was arrived.... The same day, being the 15th of December 1791, I received from Mr. Reynolds the letter ... by which he informs me of the detection of his wife in the act of writing a letter to me, and that he obtained from her a discovery of her connection with me, suggesting that it was the consequence of an undue advantage taken of her distress."

After several meetings, Reynolds still would not spell out what he wanted from Hamilton. Finally, Reynolds made a proposal in a letter which Hamilton presented to the investigating congressmen. Reynolds' letter said, "Sir I have Considered on the matter serously. I have this preposial to make to you. Give me the Sum of thousand dollars and I will leve the town and take my daughter with me and go where my Freinds Shant here from me and leve her to Yourself to do for as you think proper."

Hamilton said he had made the blackmail payment, which matched the ones Reynolds had produced for the committee. The three congressmen decided this was a personal matter; what Hamilton had said would not leave the room, they promised. According to Hamilton, "The result was a full and unequivocal acknowledgement on the part of the three gentlemen of perfect satisfaction with the explanation and expressions of regret at the trouble and embarrassment which had been occasioned to me."

Hamilton thought the matter closed, but as his power grew over the next several years and it became clear his eyes were on the nation's highest office, his enemies became desperate to stop him. In 1797 a pamphlet printed by Freneau came out with the full story of the affair.

Hamilton wrote at once to Monroe, accusing him of the leak. In turn, Monroe claimed that he hadn't released the papers but had sent them to a "friend in Virginia." Hamilton went public, saying, "My real crime is an amorous connection with [Reynolds'] wife, for a considerable time with his privity and connivance.... This confession is not made without a blush. I cannot be the apologist of any vice because the ardour of passion may have made it mine. I can never cease to condemn myself for the pang which it may inflict in a bosom eminently entitled to all my gratitude, fidelity and love."

But Hamilton was ruined. He would never again hold an important office. And who was Monroe's "friend" in Virginia? Who had leaked the affair to Freneau and destroyed a political opponent with a sex scandal?

That sage of Monticello, Thomas Jefferson.

CHAPTER 10

Duel In Weehawken

Of all the duels fought in America, the one that took place on the banks of the Hudson in Weehawken stands far above the rest in importance. Today, when political campaigns throw mud by the fistful, it is hard to believe that the vice president of the United States would challenge a former secretary of the treasury over the words "despicable character." But in the famous Hamilton/Burr duel in 1804, those were the fighting words.

The cause of the "interview," as a duel was then popularly called, was the result of a long, often heated, relationship. These two men had been enemies for years. Aaron Burr, born in Newark, came from a wealthy, well-established New York City family and attended the College of New Jersey (Princeton University). Alexander Hamilton was an orphan by thirteen, living on a Caribbean island, but he too came to New Jersey to attend school.

When the Revolution broke out, both men joined the army, and Hamilton became a close friend of George Washington. After the war he was one of the prime movers behind the writing and ratification of the Constitution. In Washington's first Cabinet, he was the secretary of the treasury and the major advisor to the president.

Burr, after leaving the army, practiced law in New York City and was elected to several local posts. His family name and the fact that he was from New York won him the 1800 nomination for vice president, with a Southern running mate, Thomas Jefferson.

Although Burr was not running for president, when the final count came in he tied with Jefferson for that office through a mistake in the Constitution and the balloting in the Electoral

College. Burr seized the opportunity and turned on his own running mate. Thirty-five times the House of Representatives voted; each time, the vote came out a tie. Finally, Hamilton convinced a delegate to vote for Jefferson because he felt Burr was not acting honorably in his attempt to become president. Jefferson won, Burr became vice president, and his real hatred for Hamilton began.

By 1804 Burr conceived a plan that seems bizarre to say the least. With a group of anti-Jefferson men from New England, he planned to get New England, New York and New Jersey to secede from the Union and start a new country with himself at its head. He planned to run for governor of New York and from this position lead the revolt.

In the spring of that year, Hamilton got wind of the proposed coup and exposed it to the public. Burr lost the election, and the plan collapsed. Burr, incensed, started looking for revenge. In June, when a newspaper article carried a story about a dinner party where Hamilton allegedly said Burr was unfit to hold government office, Burr saw his chance.

In a series of letters between the two, Burr demanded a public apology. Hamilton tried to evade the issue but finally refused. Burr challenged him to a duel to settle the issue once and for all. Over the next two weeks, as the appointed seconds worked out the details, Hamilton put his affairs in order. It seems he was morally opposed to a duel, but his pride would not let him back down. Among his farewell letters to his wife and family he wrote:

"1. My religious and moral principles are strongly opposed to the practice of duelling and it would ever give me pain to be obliged to shed the blood of a fellow in a private combat forbidden by the laws.

"2. My wife and children are extremely dear to me, and my life is of the utmost importance to them, in various views.

"3. I feel a sense of obligation towards my creditors; who in case of accident to me ... may be in some degree sufferers....

"4. I am conscious of no ill will to Col. Burr, distinct from political opposition....

"Lastly I shall hazard much, and can possibly gain nothing by the issue of the interview."

The night before the duel, he outlined his plans for the next day to his wife. "The scruples of a Christian have determined me to expose my own life to any extent rather than subject myself to the guilt of taking the life of another. This must increase my hazards and redoubles my pangs for you. Heaven can preserve me and I humbly hope will, but in the contrary event, I charge you to remember that you are a Christian. God's will be done! The will of a merciful God must be good. Once more, adieu my darling darling wife. AH."

In a letter to a friend, Hamilton spelled out his plan. "I have resolved ... to reserve and throw away my first fire, and I have thoughts even of reserving my second fire, and thus giving a double opportunity to Colonel Burr to pause and reflect."

At five o'clock the next morning, the two men crossed the Hudson to New Jersey and stood facing each other. Witnesses disagreed on whether Hamilton's gun went off when Burr's bullet struck him in the chest or if it was ever fired. But Hamilton lived about thirty hours after the interview, long enough to say goodbye to his wife and family and to say he felt no ill will to Burr.

The people, however, never forgave the vice president. New Jersey indicted him for murder; mobs in New York wanted to lynch him. Burr escaped to Spanish-held Florida, hiding out in the last days of his vice presidency. Hamilton had ended Burr's political career. The bullet that killed Hamilton also killed Burr's life in politics.

CHAPTER 11

Young America Takes a Stand at Sea

One of the most humiliating insults to the young United States took place in what is known as the Chesapeake-Leopard Affair, where the warship USS *Chesapeake* was fired on and boarded by a British man-of-war within sight of the American coast. President Thomas Jefferson, who had essentially disbanded the United States Navy after the Revolutionary War, could do little else than resort to economic warfare. In December 1807, he ordered a complete embargo.

Under the embargo, all United States ships were forbidden from leaving coastal waters, an order that virtually stopped all foreign trade on American vessels. Meanwhile, James Barron, commander of the ill-fated *Chesapeake,* was court-martialed and sentenced to a five-year suspension without pay for surrendering his ship to the British.

Younger, more aggressive officers like James Lawrence of Burlington privately vowed revenge on the British. Commander John Rogers, who was involved in the Barron court-martial, openly stated he looked forward to an opportunity to meet a British warship in a fair fight.

As time passed, the results of Jefferson's economic warfare became apparent. It was destroying the domestic economy but did not seem to have any effect on England and France. In 1808, Jefferson chose not to run for a third term as president and was succeeded by his close friend and Princeton graduate, James Madison.

Over the next several years, Madison half-heartedly negotiated with England over its practice of stopping United States ships and kidnapping sailors, known as impressment.

But Madison did little more than talk and did not enlarge the navy. It was under these conditions that an obscure event off the New Jersey coast allowed the United States to redeem itself after the disgrace of the Chesapeake-Leopard Affair.

On May 1, 1811, the coastal schooner *Spitfire* cleared Sandy Hook and set a course south along the coast. The breeze was stiff, and the seas were running rough. What the captain did not know was that just north of Barnegat Inlet was the British forty-nine-gun frigate HMS *Guerriere*.

Late in the afternoon, the *Guerriere* sighted the *Spitfire,* ordering it to stop and stand by for inspection. Once on board, the British decided that one seaman was a deserter from the British Navy and ordered him to be taken back to the *Guerriere*. The captain of the *Spitfire* accompanied the lad and told the commander of the warship that the boy was from Maine and had been born there.

The *Guerriere* captain said, "All that might be so; but he has no protection and that is enough for me."

The *Spitfire* returned to New York to report the incident and the newspapers took up the call for the release of the boy. The British captain's words "he has no protection" rang like a challenge to the infant United States Navy.

This insult was too much for even a peaceful president to endure. If the United States was to gain any respect, something would have to be done. Orders were written to Rogers to take the frigate *President* and set sail from Annapolis, Maryland, then head north to the Jersey coast. Rogers' mission was to find and inform the *Guerriere* that the sailor must be returned and that the British warship must leave U.S. territorial waters. Rogers was granted the use of all power necessary and proper to carry out this action.

Rogers reached the *President* on the seventh and spent the next three days arming the forty-four-gun ship so it would be ready to fight the moment he set sail. He would not make the same mistake Barron had. Urgent orders went to Washington and Baltimore to officers on leave informing them to return at once.

On the tenth, the *President* sailed down the Chesapeake. When she cleared Cape Henry, Rogers turned north and set a course for Barnegat Inlet. Extra watches were set to scan the horizon for ships, and about midday on the sixteenth sail was sighted. Rogers ordered his crew to run up the ensign and his broad commander's pennant.

In the distance, the strange vessel also ran up several signal flags; Rogers, not knowing their meaning, did not answer. Soon the stranger was setting more sails to pull away. As he decided to go in pursuit, Rogers ordered his men aloft to set all canvas. The *President* began to gain on the other vessel just as night fell and the wind died, leaving both ships becalmed and out of hailing distance. Finally, after eight, the *President* was close enough for Rogers to climb the rigging and with a speaking trumpet hail, "What ship is that?"

Silence.

Again he called, "What ship is that?"

This time, a flash came from the vessel's stern and a cannon ball whizzed through the rigging of the *President*.

Rogers leaped to the deck, but before he could order a shot in return, an eager sailor sent a cannon ball flying toward the stranger. The response from the mystery ship was a full broadside with musket fire from the rigging.

Rogers now acted. "Equally determined not to be the aggressor, or to suffer the flag of my country to be insulted with impunity, I gave the order to fire," he would say later. Cheers rang out from the crew as they fired a full broadside. A navy which had been disgraced and challenged off the Jersey shore was now at last able to strike back.

Rogers ordered the crew to cease firing, but the stranger continued to fight. Again Rogers opened fire, this time with a devastating effect. Again the *President* ceased fire; this time the stranger was silent. Rogers decided to let the *President* stand off and wait for daylight.

As the sun rose, Rogers could see his victim in the distance. She had suffered severe damage but still appeared to be seaworthy. Rogers sent a boat to offer assistance. The stranger, it turned out, was not the British frigate *Guerriere* but a smaller sloop of war, *Little Belt*. Rogers discovered he had killed or wounded thirty-two of her crew in the engagement. The *Little Belt* refused the American commander's offer of assistance and informed him she was going to make for the closest English port for repairs. Rogers let the ship go.

The reaction ashore was jubilant. The *Philadelphia Aurora* reported it as the "Spirit of '76" all over again. The young nation had at last stood up for its rights.

CHAPTER 12

Jersey Waters Test
Constitution

Off the beaches of Long Beach Island one hot July day, a naval battle took place
which not only changed the course of American history but also nudged an infant
United States Navy toward respectability.

The story begins with the Treaty of Paris in 1783 which ended the American Revolution.
Because of expenses, and the fact that few saw a reason for its existence in peacetime, the
navy was disbanded. Over the next decade America tried to be friendly with all nations but
learned painfully that everyone picks on a weakling. England and France routinely stopped
American merchant ships and removed sailors for their own vessels, a detested practice
known as impressment. In the Mediterranean Sea, a group of small kingdoms called the
Barbary States seized United States ships and demanded ransom.

Finally, in 1794, Congress authorized the building of six frigates to become the United
States Navy. Work was stopped, however, when a treaty was worked out to pay extortion to
the Barbary pirates rather than fight them.

President Washington wrote to Congress, arguing for a navy: "It is my experience that
the most sincere neutrality is not sufficient guard against the depredation of nations at war.
To secure respect to a neutral flag requires a naval force, organized and ready to protect it
from insult or aggression."

As war clouds gathered over England and France, Congress reluctantly voted to finish
the ships. Following the designs of Joshua Humphreys, the new frigates took shape. The

U.S. Naval Historical Center

Becalmed off the Jersey coast, the USS Constitution *is pursued by a British squadron as her crew tries to pull her out of harm's way.*

most famous was built in Boston and christened the USS *Constitution*. More than 204 feet in length and with three giant masts, the ship carried a total of thirty-six sails. She was listed as having forty-four guns, but normally carried fifty-five. Humphreys had designed a super frigate with enough firepower to sink anything of equal size and enough speed to outrun anything too big to fight.

Over the next fifteen years the *Constitution* carried the flag to all parts of the world. She eventually fought and defeated the Barbary pirates at Tripoli, and by the spring of 1812 was just finishing an overhaul at Annapolis, Maryland. Commanding the ship was Connecticut native Isaac Hull, thirty-nine years old. He had served at sea since the age of twelve and had fought the Barbary pirates on the *Constitution*.

The news that Hull received from ship captains in Washington was very distressing. Secretary of the Treasury Albert Gallatin had convinced President Madison that the American navy was no match for the British. He suggested that the *Constitution* dock in New York City, have half of her guns removed and serve as a floating fort.

As the War of 1812 opened, Hull's orders arrived. "[You] are, with the force of your command, entitled to every belligerent right to attack and capture, and to defend. You will use the utmost dispatch to reach New York ... but you are not to understand me as impelling you to battle ... unless attacked."

As Hull left to prepare his ship for sea, other captains requested to talk directly with President Madison. They argued that United States ships were built better than British vessels. They said American cannons were more accurate, American crews better trained, and the marines, who stood in the rigging with rifles to pick off enemy officers, experienced fighters. They urged that the navy be allowed to prove itself.

After several days, Madison agreed to give the navy a chance. He would make a final decision when the *Constitution* reached New York City.

Meanwhile, Hull released any sailors formerly in the British navy. If captured, the British hanged them as deserters. Next, he held training and gunning practice. On July 6, still without a full crew, Hull ordered the *Constitution* to weigh anchor. As the ship sailed down the Chesapeake Bay and word spread that she was looking for a fight, more and more sailors volunteered to join her. As soon as they were taken aboard, Hull assigned them to duty. The *Constitution's* big twenty-four-pounders could be heard for miles as the men learned to fire the warship's guns.

By the twelfth, the *Constitution* had cleared the mouth of the Chesapeake and had a full complement of four hundred fifty officers and men. Hull ordered his navigator to head north and set a course for Barnegat, New Jersey. What Hull did not know was that a British squadron of five ships, under the command of Sir Philip Bowes Vere Broke, was waiting off the Jersey coast. The flagship, the HMS *Shannon,* mounted thirty-six guns, and with it were the frigate *Guerriere* with thirty-eight guns, the sixty-four-gun *Africa,* and the *Aeolus* and *Belvidera,* each mounting thirty-two guns.

Hull stayed close to shore as he headed north in order to intercept and warn merchant ships of the declaration of war. By the afternoon of the sixteenth the *Constitution* was in twenty-two fathoms of water and in sight of the Jersey shore. At two, the cry "Sail ho!" came from the lookout, and Hull strained to identify the ships.

He hoped they were part of the navy squadron based at New York City. As the ships drew closer, the wind died and the sea became calm. By nightfall, the ships were still six to eight miles away. Hull ordered signal lights lit but received no answer. With the coming of daylight, what Hull had feared was confirmed. Six British warships were behind him and between him and the land in what is today Beach Haven Inlet.

The ship closest to the *Constitution* was the *Guerriere,* followed by the frigates *Shannon, Aeolus* and *Belvidera,* and the battleship *Africa.* The rear was brought up by the captured American ship, *Nautilus.* Against this array, the Americans had only forty-four guns.

Hull knew that to stand and fight meant certain defeat, so he ordered every sail raised and the great race was on. Unfortunately, the sea off the island was calm, and the *Constitution's* sails drooped like bedsheets. In the distance, however, the British still had some air and were steadily closing the gap. Hull ordered men aloft with buckets of water to wet down the sails. By closing the pores of the cloth with water, Hull prayed that the sails would catch even the slightest breeze. Still, nothing moved the great ship.

Finally, Hull shouted, "All hands man your boats!" and the *Constitution's* longboats were put over the side to tow the ship. Giant oars called sweeps were manned from the deck of the warship. Just then the wind died completely and becalmed the British.

Taking advantage of this reprieve, Hull ordered two large cannons moved to the stern and the rails cut away so the ship could fire at its pursuers. Guns also were run out the windows of Hull's cabin. In addition, the crew dumped 2,300 gallons of fresh drinking water over the side to lighten the ship.

As the hours passed, the *Constitution* held its distance. Then the British made their move, massing the boats from all of their ships to pull the *Shannon*. Once it engaged the American ship, the others could catch up. Hull, at his wit's end, watched as the *Shannon* crept closer. He ordered his men "Beat to quarters!" and the ship was made ready to fight.

"If they sink us, we'll go down like men," he said. He even fired the first round at the *Shannon,* but she was out of range. Just then, Hull's second in command, Lieutenant Charles Morris, spoke up: "There is one thing, sir, I think we'd better try." Hull asked what it was. Try to "kedge her off," replied Morris.

Hull agreed to give it a try. Kedging was a practice used in shallow water when a ship was becalmed. Two anchors were prepared and tied to the longest line available. The first anchor was rowed out the length of the line and dropped into the water. The anchor caught on the bottom and then the massed crew together pulled the line. As the *Constitution* was pulled to that anchor, the second anchor was being rowed out. When the first was pulled up, the second was dropped, and the entire back-breaking process was repeated over and over again.

Slowly the *Constitution* drew away, but the British were not fools. Within a short time they, too, were kedging. As the *Constitution* was kedged and towed, Hull kept all sails set in the hope of catching a breeze.

Several times a breeze sprang up, and the *Constitution* would lurch ahead. Quickly the boats were hauled in while the great ship was under way, a very difficult and dangerous procedure. But every foot counted. The British took their sails down while towing, so the sails would not act like giant brakes. When a breeze started, the *Constitution* was able to draw away as the pursuers took time to set their sails. The British also cut the rowing boats away and let the men catch up later. This extra rowing helped to wear down the British sailors.

After almost forty-eight hours, an American merchant ship was sighted. The enemy ships at once struck their Union Jacks and ran up the Stars and Stripes to lure the defenseless merchantman closer. Hull in turn ran up the Union Jack and fired on the merchant ship which veered away.

Finally, Hull could see the dark clouds of a thunderstorm approaching. The storm would reach the *Constitution* first, and Hull decided on one last gamble. As the sky darkened, he sent his crew aloft to take in the sails and make it look like a severe storm was blowing in. A few miles away, the British, not wanting to be caught off guard, also prepared for a gale.

As soon as the front reached the *Constitution* and the rain obscured it from the British, Hull set all sails and was off at eleven knots. By the time the British squadron realized the storm wasn't severe, the *Constitution* was gone.

A jubilant Hull now made a decision. The waters off New Jersey had been a proving ground for his crew. He had confidence in them, and the crew believed in him; they would follow him anywhere. These men and this ship deserved better than to spend the war tied up to some New York City dock, he thought. He decided to disobey his orders and sail to Boston, not New York.

In Boston, Hull and his crew met with a strange reception. While they were received warmly and praised for their great seamanship, they were also targets of abuse. New Englanders objected to the war with England, and many people openly supported the British. There were even plans for a meeting to discuss New England's secession from the United States.

Hull had problems getting supplies for his ship. Merchants actually refused to give the government credit. Finally, Hull borrowed money from a merchant who supported the government and resupplied his ship.

Hull had been waiting for new orders from President Madison, but since the attitude of Boston was affecting the morale of his crew and he wanted to test the *Constitution* in battle, he set sail without orders, dangerous action for a career naval officer, but a lucky choice for the history of the United States Navy.

After the *Constitution* left, orders arrived from Madison telling Hull to stay in Boston and not to engage any British warships. Over the next few days, however, Hull and the *Constitution* prowled the coast as far north as Nova Scotia, looking for any British craft heading for Canada. He found several unarmed merchant ships which he captured and set on fire after seizing their crews. Then, on the night of August 18, a sail was sighted in the distance. Hull ordered all sails set and went in pursuit. After several hours, the *Constitution* discovered that her prey was an American privateer, the *Decatur.* Hull learned from the captain that there was a British frigate nearby which had chased the *Decatur* only hours before. Hull now made all speed in the direction of the reported enemy ship.

The next afternoon the call "Sail ho!" came from the lookout. Slowly the *Constitution* gained on the ship until Hull, through his glass, could make her out. She was the HMS *Guerriere,* a sight which must have made Hull smile to himself.

In the years before the war, the *Guerriere* and the *Constitution* had both been at anchor in Delaware Bay. One evening ashore, Hull had met the *Guerriere's* captain, James Dacres. The two started talking with a great deal of pride about their respective navies and ships. Hull is reported to have said, "Well, you may just take good care of that ship of yours, if I catch her in the *Constitution,*" to which the British captain offered to make a wager, if they should ever meet. Hull replied, "No, I'll bet no money on it, but I will stake you a hat that the *Constitution* comes out victorious." "Done," answered Dacres.

Now Hull ordered his drummer to "beat to quarters." At once the ship became a living thing as men prepared for combat. Marines climbed into the rigging to pick off enemy officers and to throw hand grenades if the ships came close enough. Surgeons and their assistants brought up buckets of sand to throw on the decks to keep men from slipping in puddles of blood. "Powder monkeys," boys of ten and eleven, were ready to dash about the ship carrying gunpowder for the cannons.

As the *Constitution* closed in on the British, *Guerriere* opened fire. Hull shouted to his crew, "Men, now do your duty. Your officers cannot have entire command over you now. Each man must do all in his power for his country." He then turned to the man at the wheel of the great ship. "You shall have her as close as you please, Sailing Master! Lay her longside!"

The *Constitution* crossed in front of the enemy ship like crossing a "T." As each gun came into play, it was fired down the length of the *Guerriere's* deck, each a double load with a large cannon ball to damage the ship and dozens of marble-sized grapeshot to annihilate the crew.

Within fifteen minutes, the *Guerriere's* mizzenmast, the most rear of the three masts, was shot away and dragging in the water. A sailor on the *Constitution* wrote, "As we came up she began to fire.... We came so near on one tack, that an eighteen-pound shot came through us under the larboard [port] knight-head striking just abaft the breech of the gun to which I belonged. The splinters flew in all directions; but no one was hurt. We immediately picked up the shot, and put it in the mouth of long Tom, a large gun loose on deck — and sent it home again, with our respects."

As the *Constitution* tried to cross the "T" again she got too close and the bowsprit of the *Guerriere* became tangled in the rigging of the *Constitution's* mizzen. Now the marines poured in their deadly rifle fire. When the two ships pulled away, the *Guerriere's* fore and main masts came crashing down, making her a helpless wreck. As the *Constitution* approached again, Dacres ordered a signal shot fired and struck his colors.

The *Guerriere* was so badly damaged that Hull ordered her crew taken aboard and the British ship set afire. Hull offered his hand to Dacres and said to him, "Dacres, my dear fellow, I am glad to see you on board."

"Damn it, Hull," responded Dacres, "I suppose you are." Unbuckling his sword, he offered it to his captor.

"I will not take a sword from one who knows so well how to use it," said Hull, "but, I tell you, Dacres, I will trouble you for that hat."

The *Constitution* headed for home. Hull had the proof he needed to convince the politicians that the United States Navy could fight. Besides its victory, the *Constitution* also had something else as it returned to Boston. During the height of the battle when the British were only a few feet away, they fired a cannon at the *Constitution's* side. The cannon ball hit the American ship's heavy oak planks and bounced off. An American sailor shouted across to the British, telling them to give up, that the *Constitution* was too strong for them to hurt. "Her sides are made of iron!" he shouted.

Hull had the first great victory for the navy, and its most famous ship had her nickname, "Old Ironsides."

CHAPTER 1

Antislavery Crusade Launched at Shore

Slavery in New Jersey? For most of us that sounds strange. New Jersey was a Northern state; of course there wasn't any slavery. However, prior to the Revolution almost 10 percent of the state's population were slaves. Perth Amboy was a major slave trade center where the Royal African Company brought shiploads of misery to America.

The first black Africans were brought to Jamestown, Virginia, in 1619 on a Dutch ship. They came as indentured servants, not slaves, and they were set free after a prescribed period of work. But gradually the demand for workers overtook the supply; by the mid-1600s, the colony of Virginia began to distinguish between blacks and whites. The Assembly declared "that all children born in this country shall be held bond or free only according to the condition of the mother."

By this time the Dutch had also established slavery in New Jersey. In 1680, Richard Morris of Shrewsbury kept more than sixty slaves to operate his mill and plantation.

The Quakers who settled in West New Jersey had attempted to ban the practice in 1676 saying, "That all, any, every person and persons inhabiting the said province shall, as far as in us lies, be free from oppression and slavery." But this was not to last.

When Queen Anne united East and West Jersey into the royal colony of New Jersey, she encouraged slaveholding by urging trade with the Royal African Company of Stockholm, Sweden, which was said to "have a sufficient supply of merchantable negroes at moderate rates."

The East Jersey capital of Perth Amboy became the center of a flourishing slave trade; by 1737, with the colony's population at about 47,000 people, there were more than 3,900 slaves, about one slave for every twelve citizens.

What ended the practice of slavery in New Jersey? The credit for this humanitarian crusade that eventually spread around the world — this was a global cause — can be traced to one humble man from Burlington County.

John Woolman was the fourth of thirteen children born to a devout Quaker couple who lived just outside Mount Holly. John's formal education began at age four and lasted until he was about fourteen; he was then encouraged to continue reading on his own. At twenty-one, he left the farm and opened a store in Mount Holly. He soon prospered, but this made him uneasy. Prosperity was not Woolman's goal in life, and he found that the more money he made, the more he craved.

As a Quaker, Woolman longed for the simple life, so he gave up storekeeping and became an apprentice tailor. To supplement his income, he did various odd jobs — surveying, teaching, and grafting and raising apple trees. Each Sunday, Woolman attended the Quaker meeting, looking for an inner light, a calling.

It was during this time that a minor incident took place which helped guide Woolman. As he later recalled, "My employer, having a Negro woman, sold her and directed me to write a bill of sale, the man being waiting who bought her. The thing was sudden and though the thoughts of writing an instrument of slavery for one of my fellow creatures felt uneasy, yet I remembered I was hired by the year, and it was my master who directed me to do it, and that it was an elderly man, a member of our Society who bought her; so through weakness I gave way and wrote it, but at the executing [of] it, I was so afflicted in my mind that I said before my master and the Friend that I believed slavekeeping to be a practice inconsistent with the Christian religion. This in some degree abated my uneasiness, yet as often as I reflected seriously upon it I thought I should have been clearer if I had desired to be excused from it as a thing against my conscience, for such it was."

The incident stayed with him. Could he stand by unprotesting? A short time later, "a young man of our Society spake to me to write an instrument of slavery, he having lately taken a Negro into his house. I told him I was not easy to write it, for though many kept slaves in our Society, as in others, I still believed the practice was not right, and desired to be excused from writing [it]. I spoke to him in good will, and he told me that keeping slaves was not altogether agreeable to his mind, but that the slave being a gift made to his wife, he had accepted of her."

As Woolman's doubts about slavery grew, so did his feeling that his calling was to his faith. Quakers had no paid ministers; they met in silent prayer. Anyone who felt called could rise and speak. Some who spoke more often could receive a certificate from the other members to be a "recommended minister."

Woolman received a certificate, and soon he made his first pilgrimage to Perth Amboy to meet other Friends. Over the next twenty-nine years, he would make trips all over New Jersey and to other colonies. Woolman kept a journal which he eventually published. As he traveled, he witnessed slavery firsthand and made an uncanny prediction on a visit to Virginia.

"[Slavery] appeared to me as a dark gloominess hanging over the land; and though now many willingly run into it, yet in future the consequence will be grievous to posterity!"

In 1746, Woolman began writing *Some Consideration on Keeping of Negroes,* the book that would eventually change America and most of the world. The abolitionists of the nineteenth century would find it contained all the moral arguments they would need to start the crusade against human bondage.

Woolman first looked at slavery from a religious point of view. "To consider mankind otherwise than brethren, to think favours are peculiar to one nation and exclude others, plainly supposes a darkness in the understanding for as God's love is universal ... again to conclude a people forward, perverse, and worse by nature than others ... will excite a behavior toward them unbecoming the excellence of true religion."

Woolman then wrote that the practice also degraded the master.

"It may be objected there is cost of purchase and risk of their lives to them who possess them.... If I purchase a man who hath never forfeited his liberty, the natural right of freedom is in him. And shall I keep him and his posterity in servitude and ignorance? How should I approve of this conduct were I in his circumstances and he in mine?"

As Woolman worked on his book, he decided to take up the cause as his own and to convince Quakers to set their slaves free. If charity begins at home, he thought, then the crusade against slavery should begin in New Jersey.

"I felt an increasing concern for Friends on our seacoast. And on the 8th day, 8th month, 1746, with the unity of Friends and in company with my beloved friend and neighbour ... we set forward and visited the meetings generally about Salem, Cape May, Great and Little Egg Harbor, and had meetings at Barnegat, Manahawkin and Squan, and so to the yearly meeting at Shrewsbury. Through the goodness of the Lord, way was opened, and the strength of divine love was sometimes felt in our assemblies, to the comfort and help of those who were rightly concerned before him. We were out 22 days and rode by computation 340 miles."

Woolman would start his crusade at the Jersey shore. Success there and in the rest of the state led him to travel throughout the Colonies and into the Deep South where slavery was even more firmly entrenched.

Woolman told of an encounter with a militia colonel who defended slavery, pointing out that "the lives of the Negroes were so wretched in their own country."

On another trip Woolman answered that reasoning. "And I may here add that another person some time afterward mentioned the wretchedness of the Negroes occasioned by their intestine wars an argument in favour of our fetching them away for slaves, to which I then replied: If compassion on the Africans in regard to their domestic troubles were the real motives of our purchasing them, that spirit of tenderness being attended to would incite us to use them kindly."

By the time of Woolman's death in 1772, on the eve of the American Revolution, his crusade started to bear fruit. Quakers had begun to free their slaves, and a new idea first heard at the Jersey shore, that "all men are created equal," flickered to life. Quakers whom Woolman had converted to his cause pushed the moral issue of slavery to national prominence.

When Thomas Jefferson wrote the Declaration of Independence, he attempted to condemn the slave trade. Heated opposition from the Deep South forced Jefferson to drop the offending passage but the words "All men are created equal" eventually would have the same effects.

When the state of Vermont was formed in 1777, it was the first to ban slavery. Slowly, other Northern states banned the practice, although many Northerners still profited by the slave trade. In New Jersey, the issue of what to do with the state's thousands of slaves was publicly debated. John Cooper, a Quaker from Gloucester, wrote about the situation in 1780, in the *New Jersey Gazette*.

"Whilst we are spilling our blood and exhausting our treasure in defence of our own liberty, it would not perhaps be amiss to turn our eyes towards those of our fellow-men who are now groaning in bondage under us," Cooper wrote. "We say 'all men are equally entitled to liberty and the pursuit of happiness'; but are we willing to grant this liberty to all men?... But if after we have made such a declaration to the world, we continue to hold our fellow creatures in slavery, our words must rise up in judgement against us, and by the breath of our own mouths we shall stand condemned."

Despite Cooper's writings, abolition was not a sure thing in New Jersey. Twelve percent of the state's population were slaves, and they represented a tremendous amount of capital. In response to calls for abolition, the *New Jersey Gazette* ran the following:

"I think ... it may be right and highly praiseworthy to set free the children of slaves to be born after a certain time, there are many weighty reasons of policy against freeing the present race of slaves at this crisis.... That as all slaves are in reality as much the property of their masters as the gold and silver for which they were bought ... they [the owners] cannot be deprived of them without being paid the value, which will be a new and heavy tax upon the publick.... That there will be a considerable number of superannuated, diseased, and vagabond slaves to be maintained at the publick cost, which will also be a heavy tax.... Because they are treated with a humanity unknown in other parts of the world, and are better off than the generality of white poor, who are obliged, those who have families, from their necessities to work harder than the slaves in general in this state."

Considering the amount of money invested and the fear of thousands of unemployed former slaves, a compromise was proposed: a gradual emancipation. Pennsylvania had passed such a law in 1780. But in New Jersey the Legislature tabled a similar bill in 1781, and the issue of slavery again was put on the back burner for more than twenty years. Slowly, the abolitionists chipped away at the practice. In 1786, importing slaves into New Jersey was forbidden, and punishment for mistreating a slave was increased. But it was a long road. It was not until February 15, 1804, that New Jersey finally passed its ordinance for gradual abolition.

"Sec. 1. Be it enacted by the Council and General Assembly of this State, and it is hereby enacted by the authority of the same. That every child born of a slave within this state, after the fourth day of July next, shall be free; but shall remain the servant of the owner of his or her mother, and the executors, administrators or assigns of such owner, in the same manner as if such child had been bound to service by the trustees or overseers of the poor, and shall continue in such service, if a male, until the age of twenty-five years, and if a female until the age of twenty-one years."

This law would mean that any slave born before July 4, 1804, would be a slave for life. Under the law, New Jersey would have slaves even during the Civil War, sixty years later. In an attempt to encourage voluntary emancipation, the same act stated, "And be it enacted, That the person entitled to the service of any child born as aforesaid, may, nevertheless within one year after the birth of such child, elect to abandon such right; in which case a notification of such abandonment, under the hand of such person, shall be filed with the clerk of the township...."

Woolman's cause took more than a century to succeed, but its goal in this state was achieved without bloodshed. This, more than anything else, would have pleased New Jersey's forgotten crusader.

CHAPTER 2

Champion of the Forgotten

W hat Dorothea Lynde Dix found in New Jersey in the mid-1800s was appalling. The state's care of the homeless, poor and insane was possibly the worst in the nation, a fact that made her even more motivated to improve treatment for the needy. But it wouldn't be easy. Getting the taxpayers to support a public hospital would be difficult, particularly since Dix was a wealthy, out-of-state socialite.

Born in 1802 into the family of a strict minister, Dix ran away from home at age twelve to live with her widowed grandmother in Boston. At nineteen she opened a school for girls, teaching math, reading and writing to the daughters of wealthy Bostonians. After publishing several literary books, she visited Europe for her health. In 1837 her grandmother died, making Dix a wealthy woman.

For the next few years Dix lived the life of an aimless socialite until a friend recommended she teach Sunday school at the East Cambridge House of Correction. The conditions she found among the prisoners were shocking enough, but she also discovered that the mentally ill were placed among the convicts. As she later described in an official report, "Long before reaching the house, wild shouts, snatches of rude songs, imprecations and obscene language, fell upon the ear, proceeding from the occupant of a low building, rather remote from the principal building to which my course was directed. Found the mistress, and was conducted to the place which was called 'the home' of the forlorn maniac, a young woman, exhibiting a condition of neglect and misery blotting out the faintest idea of comfort, and outraging every sentiment of decency.... There she stood with naked arms and disheveled hair, the unwashed frame invested with fragments of unclean garments, the air so extremely offensive, though ventilation was afforded on all sides save one, that it was not possible to remain beyond a few moments without retreating for recovery to the outward air. Irritation of body, produced by utter filth and exposure, incited her to the horrid process of tearing off her skin by inches. Her face, neck and person were thus disfigured to hideousness."

The experience launched the heiress on a lifelong commitment to help the mentally ill by building state-supported institutions separate from prisons. Dix recruited other members of Boston society to take up the cause, and soon her crusade expanded throughout New England and even into New York.

New Jersey had its own way of handling the mentally ill. Counties operated jails, poorhouses and farms. The homeless and mentally ill were either put on a farm where they could support themselves or, if dangerous, confined to prison. Some were sent to Pennsylvania or New York which had hospitals.

The New Jersey Medical Society urged the state to build an asylum, and a legislative committee proposed that a state hospital be built, but the proposal died because the Legislature claimed it could not justify raising taxes to support the poor.

So Dix set her sights on New Jersey; a victory here, she believed, would impress the entire nation. She toured the state gathering facts and in Salem County found particularly shocking conditions. "She noted, besides several epileptics and persons of 'infirm mind' kept there, eight insane inmates. One middle-aged woman had been unbalanced for seventeen years. Two of the patients were in chains, and one man, who had been mentally ill for nearly thirty years, had been out of his small apartment but 'ten times ... in nineteen years.' "

In Pemberton, Dix toured the Burlington County Poorhouse where she found "twenty-two insane persons, ten of them occupants of the cells in the cellar or 'low basement.' She found these quarters to be 'strange and woeful contrast to the rooms above.' The dreary confined cells of the low basement were 'insufficiently lighted, insufficiently warmed, and pervaded with foul air to an intolerable degree.' "

In Monmouth County, she heard that one "crazy man" periodically wandered into the woods until hunger again forced his return. Finally one day, he did not return at all.

"A local official told her that perhaps, 'he has gone home to friends — we lay out to write; we have talked of it for some time.' Dix was outraged at the horror of a 'feeble insane man gone three months from the watch of those who had, officially, the care of him' but who had neither made a diligent inquiry about him nor instituted a search."

At the Morris County Poorhouse, she found "violently excited maniacs. It contained two cells constructed of plank and boards. These dreary places were seven and a half feet high, by eight square; dark, damp and unfurnished, unwarmed and unventilated — one would not hesitate, but [to] refuse to shut up a worthless dog [there];... A small aperture cut at the end of one of these cells, some time ago occasioned the involuntary death of the crazy tenant, who thrusting his head through his eagerness to escape, could not withdraw it, and hanging there died. A female maniac died in the adjoining cell."

Armed with her facts, Dix prepared a "Memorial to the State of New Jersey." A supporter, Senator Joseph S. Dodd of Essex County, presented it to the Legislature on a cold January 23, 1845.

Wrote Dix: "I come to solicit your attention to the condition and necessities of idiots, epileptics, and the insane poor, in the state of New Jersey.

"I ask your consideration of the claims of this large and much neglected class of sufferers.... I come to ask justice of the legislature of New Jersey, for those who, in the providence of God, are incapable of pleading their own cause, and of claiming redress for their own grievances."

Dix reported on her tour of the state and explained each horrible stop. "Attached to the Shark River Poorhouse, in Monmouth County, is a farm of nine hundred acres, one hundred of which are cultivated.... There is no infirmary or hospital department connected with the establishment. The sick, the infirm, and the imbecile are indiscriminately distributed and associated. The house, which is built of wood, is very old and inconveniently constructed for the purpose for which it is occupied. It contains, in winter, about sixty paupers, gathered from three townships; in the spring, a portion of these seek maintenance elsewhere....

"In the vicinity of the main dwelling is a small brick building, containing on the first floor two poor cells, from eight to nine feet square, warmed in cold weather by a stove set into the dividing wall, or partition. A straw bed and blanket, spread upon the floor, constitute the furniture, if one excepts the ring-bolts and iron chains for securing the patients!...

"I heard in this township of three wandering insane persons, but learned nothing special of their history; little interest was expressed for them. Where they belonged, to whom they were allied, or what their name and degree, were facts equally obscure and equally uncared for."

According to Dix, Monmouth was perhaps the most progressive county in the state! The report ended, "Permit me, in conclusion, to urge that the delay to provide suitable asylums for the insane produces miseries to individuals, and evils to society.... Shall New Jersey be last of 'the Thirteen Sisters' to respond to the claims of humanity, and to acknowledge the demands of justice?"

The proposal to build a state-sponsored hospital was sent to a committee where it was reported out favorably. A major argument used by Dix and Dodd was that by centralizing, one state hospital would actually save taxpayers money by eliminating bureaucracy and paperwork. The committee stated the hospital should be built "both on the ground of duty and economy ... without any additional tax, without feeling it to be a burden."

But not all were convinced. Some in the Assembly saw a danger.

"Sir," said one critic, "I do believe that if that Miss Dix had been paid $500 or $600, and escorted over the Delaware or to Philadelphia, or even $1,000 and taken to Washington City, and, if you choose, enshrined in the White House, it would have been money well laid out."

As Dix learned the real world of politics, she became the state's first lobbyist. To a friend, she wrote, "At Trenton, thus far, all is prosperous, but you cannot imagine the labor of conversing and convincing. Some evenings I had at once twenty gentlemen for three hours' steady conversation. The last evening, a rough country member, who had announced in the House that the 'wants of the insane of New Jersey were all humbug,' and who came to overwhelm me with his arguments, after listening an hour and a half with wonderful patience to my details and to principles of treatment, suddenly moved into the middle of the parlor, and thus delivered himself: 'Ma'am, I bid you good-night! I do not want, for my part, to hear anything more; the others can stay if they want to. I am convinced; you've conquered me out and out; I shall vote for the hospital.' "

On March 25, Dodd wrote to Dix, "I am happy to announce to you the passage unanimously of the bill for the New Jersey State Lunatic Asylum. The Senate vote was 18-0 and the General Assembly vote was 41-8."

Three years later in Ewing Township, near Trenton, the doors opened to the state "Lunatic Asylum." Dix would treat the facility like a first child, always watching over it. She would go on to other triumphs, carrying her humanitarian arguments to Europe and serving as Superintendent of Women Nurses in the Civil War, but she would return to New Jersey. In October 1881, a weakened Dix came back to her firstborn. The last five years of her life were spent outside Trenton. The trustees of the hospital Dix fought to build voted that she be treated as an honored guest, and an apartment was set up for her.

On July 18, 1887, Dix's long crusade as an educator and social reformer ended. She was buried in Boston with only her name on the tombstone. Her epitaph was her work.

CHAPTER 3

New Jersey to the Rescue

The history of the Jersey shore is filled with shipwrecks. The mere mention of the word brings to mind howling winds, roaring surf, a bearded captain shouting orders over the din.

It was visions like this that inspired two Ocean County men to make travel by sea safer. Both would work separately, but their ideas would eventually form the foundation for the United States Coast Guard.

During the early 1800s, New Jersey's bays and small rivers were lined with shipyards turning out sailing ships to carry on the commerce of the East Coast. Most of the ships were two-masted, square-rigged vessels called brigs. Other shipyards built shallow water craft, including the famed Barnegat Bay sneakbox.

One of these shipbuilders, Joseph Francis of Toms River, specialized in smaller craft. In 1830 he designed and built a rowboat for the czar of Russia who used it at the Cowes Regatta in England. As Francis' business increased, he turned to dealing with a major nautical problem of the day, lifesaving equipment.

While a lifeboat may look like little more than a rowboat, it is specially designed for its lifesaving duty. It must withstand rough seas and carry a large payload without capsizing or filling with water. Francis started by taking an existing whaleboat common in that day and trying to make it safer.

He put compartments in the bow and stern and filled them with cork; under each seat he put airtight compartments, a design used today in most unsinkable craft. With the floats to hold up the boat, drains were placed in the sides to allow water from a crashing wave to return to the sea.

In 1841 Francis took his lifeboat to the foot of Wall Street for a demonstration. As he cut the boat loose, it crashed end first into the water, then came to the surface upside down. To the crowd's amazement, it righted itself and the water in the boat seemed to disappear.

In a time when shipping ruled trade, Francis' Improved American Life-boat brought praise from Queen Victoria of England and Emperor Nicholas of Russia. But Francis was still dissatisfied with a boat that could be splintered in a storm surf. By 1843, he had designed a lifeboat made from corrugated metal.

Again Francis was heaped with praise for his invention, but still he was not happy because even the strongest lifeboat could be battered to pieces or its occupants swept overboard.

By 1844 Francis had perfected the Francis Life Car, an enclosed bullet-shaped craft with rings at both ends. Shipwreck victims would get inside and close the hatch, then one line on the front would be pulled from shore, while another from the rear would be let out. The process was reversed to send the empty car back to the stricken vessel.

Twin Lights Historical Society and Museum

A Francis Life Car would be used to rescue victims of a shipwreck after a line had been fired to those in distress.

But on February 14, 1846 a northeaster struck the Jersey shore and pointed out the Life Car's two fatal weaknesses. The packet ship *John Minturn* was driven ashore near Point Pleasant. The ship's passengers were just a hundred yards from safety, but that turned out to be too far for most. Twice the crew tried to launch boats to bring a line ashore, and both times they failed. From shore, rescuers were driven back by wind and waves as they tried to launch a boat.

For the next eighteen hours, the crowd on shore watched helplessly as the storm battered the wooden ship. Passengers held onto the rigging in the snow and freezing rain as long as they could before dropping into the frigid ocean. Late that night the *John Minturn* broke up and the last of her victims fell into the water. Thirty-nine bodies washed up; thirteen passengers made it to shore alive.

That same storm drove nine other ships onto New Jersey beaches and newspapers called for action. The Francis Life Car seemed like a good idea except that a line often could not be taken out to a shipwreck. These problems, however, were soon taken up by a physician from Manahawkin, William A. Newell.

Newell grew up in Freehold. After graduating from Rutgers University, he attended medical school and earned his degree in 1839. As was customary at the time, a graduate practiced under a licensed doctor for a year; Newell chose his uncle, Dr. Augustus Hankinson of Manahawkin.

As the only doctors in southern Ocean County, Newell and his uncle were on call for all emergencies. On the night of August 12, word came that a ship had grounded on Long Beach Island near what is now Surf City. Newell made the trip across the bay and stood on the beach where he could see the Austrian brig *Count Perasto* grounded hard on a sand bar.

All attempts of sending a lifeline out to the brig fell short, and Newell and the other volunteers watched as the ship's crew futilely tried to launch lifeboats. When the ship finally broke up, Newell had the unpleasant task of pronouncing the captain and thirteen crew members dead as they washed ashore.

The young doctor decided to put his mind to the problem of getting a line to an offshore wreck. He used everything from rockets to bows and arrows to send a light line over a great distance. Finally, using a small cannon from the brig's wreckage he succeeded in shooting a line far enough to aid stricken mariners.

During this time, Newell had finished his stay in Manahawkin and moved to Allentown where he set up his own practice. Once established, he became interested in politics and rose through local offices until 1847 when he won a seat in Congress.

In a proposal before Congress in January 1848, Newell outlined a system in which the government would provide the lifesaving equipment for local volunteers to rescue wreck victims. The proposal was supported by former President John Quincy Adams from Massachusetts and even by a young Illinois congressman, Abraham Lincoln, who said, "It is good. I hope it will prevail. I will help you."

But the powers that be refused to spend federal money to help make the Jersey beaches safer. As the doctor made his rounds of Congress trying to win support for the lifesaving stations, he was not idle.

He learned that he was not the only one involved in trying to save mariners' lives. In fact, the English were far ahead. They already had lifesaving stations set up on their coast and had perfected a mortar known as the Manby Gun, which could fire a ball several hundred yards with a line attached.

By August, Newell still had not won support and addressed Congress again. By his records, Newell said, the coast from Sandy Hook to Little Egg Harbor over the last nine years had claimed twenty-five ships, forty-eight brigs, seventy-three schooners, eight barques, two sloops and two pilot boats.

Six days later, as a rider to a lighthouse bill, Congress voted $10,000 "for providing surfboats, rockets, cannonades, and other necessary apparatus for the better preservation of life and property from shipwrecks along the coast of New Jersey, between and Little Egg Harbor.... "

Eight stations were erected and included the inventions of Francis and Newell. Each station had a substantial frame house furnished with galvanized surf boats with ten separate air chambers, 320 yards of hawser, 720 yards of hauling line, 600 yards of rocket line, rockets, and other lifesaving equipment. In addition to the surf boats, it was proposed that each station have a Life Car.

Only one station, however, had a Francis Life Car — the rest were on order — plus the line-throwing gun. If the system worked, it would be expanded, but if it failed, sailors would be back to "every man for himself." Now all that was needed was a test.

With winter storms common along the Jersey coast, the lifesavers did not have long to wait.

Early in December the Scottish brig *Ayreshire* set sail from Newry, Ireland, under the command of Captain J. P. M. McGlew, carrying 166 immigrants and a crew of thirty-five. As the ship approached the Jersey shore, she was caught in a winter gale and pushed dangerously close to the Barnegat shoals.

One of the passengers, Mrs. A. E. Bell, remembered: "It was blowing almost a hurricane and the vessel had been tossing and rolling under short sail for the 24 hours previous. Not much sleep had the passengers indulged in, but those who had slept were rudely awakened at midnight by a terrible, ominous shock. The ship stood upright and perfectly still for one awful moment. After that it monotonously pounded on the shore. Most of the passengers kept cool and appeared to know better what to do than did the captain, officers and crew." The *Ayreshire* had grounded fast on the bar near Squan Beach and Life-Saving Station No. 5, with Captain John Maxson in charge. By luck, this was the station that had been chosen to house the mortar and the Francis Life Car.

Maxson assembled as many of his volunteers as he could find and set off for the wreck. By now it was snowing heavily, and the breakers prevented launching a surf boat. This left Maxson only one choice, the untried mortar and Life Car.

The mortar was loaded and the untrained gunner fired. The first shot cleared the ship and her jib boom and landed in the water.

Maxson and his lifesavers hauled in the line and tried again. The second shot went through the *Ayreshire's* quarter house and landed in the mate's stateroom. The lifeline was secured aboard just after midnight.

On the *Ayreshire,* Mrs. Bell later recalled, "It was about 1 or 2 o'clock when we saw a flash from the shore, followed by a report and a line which fell across the ship, through which means the life car was afterward hauled back and forth from the ship to the shore. The line was attached to a shot which was fired from a mortar...."

Once the light line reached the ship, a large rope was hauled out and secured to the mast. The passengers then began a horrifying ride ashore in a metal cylinder not much bigger than a bathtub. But anything was better than staying on the ship, as Mrs. Bell remembered.

"All the passengers, who were down below when the ship struck, were obliged to come to the upper deck in the freezing weather with scant clothing on them, on account of the water coming in from below. About 50 of the women and children were in the mate's house on deck, a room hardly 20 feet square, and the water got in there after awhile so that the children had the water up to their knees.

"The ship lay over so that one side was almost under water and men were compelled to come and pass strips of blankets and ropes around the women for fear they would slip overboard. The waves beat against the weather side of the vessel with fearful force, keeping a continual shower of water flying over everybody who was on deck."

Over two days, carrying four or five people at a time, the Francis Life Car proved its worth. Of 201 passengers and crew, there was only one fatality, a father who tried to ride to shore holding onto the outside with his family safe inside the car. As the car was pulled through the surf, the man was swept off to his death.

But the rescue system worked. After an exhibition tour of Europe, the Life Car was retired with honors in the Smithsonian Institution in Washington, D.C.

CHAPTER 4

Night of Horror on Long Beach Island

The Jersey coast has had more than its share of shipwrecks, many of them in an area off Long Beach Island known as the "graveyard of the Atlantic." Stories have been told and retold of rescues and bravery — and cowardice — but the largest shipwreck in the island's history has gone almost unnoticed. One reason is that facts about the wreck are scattered like flotsam from Maine to Washington, D.C., but each bit of information gives a little more insight into the wreck of the *Powhattan*.

Built in 1835, the *Powhattan* became the pride of Baltimore, Maryland, the largest ship registered there. Owned by Alex Brown and Sons, she took part in the booming trans-Atlantic trade, visiting important ports on both sides of the ocean.

As more ships made the run from Europe to America and New York Harbor, the coast of New Jersey became more dangerous for mariners. Ships from Europe would sail north up the Jersey coast, bound for the Hudson River. If a northeast storm struck while a vessel was off the coast, wind and tide could drive a hapless ship onto the beach where waves would quickly pound a wooden hull to splinters.

One such disaster was witnessed by a Manahawkin doctor, William A. Newell, who treated shipwreck victims. Later, Newell was elected to Congress and introduced a bill that established "houses of refuge" on the coast between Sandy Hook and Little Egg Harbor. They were little more than barns that housed lifesaving equipment — surf boats, line-throwing mortars, and the Francis "life car." A nearby resident held the keys to a house of refuge; in the event of a wreck, the local people were supposed to provide the courage and take the risks free of charge. This was strictly a volunteer group; not even the state-appointed wreck master, who oversaw salvaging efforts, was paid. By 1854, Long Beach Island had two houses of refuge. One stood at the southern end where hotel owner Thomas Bond directed rescue efforts. The other was located in Harvey Cedars under Samuel Perrine.

As the year began, the *Powhattan* left for France where she picked up 311 German immigrants bound for New York City. These were not the poor, huddled masses of the Irish potato famine. They were prosperous Germans leaving the political instability of Europe.

When the *Powhattan* set sail from Havre on March 1, her passengers were looking forward to a new life in America. Samuel Liff carried an American eagle gold coin, and Johanne Schroeder held a train ticket for her family on the Erie Railroad.

Ironically, the America they were traveling to was in the midst of an onrushing political storm. As the *Powhattan* headed westward, signs of trouble were beginning to show. In New York City, the longest-running play was "Uncle Tom's Cabin" with 298 performances. In Trenton, Senator Stephen A. Douglas was hung in effigy during a public meeting for his proslavery stand in the controversial Kansas-Nebraska Bill. But all of this lay ahead. The *Powhattan* and its captain, James Myers, had their own problems.

The weather was unusually cold which made life on board uncomfortable. As March drew to a close, another problem appeared in the form of icebergs in the shipping lanes. One ship recorded forty to fifty large icebergs, while another saw a three-hundred-foot-high, two-mile-long berg off the coast of New Jersey.

On Friday, April 14, barometers on the East Coast plummeted as a tremendous storm approached. Telegraphs from Washington, D.C., and Baltimore relayed news of a freakish springtime snowstorm. Several inches had fallen in Philadelphia, and on Long Beach Island the blinding snow was driven out of the east by a gale. In Manahawkin, Captain Edward Jennings wrote, "On Saturday the wind blew with great violence from the northeast. The sea ran very high all day, and I supposed that there would be many a wreck along the coast from Barnegat to Egg Harbor...."

As Jennings waited, ships were in trouble all along the mid-Atlantic coast, but none was in a worse position than the *Powhattan.* Less than a mile off Long Beach Island, she had lost her forward mast and was in the grip of the giant northeaster driving relentlessly toward the beach.

"A violent storm of rain and snow commenced here on Friday afternoon, and has continued with considerable violence up to the time of our going to press. We understand that a large vessel is ashore on the outer bar opposite Manahawkin," reported *The Ocean County Emblem.* Little did the editor know that a life-and-death drama was being played out on that sand bar. Late on Saturday, the 127-foot *Powhattan* had grounded fast just south of today's Ship Bottom, about six miles from the nearest house of refuge.

Knowing the severity of the storm, Edward Jennings wasn't surprised when he looked from Manahawkin toward the island early Sunday morning and saw the *Powhattan's* masts silhouetted against the sky. Jennings and Captain Stacy Hazelton rowed across the bay and made their way to the beach where they found the ship in serious trouble. She had swung around and was parallel to the beach, her bow pointed south. Each mountainous wave hit her broadside, raising frightened screams from the passengers crowding the deck.

Several attempts by the ship's crew had already failed to get a line ashore. The *Powhattan* carried no line-throwing mortar and was too far out to snag a rope thrown from shore by hand. The other method of the day, tying a rope to a barrel and floating it from the ship, could not succeed because the current was ripping parallel to the beach, southward.

The only chance the passengers had was the Francis Life Car. On Jennings' orders, Hazelton and three volunteers headed north to get the car from the Harvey Cedars house of refuge, finally reaching the lifesaving building around midafternoon. Here they found Captain Sam Perrine and told him about the wreck and the need for the life car. They also told Perrine that the ocean had breached the island in several places and that moving the equipment under such conditions with the few men at hand would be almost impossible.

Perrine decided to launch the lifeboat in the bay, row south to a point opposite the wreck and then haul the boat and life car across the dunes to the sea. "By the time the boat was brought a short distance to a convenient place for launching her, it was five o'clock, and it was feared that in a fierce gale they could not reach the place that night as the channel is intricate. They concluded therefore to wait until morning," went reports of the rescue effort.

Back at the *Powhattan*, Jennings stood his lonely watch. "During the day the ship's deck was crowded with passengers," he noted, "and when the surf ran out I could get within 75 yards of the vessel." Jennings even got close enough to shout to Myers, but seventy-five yards of freezing ocean and raging seas kept the panic-stricken immigrants from swimming to safety. By now, waves were beginning to wash over the deck. The stronger passengers climbed into the rigging for safety; the weaker ones washed overboard.

"Captain Myers hailed me through his speaking trumpet, and asked me for God's sake to try and save some of those who might come ashore," Jennings would later testify. "I told him I had went down to the beach to where the bodies came on shore, but found them all dead, and it was of no use trying to save them as they were all drowned before they got half way to the beach. Captain Myers asked me just before this if any aid would soon reach them. I said I hoped so, as four men had been sent down to the government station for that purpose."

Myers called out again to try to help those in the water. Said Jennings, "I replied that I would see to it, and went down about 200 yards on the beach where the bodies were being washed ashore. Women and children came on shore first."

All were dead, frozen in the icy water. The only chance for any survivors would be the life car. Then, just before dark, Jennings reported that "the sea rose to a great height, and one large wave, fully a hundred feet high, struck the unfortunate vessel."

His report continued, "The sea was running mountain high and completely hiding the vessel from my view, I could no longer hold any communication with the Captain. I never saw him since. The main and mizzen masts soon went by the board, and bodies appeared floating in the surf in great numbers. Some twenty-five dead bodies, mostly women, came on shore about a mile south of the wreck ... and on one moment the hull was scattered into fragments which tossed wildly through the surf. The shrieks of the drowning creatures were melancholy indeed, but I could render them no aid, as the sea ran so high I could not get near the unfortunate people. In a few moments all disappeared beneath the surface of the water, except a few fragments of the wreck."

The monstrous wave had crushed the ship like an eggshell, spewing what was left of her passengers and crew into the surf. Ashore came a "Girl about 11 years of age. She was in her bare feet, her right eye knocked out, and the right side of her face black and blue," from being pounded against the side of the ship. The body of a twenty-year-old woman also washed up. "On her finger she wore 2 rings, one plain and the other having a heart attached to it, they were marked P.S. and B.S. 1854."

Of the bodies recovered, fifty-eight had washed over the island and into the bay. But for Jennings, the nightmare was not over. As he ran along the beach trying desperately to pull someone out of the surf alive, he looked up and, to his horror, saw in the distance another ship grounded on the bar. Realizing there was nothing more he could do for the unfortunates of the *Powhattan*, Jennings headed for the second wreck and was able to hail the *Manhattan*, a schooner from Bangor, Maine.

Captain Fields and his seven-man crew had been bound for Philadelphia with a load of stone coal when they had been caught by the storm. Unlike the *Powhattan*, the schooner had a shallow draft and was soon driven over the bar and into the surf just off the beach.

As the tide went out, Jennings hailed Fields and proposed a simple plan to get off the vessel safely. The *Manhattan* was close enough to the beach so that if the jib boom was swung out it would cover the distance from the vessel to the sand. Jennings reasoned that Fields and the crew could climb out on the jib and, by rope, lower themselves to the beach and safety.

But Fields refused to abandon his ship. Because Jennings was a wreck master, it meant that Fields, as owner, could lose title to the *Manhattan* if he abandoned ship. Fields also believed that the schooner could weather what was left of the storm.

Fields and the crew took refuge in the after cabin, but when the tide rose, the waves raced over the bar and destroyed the vessel. Too late, Fields ordered his crew to abandon ship. Now, at high tide, too far from the beach to use the boom, five men tried to float ashore on a spar, but the icy water took its toll. Only one seaman was able to hang on long enough to make it to shore.

The next morning, Hazelton, Perrine and the rest of the men Jennings had sent to Harvey Cedars finally returned with the lifecar, but for them there only remained the grim job of piling up the frozen bodies like logs and salvaging baggage and papers.

Now came the cleanup and mostly futile attempts at identification. Bodies washed up as far south as Absecon and Brigantine beaches, fifteen miles down the coast. Some were buried at Smithville where a commemorative plaque on Route 9 still marks the site. The bodies found on the island's beaches were rowed to Manahawkin. One hundred twenty-eight unidentified victims were laid together in a long, shallow trench in the graveyard of the old Baptist church on Main Street.

New York newspapers demanded an investigation. Rumors of "Barnegat pirates" arose, charges that the avaricious islanders had stood by, waiting for the *Powhattan* to break up. In May, the federal government sent James Biddle to investigate the sinking. He visited the rescuers and the houses of refuge and made several recommendations.

Biddle concluded that the island needed more lifesaving stations, notably one at Barnegat Light. He also found that the lifesavers had done all in their power to get to the *Powhattan*. Finally, Biddle recommended that each station have a full-time officer to take care of the equipment and that a bounty system be set up to pay the local men who risked their lives to come to the aid of those in danger. It would take the United States government almost twenty years to act, but when it did, it was basically Biddle's plan which was used as a model for what became the United States Life-Saving Service. In 1915, the Life-Saving Service joined with the Revenue Cutter Service to become the modern-day Coast Guard.

In 1904, the state of New Jersey erected a monument at the Baptist church to the *Powhattan* victims, "For the unknown of the sea." Down through the years, it has been said by many that if you enter the churchyard during a northeast storm, you can hear the wind in the ship's rigging and muffled cries that sound like a foreign language.

CHAPTER 5

New Jersey Split Over Civil War

By fall 1862, New Jersey had twenty-seven regiments, more than thirty thousand men in the Union Army. They had joined to preserve the Union and protect the Constitution. But in September of that year Abraham Lincoln made an announcement which threatened to split the state and maybe the North.

Lincoln was losing the war; in a gamble to keep England and France neutral and add troops to the North and weaken the South, he issued the Emancipation Proclamation, "freeing the slaves in the seceding states."

Issued on September 22, the proclamation became a major issue in the New Jersey state election. Republicans supported the president, while antiwar Democrats, known as Copperheads, demanded immediate peace. The *Newark Journal* described Lincoln as "a perjured traitor who betrayed his country and caused the butchering of hundreds of thousands."

The role of New Jersey in the Civil War was one of contradiction and confusion. The state had abolished slavery in 1804, but it was the only northern state to vote against Lincoln twice. Thousands of its sons died on the battlefields, but it refused to ratify the Thirteenth Amendment which ended slavery.

En route to his inauguration in 1861, Lincoln had stopped at Trenton, where he told the New Jersey Legislature, "This Union, the Constitution, and the liberties of the people shall be perpetuated.... The man does not live who is more devoted to peace than I am. None would do more to preserve it. But it may be necessary to put the foot down firmly.... And if I do my duty, and do right, you will sustain me, will you not?"

Initially, it appeared that New Jerseyans would "sustain" the president. When the Confederacy fired on the American flag at Fort Sumter in April, reaction in New Jersey to the shelling would have pleased Lincoln.

"Thousands of people gathered in the streets, mournfully discussing the imperfect items and conjecturing as to the result," wrote Republican Charles Smith the day after the shelling. "Suddenly there flashed over the wires, 'The Flag is down, and the Fort is in flames!' Then burst forth the long-pent patriotic enthusiasm! The cities suddenly became resplendent with flags! The women and children vied in displaying the national Colors, in badges, rosettes, and in every possible manner. Crowds paraded in the streets, with drums and shouts, visiting the residences of supposed disloyalists and demanding that they show their colors."

The issue was clear: union or disunion. New Jerseyans swarmed to join the armed forces. Four regiments paraded through Washington, D.C., on May 6, the first major group of troops to arrive, but Lincoln's actions began to cause problems to many in the state.

The president had ordered the suspension of habeas corpus in critical areas, most notably Maryland. The U.S. Supreme Court ruled against Lincoln, but he simply ignored the judiciary. He was fighting a war to save the Constitution by ignoring the Constitution. In New Jersey, the Democratic mayor of Burlington, Colonel James W. Wall, was suddenly arrested by federal marshals after he criticized Lincoln for censoring newspapers. Wall was jailed for several weeks. He was never formally charged, nor was any explanation ever given.

Wall was released only after he swore allegiance to the United States. This forced oath turned many a New Jersey citizen against Lincoln and the war.

To galvanize the anti-Lincoln feelings, the Copperheads ran a ticket headed by Wall. The strategy succeeded and the Copperheads were swept into office. The new governor, Joel Parker, was supported by a Copperhead-controlled Legislature, and Wall was sent to Washington as a senator.

News from the battlefield that the Cumberland County regiment had lost 160 men at Fredericksburg further fueled New Jersey's antiwar mood. When the Lincoln administration proposed drafting men to fight in the war, the Copperheads passed their Peace Resolutions in March 1863. The faction believed that Lincoln was not waging war to protect the Constitution, that Lincoln's acts were "without warrant or authority, and if permitted to continue without remonstrance, will finally encompass the destruction of the liberties of the people and the death of the Republic."

Most notably, the state of New Jersey wanted to protest "against the power assumed in the proclamation of the President made January first, 1863, by which all the slaves in certain States and parts of States are forever set free; and against the expenditures of the public moneys for the emancipation of slaves or their support at any time, under any pretence whatever."

Finally, there came a hint that New Jersey might withdraw from the Union, but even before the resolutions passed, loyal New Jersey troops began to take sides. The vast majority followed the example of the Eleventh New Jersey Volunteers.

"The Legislature of our native State ... has sought to tarnish its high honor, and bring upon it disgrace, by the passage of resolutions tending to a dishonorable peace.... We, her sons, members of the Eleventh Regiment New Jersey Volunteers, citizens representing every section of the State, have left our homes to endure the fatigues, privations, and dangers incident to a soldier's life, in order to maintain our Republic in its integrity, willing to sacrifice our lives to that object; fully recognizing the impropriety of a soldier's discussion of the legislative functions of the State, yet deeming it due to ourselves, that the voice of those who offer their all in their country's cause be heard when weak and wicked men seek its dishonor."

The troops went on to condemn the Copperheads.

"We consider the passage, or even the introduction of the so-called Peace Resolutions, as wicked, weak, and cowardly, tending to aid by their sympathy, the rebels seeking to destroy the Republic.... We regard as traitors alike the foe in arms and the secret enemies of our Government, who, at home, foment disaffection and strive to destroy confidence in our legally chosen rulers."

At another rally, an officer of the Twenty-fourth Regiment told his men, "It is a matter of regret and shame that as we endure the perils and sufferings of war ... these traitors at home should be striving to outstrip each other in the haste to throw themselves at the feet of the slave power."

These reactions blunted the major antiwar movement in the state, but there would be riots in Newark against the draft. New Jersey would again vote against Lincoln in 1864 and the following year would refuse to ratify the Thirteenth Amendment to the Constitution. Despite all this, the crusade which had started at the Jersey shore with the work of John Woolman, a simple Quaker minister, had succeeded after 119 years: Slavery in New Jersey and America was finally ended.

CHAPTER 6

Civil War Soap Opera

He was a little-known carpenter from Cape May, but there would be a moment in time when he would be at the center of a whirlwind. Presidents would negotiate and threaten. A newspaper war of editorials would make his name a household word. And the people of our divided nation would follow his fate like a soap opera.

The story of Captain Henry Washington Sawyer begins in October 1861. The American Civil War had seen its first battle at Bull Run. Desperate to put down the South, President Abraham Lincoln suspended the writ of habeas corpus, empowering the army to seize and hold civilians and imprison or execute them without using civilian courts.

Under this authority, two Confederate officers, William Corbin and T. G. McGraw, were arrested in Kentucky for trying to recruit soldiers. Taken to the headquarters of General Ambrose Burnside in Sandusky, Ohio, the two captains were tried as spies and sentenced to death. A sister of one of the men wrote to Burnside, begging him to spare the life of her brother. Burnside replied that the executions would be carried out on time and stated he and the North "had quit handling the rebellion with gloves."

The publication of the letter and the ensuing executions enraged Southerners who demanded satisfaction. Meanwhile, a Mr. Henry Sawyer had joined the First New Jersey Cavalry and had risen from first lieutenant to captain of Company K. On June 9, 1863, the First New Jersey engaged the forces of Jeb Stuart at the Battle of Brandy Station. A survivor recalled the battle.

"The rebel traitors poured down upon us. Then Colonel Broderick gave the order 'charge' and instantly every man drove his spurs deep into his horse's flanks, and with a yell as only the 1st New Jersey boys can give, we rode upon the rebels. Colonel Broderick led the charge.... The rebels were armed and used the pistol principally; our boys generally the sabre. It was a regular hand-to-hand encounter, and in less than a minute the whole regiment was engaged.... The noise and din of pistol shots, and clash of sabres was perfectly deafening, and the curses and yells on both sides rent the air."

The colonel was killed. Riding with him was Captain Sawyer, who was wounded and captured. Eventually he was taken to infamous Libby prison in Richmond, Virginia.

On July 6, Confederate President Jefferson Davis ordered the honor of the South to be avenged. The seventy-four Union captains at Libby prison would be assembled. Two would be selected by lot "to be shot in retaliation" for the executions of the two Confederate captains. The *Richmond Dispatch* reported the scene.

"Amid a silence almost deathlike, the Reverend Joseph T. Brown performed the drawing. The first name read was Captain Henry Washington Sawyer, First New Jersey Cavalry; the second, Captain John Flinn, Fifty-first Indiana. When the names were read out, Sawyer heard it with no apparent emotion, remarking that someone had to be drawn and he could stand it as well as anyone else. Flinn was very white and much depressed. Sawyer asked permission to write a letter home, while Flinn said he had no letters to write home, and only wanted a priest."

Sawyer's letter to his wife appeared on the front page of every major Northern newspaper.

"The Provost General, J. G. Winder, assures me that the Secretary of War of the Southern Confederacy will permit yourself and my dear children to visit me before I am executed.... My situation is hard to be borne and I cannot think of dying without seeing you and the children.... I am resigned to whatever is in store for me, with the consolation that I die without having committed any crime. I had no trial, no jury, nor am I charged with any crime, but it fell to my lot."

As Sawyer prepared for death, he told his wife he would go like a man. "Bring with you a shirt for me." His concern for his wife and children's future was clear. He told her she was due his back pay, plus "Capt. B___ owes me fifty dollars — money lent him when he went on furlough. You will write him at once, and he will send it to you."

Finally, he wrote, "My dear wife, the fortune of war has put me in this position. If I must die a sacrifice to my country, by God's will, I must submit; only let me see you once more, and I will die as becomes a man and an officer; but for God's sake do not disappoint me....

"I have done nothing to deserve this penalty. But you must submit to your fate. It will be no disgrace to myself, you or the children; but you may point with pride and say, 'I gave my husband'; my children will have the consolation to say, 'I was made an orphan for my country.' "

Now it was the turn for Northerners to be enraged; by mid-July New Jersey papers dropped hints about the tactics used by President Lincoln to win the release of the two captains. The *New Brunswick Daily Fredonian* reported, "Notice has been given that such execution would be retaliated severely," then just two days later wrote that "our Government will retaliate by hanging officers two or three degrees higher in rank."

Lincoln had ordered a search of the list of names of all Confederate prisoners; he wanted the two most important men he could find, and what he found pleased him. The first was a twenty-six-year-old Harvard graduate who had risen to the rank of colonel in the Ninth Virginia Cavalry. He, like Sawyer, had been wounded at Brandy Station and captured when Union troops attacked the house where he was convalescing. The colonel was William H. Fitzhugh Lee, second oldest son of Confederate General Robert E. Lee.

The second was Captain W. S. Winder, son of the Confederate officer who had selected the two Union officers for death and whom the *Fredonian* called "the notorious jailer of Libby Prison." Soon the newspaper proudly proclaimed the reason behind the search of the prison records, quoting the president on July 20, "as Jefferson Davis does by Sawyer and Clunn [sic] so shall we do by Lee and Winder."

That same day, Sawyer wrote to a friend from prison. "I have been upon many hard-fought fields of battle, where death seemed to stare me in the face; but, sir, all that is nothing compared with what I experience every hour. It is a great inconvenience to which prisoners of war are in all cases subjected, to have their letters inspected; but this is the rule in all countries. A third person, cold-blooded at best, if not what is worse, with an inclination [to] hold up to ridicule the expression of grief or affection, is permitted to have the reviewing of a man's heart toward a beloved wife and children, a dear old mother or friend."

But the publication of these letters had little effect on the South. A Confederate officer wrote in his diary, "The two officers write somewhat lugubriously, in bad grammar and execrable chirography." Furthermore, he alleged, the two Yankees were far from gallant when they said they had never served under General Burnside, who had executed the Confederates, so "they should not be made to suffer for his deed. They say we have two of Burnside's captains at Atlanta [and they give their names] who would be the proper victims."

As the long hot summer wore on, the people of New Jersey had their own soap opera.

Meanwhile, it seemed that the South was unmoved when Lincoln announced his threat to shoot Winder and Lee. The *Richmond Examiner* printed the typical Confederate reply.

The Confederacy "will not be intimidated.... It is hoped that the Executive [Jefferson Davis] will see fit to give the order for the execution [of Sawyer and Flinn] immediately; and as we now have over 500 federal officers in our hands, besides 5,000 or 6,000 privates, it is in the power of the Government to carry retaliation to a very bitter extreme. The people call for death of these two Yankees, and it is useless to delay their deaths any longer."

As Sawyer awaited his fate he was told his wife would be allowed to visit him. She traveled from Cape May to Union-held Fortress Monroe near Norfolk. From there she was to proceed under a flag of truce up the James River to Richmond and Libby prison. But even Sawyer's wife became a pawn in the political struggle. The New Brunswick `American

Standard's headline read, "Evidence of atrocious vindictiveness on the part of the rebel leaders." The paper went on to explain what happened.

"Mrs. Sawyer ... on arriving at City Point, on the flag of truce boat, made application to the Confederate authorities to be permitted to visit Richmond ... [but] the authorities denied her permission, and she returned on the same boat."

Mobs gathered outside Sawyer's cell and chanted for his execution, but the events on the battlefield began to have an effect on the political leaders. Vicksburg fell to the Union as the Confederates were defeated at Gettysburg. The hostage stories faded from the front page. Secret negotiations took place. Finally, in March 1864, instead of shooting captain for captain, the two sides agreed to a prisoner exchange.

Lee and Winder returned to fight with the Army of Northern Virginia. Flinn went back to the Army of the Potomac. For Sawyer, Lincoln had one important mission: 1864 was a presidential election year, and New Jersey was a key state. Sawyer, now a symbol of Northern manhood and strength, campaigned for Lincoln and his policies.

In May, *The Salem Standard* reported that Sawyer had been exchanged and would "deliver an address in the Town Hall, Millville.... The Major in a neat and patriotic speech ... said that he had originally disapproved of the Emancipation Proclamation, and Negro enlistments, but from his education among the rebels he had been taught to see the wisdom of both, because both were calculated to injure the rebels. He thought the interest of the country demanded the reelection of Mr. Lincoln."

In the fall election Lincoln again failed to carry New Jersey. Sawyer left both the Army and politics to take up a successful career as a hotel owner in Cape May. Today, in the town's historic district, a bronze plaque marks Captain Sawyer's moment in time when he was the nation's most famous hostage.

PART THREE

CHAPTER 7

Jerseymen Fight at Appomattox

The First New Jersey Cavalry was made up of volunteers who had answered President Lincoln's call in 1861 at the start of the Civil War. Four years later they had been battle tested in nearly ninety skirmishes and campaigns. Now they were in the vanguard of a dash to end America's bloodiest war.

Philip Sheridan, commander of the Union cavalry, was in a race to the west. He was trying to prevent Robert E. Lee and the Army of Northern Virginia from getting around him and linking up with General Joseph Johnston and his force in North Carolina.

Lee had gambled everything on this one move. Hoping to keep the Confederacy alive and continue the war, he had abandoned Richmond on April 2 and taken every able-bodied man with him. The first leg of the race was won by Lee and his half-starved army when they reached Amelia Court House ahead of Sheridan. Here they were to meet a trainload of supplies, but it never arrived. Lee, desperate, held the army there for a day as he tried to get food to his hungry men and animals.

The day had not been wasted by Sheridan's cavalry. They arrived at Jetersville, about ten miles south of Amelia Court House, on April 4 and immediately sent out a reconnaissance. The force, under the command of Captain Samuel Craig and with companies A and B of the First New Jersey, captured twenty-two rebel soldiers. From the prisoners Craig learned that Lee was still at Amelia Court House and that the Union forces now blocked Lee's route of escape southward toward Johnston.

Sheridan prepared to concentrate his forces at Jetersville, calling back the division heading in the direction of Amelia Court House and bringing in reinforcements. The first of these men arrived that evening, and the combined forces prepared for Lee to attack. Sheridan sent a message to General Ulysses Grant evaluating the situation: "If we press on we will no doubt get the entire army."

Early on the fifth, Lee abandoned any idea of heading due south, knowing it would be suicide to attack Sheridan's entrenched forces at Jetersville. However, he could not stay at Amelia Court House because his men faced almost certain starvation. His only hope now was to head west toward Lynchburg, where he might receive supplies, then to either cross the Blue Ridge Mountains to Lynchburg or make another attempt to get around Sheridan.

As the sun rose, the Union forces awaited Lee's attack, but as time passed it became apparent that something was wrong. Sheridan ordered General Henry Davies to move his brigade to make a reconnaissance to the rear of the enemy. During this mission Davies learned that Lee's wagon trains were passing a point about four miles from the town. He ordered the brigade to a gallop to intercept them.

Catching the wagon train by surprise, the lead regiment, the First Pennsylvania, gave a fox hunting cry and led the brigade in a charge through a swamp. They captured five pieces of artillery before the Confederates could get the guns ready to fire. They also took about 750 prisoners and eleven battle flags. Davies ordered the horses and prisoners taken back to Jetersville, but the captured wagons were burned because of the approach of a large body of Confederate cavalry under General Martin Gary.

A running battle began between Gary's forces and Davies' rear guard, the First New Jersey, under the command of Lieutenant Colonel Hugh Janeway. Davies ordered Janeway to hold the town of Painesville for a half hour while the horses and prisoners were withdrawn to Jetersville. The regiment repelled several charges by Gary's men but was finally routed and driven back. This rebel advance was stopped when the Jersey troops were reinforced. During the series of charges that followed, Janeway was shot in the head and died almost instantly.

The discovery of the wagon train was crucial to Sheridan. It meant that Lee was trying to avoid a battle by escaping to the west, and the Union general wanted to attack immediately.

At about midafternoon, General George Gordon Meade arrived south of Jetersville. Meade had been forced to travel by ambulance because he was too ill to ride. Hearing Sheridan's plan for an immediate attack, Meade decided to be more cautious, delaying any action until morning so more troops could arrive. Since Meade was the senior officer, Sheridan decided to take his case to Grant.

Sheridan wrote a message detailing Davies' raid and expressing his wish that Grant were at Jetersville saying, "I feel confident of capturing the Army of Northern Virginia if we exert ourselves."

When Grant read the dispatch he knew Lee had been stopped at Jetersville. Grant and a small party set out for Sheridan's headquarters where the two generals conferred late that night with Grant finally sending a message to Meade. "I would go over to see you this evening, but I have ridden a long distance today. Your orders directing an attack tomorrow will hold in the absence of others, but it is my impression that Lee will retreat during the night, and, if so, we will pursue with vigor."

As Meade's dawn attack began, it became apparent that Lee had escaped to the west. At about this time Meade also learned that Lee was to meet a ration train at Farmville, about fifteen miles west of Jetersville.

The race to the west was on again, with Grant's strategy shaping up on the move. First, Grant would try to beat Lee to Farmville and destroy the bridges over the Appomattox River. Meanwhile, Sheridan would parallel Lee's route, making constant flanking attacks to slow him down. Finally, Major General Andrew Humphreys would follow Lee, giving him no rest.

The morning and early afternoon of the sixth had been a series of delaying actions fought by Lee's rear guard. Sheridan's big chance finally presented itself at about three o'clock as Lee's columns began crossing Sayler's Creek. A gap formed in the Confederate line when one general received orders to cross the creek, but two other generals did not.

George Custer, the general leading Sheridan's advance division, spotted the gap. Custer's men came on an unprotected wagon train and attacked, smashing wagon wheels with axes, cutting traces and driving off the teams. Custer called for reinforcements, and Davies arrived to support him. Sheridan, seeing that he had cut off a large portion of enemy, sent at once for more men.

While the cavalry waited for reinforcements, a mix-up in orders nearly caused disaster. While Custer's division was ordered to withdraw, Colonel Walter R. Robbins, the new commander of the First New Jersey, received orders to charge. For a few moments, the lone Jersey regiment came under the concentrated fire of the entire rebel line and was driven back with heavy losses.

About two hours later, a combined attack was made. Davies' men jumped the Confederates' breastworks and captured about a thousand prisoners, along with two guns and two battle flags. In all, almost eight thousand prisoners were taken at Sayler's Creek. Lee, who had ridden back and saw the end of the battle from a hilltop, said, "My God, has the army been dissolved?"

Lee continued his march to Farmville where his army got rations for the first time in four days. He planned to get his men north of the flooded Appomattox River by crossing two bridges at Farmville, then destroying them to prevent Grant from following. The job of destroying the bridges was given to the chief engineer, Colonel T. M. R. Talcott.

As the last Confederates crossed the bridges, Talcott could not start the fires because he had not received his orders. The delay would prove fatal for the Confederacy. When the fires were finally lit, the pinewood railroad bridge burned well, but the wagon bridge, which was hardwood, would not catch. Union troops captured the bridge and began crossing in force. With the failure to destroy the bridges, Lee lost any chance to rest his army and was forced to order an immediate march in the direction of Cumberland Church.

After crossing the river, Union troops attacked what was thought to be an unprotected wagon train south of Cumberland Church. The wagon train turned out to be a trap with twelve guns of the New Orleans Artillery opening fire on the troops immediately. The charge was repelled in complete disorder.

Davies, seeing that the rout might carry to the following brigades, ordered Robbins' First New Jersey to the left of the road in a flanking attack. The Jerseyans did this with great success, stopping the Confederates' advances and checking the retreat. The rebel trap had succeeded only in holding up the cavalry chase, since the cavalry stopped until the infantry could arrive.

On the night of the seventh, Grant was in Farmville. It was from here that he sent his first call to Lee asking for a surrender.

The eighth was a day of communication between Lee and Grant, but for the armies it was just another day of hard marching. Lee's men, north of the Appomattox, marched west toward Lynchburg. Grant's force divided in two. The infantry followed Lee; the cavalry stayed south of the river and tried to get ahead of him.

Sheridan, learning that a rebel supply train was at Appomattox Depot, sent Custer ahead to destroy it and tear up track. This action drove the Confederates northeast toward Appomattox Court House. Late in the afternoon, the rest of the Union cavalry arrived, blocking the road west.

That night, Lee met with his commanders and decided to attack at first light, calculating that if they were opposed only by cavalry a breakthrough might be accomplished. They also knew that if the Union infantry arrived, there would be no other choice but surrender.

Shortly after dawn, Lee's men advanced. Davies' brigade, including the First New Jersey, was on the extreme left of the Union line. Just as Lee had hoped, the Union cavalry was driven back toward Appomattox Depot and it looked as if his plan to escape might succeed. But Union infantry arrived and rallied the cavalry, repulsing Lee's last-gasp attack.

Sheridan ordered the infantry to the middle of the Union line to face Lee and put the cavalry on the flanks. The First New Jersey was ordered to the extreme left of the line and formed up as skirmishers. As Sheridan readied his men for a final charge, a lone rider with a white flag emerged from the Confederate forces and rode toward the Union line. It was over.

In this final major encounter of the Civil War, the First New Jersey was the last unit to receive word of the cease-fire and claimed to have the last man wounded before Lee's surrender. The war's human cost for the Union was 360,220. More than six thousand of these were Jerseymen.

CHAPTER 8

The President Dies in Long Branch

During the last few hours of his life, Charles Guiteau was concerned about his place in history. He wrote that his life story should be called "The Life and Work of Charles Guiteau." Confident that this would secure his fame he added, "If at any time hereafter any person or persons shall desire to honor my remains, they can do it by erecting a monument whereon shall be inscribed these words: 'Here lies the body of Charles Guiteau, Patriot and Christian. His soul is in glory.' "

But there are no statues or monuments to Charles Guiteau, and the name isn't even familiar to most students of history. The one thing that *is* known is that Guiteau did change its course.

Born in Illinois in 1841, Guiteau had an unhappy childhood. His mother died when he was seven, and his father, a stern and extremely religious man, whipped him repeatedly for a speech impediment. The boy became more unruly and eventually was raised by an older sister and her husband.

Guiteau had an aversion to physical work but appeared brighter than normal. Unfortunately, deluded by his own importance, he led an aimless life, always looking for an easy way to make money. In 1880 he claimed to have supported James A. Garfield for president, moved to Washington and began to make appointments with the secretary of state and even Garfield himself to ask for jobs.

James Abram Garfield was ten years old when Guiteau was born. Garfield's family was very poor, but James was a hard worker and graduated from Williams College in Massachusetts in 1856. For a time he taught school in his hometown in Ohio where he was also a lay preacher in his church. His ability at public speaking led him into politics and in 1859 as a Republican he was elected to the Ohio state senate.

With the outbreak of the Civil War, Garfield joined the Union Army and rose to the rank of major general. He resigned in 1863 after being elected to the House of Representatives where he served for the next seventeen years. On March 4, 1881, Garfield was inaugurated as the twentieth president of the United States, and Charles Guiteau moved to Washington.

During the first weeks of Garfield's presidency, Guiteau was constantly at the White House seeking an appointment as American consul to Paris or Vienna. He took his case to the State Department where he finally got to see Secretary of State James Blaine who told Guiteau there was "no prospect whatever" for a job. On April 26 he somehow got into a White House reception hosted by First Lady Lucretia Garfield and tried to enlist her support. By May, White House ushers were told that Guiteau "should be quietly kept away."

A disgruntled Guiteau had a vision which came to him "like a flash." He said it was a message from God: Somehow, Vice President Chester A. Arthur must be made president. On May 23, Guiteau tried one last time for an appointment with Garfield, writing, "I have been trying to be your friend."

After waiting for a response from the White House, Guiteau purchased a .44-caliber revolver and a box of cartridges. Twice he went down to the Potomac River and practiced firing the gun. On the twelfth he waited outside a window of the church where Garfield was attending services, but he could not get a clear shot.

On June 18 the president accompanied his wife to the railroad station to see her off on a visit to the Jersey shore. Guiteau, shadowing Garfield, lost his nerve again when he saw Mrs. Garfield, "a thin, delicate, sickly lady." Next he followed the president as he walked the streets of Washington, and on June 28 followed Garfield and Blaine as they took a walk in a park. Again Guiteau could not find the courage to shoot.

By July 2, Guiteau was desperate. Garfield was leaving for an extended vacation on the Jersey shore at Long Branch. He prepared a note explaining his actions: "The President's tragic death was a sad necessity, but it will unite the Republican party.... It will be no worse for Mrs. Garfield, dear soul, to part with her husband this way than by natural death. He is liable to go at any time anyway.... I had no ill will towards the president. His death was a political necessity. I am a lawyer, a theologian, a politician.... I have some papers for the press ... all the reporters can see them. I am going to jail."

As Garfield and Blaine walked through the railroad station waiting room, Guiteau waited for them to pass, stepped up and drew his revolver, pointed it at Garfield's back and fired two shots at point-blank range. The first shot hit the president's right arm; the second entered the body three and one-half inches to the right of the spinal column between the tenth and eleventh ribs. Blaine turned to Garfield who threw up his arms and gasped, "My God, what is that?"

As Guiteau turned to make his way to a waiting taxi, a police officer rushed up and grabbed him. "I did it and will go to jail for it. I am a Stalwart and Arthur will be President," he shouted.

Garfield was taken to a nearby room where Dr. William Bliss of Ohio took charge of the president's care. Bliss first probed the wound with his finger, then a long metal probe — neither of which had been washed or sterilized — but could not find the bullet. Garfield beckoned to an aide and said, "I think you had better telegraph Crete," his wife, who was already in Long Branch. Then the president told the group, "I think you had better get me to the White House as soon as you can."

Garfield was carried back over the spot where he had been shot to a horse-drawn ambulance which began the ride over Washington's rough, cobblestone streets. By now a large crowd had gathered outside the station, and hundreds followed the conveyance to the White House.

When word reached Mrs. Garfield, a special train was arranged and a wild ride followed through New Jersey, Pennsylvania and Maryland. That evening, Mrs. Garfield, "frail, fatigued, desperate, but firm and quiet and full of purpose to save," was by her husband's side.

As the president lay in the White House, the best medical team available was assembled to try to save him. Unfortunately, most American doctors of the time ridiculed the works of Joseph Lister and scoffed at the idea that sanitation had anything to do with infection. Secondly, most of the president's doctors were homeopathic physicians who believed in treating patients by giving them medicines which caused reactions similar to the symptoms.

And so it would be that the president would be subjected to more unwashed fingers and dirty probes stuck into his wound as the doctors tried in vain to locate the bullet. As the nation watched and read the bulletins on Garfield's condition, a sad Fourth of July passed as the president developed a fever. Two days later, a Washington astronomer named Simon Newcomb suggested locating the bullet through an electrical device.

When the theory was printed in the newspapers, it was read by Alexander Graham Bell, the inventor of the telephone, who at once volunteered his Boston laboratory. Now began a life-and-death race between Bell and the infection in Garfield's body. His first experiments were based on placing a large light behind a person to cast an outline of the bullet, much like holding your hand over a flashlight, but this method failed because of the location of the bullet and the strength of light needed.

Bell then turned to a phenomenon produced when two overlapping flat spiral coils are positioned in a certain way. By passing an electric current through them, Bell found that an audible signal could be produced when the device was held near metal.

By the fourteenth, Bell moved his experiments to a laboratory in Washington. It had been twelve days since the president had been shot, and he was weakening. At a frantic pace, work continued in Boston, Washington and Baltimore with Bell coordinating everything by telegraph, but by the twenty-third, the president had taken a serious turn for the worse. His temperature was 104 degrees and the city was sweltering in a heat wave: From around the country, suggestions poured in on how to cool the president's room. On the twenty-fifth a condenser was added to Bell's invention, increasing by a half inch the depth at which it could detect a bullet. Bell was now ready.

The following day, Bell described Garfield. "His face is very pale — or rather it is of an ashen gray color which makes one feel for a moment that you are not looking upon a living man. It made my heart bleed to look at him and think of all he must have suffered to bring him to this."

The experiment was disappointing. The sound was not localized. "That horrid, unbalanced sputtering kept coming and going.... I feel woefully disappointed and disheartened," observed Bell. He returned to the lab to discover that the wiring had been hooked up incorrectly. He made several improvements and tried again.

Word was sent to have an adjoining room ready for the equipment and to remove all metal from Garfield's bedroom. Again Bell listened as the doctors passed the metal detecting paddles back and forth over the president's body. This time there was no local sound, but a strong background of metal detected everywhere.

A dejected Bell finally left, unable to explain the failure of his device. It was later discovered that when the doctors and a maid had cleared the room of all metal objects, they had neglected to look in one very important place. It seems the president had a modern bed, one supported on iron springs.

By the time of the discovery and further improvements to the device, the president was too weak to survive surgery even if the bullet could be located precisely. Although Bell's invention would not help Garfield, it would eventually save countless lives and also become a familiar device on New Jersey beaches as, respectively, the mine detector and the metal detector of today.

The oppressive heat only added to Garfield's suffering. Only once could he even dictate a letter. "Dear Mother: Don't be disturbed by conflicting reports about my condition. It is true I am still weak, and on my back, but I am gaining every day, and need only time and patience to bring me through. Give my love to all the relatives and friends and especially to sisters, Hitty and Mary. Your loving son, J. Garfield."

As August drew to a close with no break in the weather, Garfield, who had lost close to one hundred pounds, feebly asked if he could be taken to the Jersey shore. He had already planned to make his summer White House at Francklyn Cottage in the Elberon section of Long Branch. Finally, in early September the doctors agreed that the "good air" of New Jersey was the president's last and only hope.

By the fourth preparations were under way for the move with two special railroad tracks laid, one from the White House to the main rail line, the other from the Long Branch station to Francklyn Cottage. Three hundred men worked all of the day and well into the night to put down the smoothest track they could to keep Garfield comfortable. On the sixth, the president began his ride on rails that had been oiled to make the trip as smooth as possible. Wrote the president's secretary, "One of the pleasantest things about the whole trip ... was the admirable conduct of the people along the entire route from Washington to Elberon. Everybody in every town and hamlet seemed to know the train was coming, and at every station and farmhouse people lined the track; but they seemed to feel that noise was not good for the president, and so, instead of cheering, as one might naturally expect them to do, they simply took off their hats and stood in silence as the train went past. Even the street urchins in Washington were quiet as we left the city. In Baltimore and Philadelphia there were great crowds, mostly of laboring men and nearly every man stood with uncovered head while we were passing. I helped carry the president to the express wagon at the White House ... and it was the first time I had seen him for 17 days. His face was much less emaciated than I had expected to find it. After we got him into the car and during the trip the president took considerable interest in what was going on. There were scarcely any incidents worth mentioning on the train. One of the most touching things was the manner of the people at the few places where we stopped to take in coal and water for the engine. The people would crowd up around the train and whisper to us, 'How is the president? How does he stand the ride?' and similar questions, but they were always asked in whispers. No one would talk loudly and everybody seemed anxious not to do anything that could possibly disturb Mr. Garfield...."

For the next several days there was hope in the air. Garfield was even able to be moved to a reclining chair and look toward the beach and say, "Oh, the beautiful sea." But soon he began to slip. By the sixteenth, the secretary of state cabled from Long Branch, "A sensible increase in anxiety." By the eighteenth, he talked of "grave apprehensions."

On the morning of the nineteenth, Garfield asked to see his children. By now he was very weak. That evening he spent some time with his wife talking of their farm in Ohio and of the good times they had shared. At about ten, Garfield woke with a gasp and said to General Wager Swain, a longtime friend, "Oh Swain, Swain! I am in terrible agony, can't you do something to relieve me? Oh my heart! The terrible pain." Seventy-nine days after being shot, James A. Garfield died.

"Mrs. Garfield sat in a chair shaking convulsively, with the tears pouring down her cheeks, but uttering no sound. After awhile she arose, and taking hold of her dead husband's arm smoothed it up and down. Poor little Mollie threw herself upon her father's shoulder on the other side of the bed and sobbed as if her heart would break. Everybody else was weeping slightly."

At his trial Charles Guiteau claimed he was not responsible for the president's death since he lived so long after the shooting; it was the doctors' malpractice which caused death.

He also claimed he couldn't be tried because Garfield had died in New Jersey, not Washington where the trial was held.

On June 30, 1882, after condemning Chester Arthur for ingratitude since the assassination had made him president, and with the words of a hymn on his lips, Guiteau was hanged.

While the Washington theater where Abraham Lincoln was shot is a national historical site, the railway station where Garfield was shot was torn down for another building. The house where Lincoln spent his last few hours has been preserved as it was at the moment he died. The house where Garfield spent his last weeks was leveled in the 1950s.

CHAPTER 9

The Blizzard of 1888, Jersey Style

On March 10 in Washington, D.C., weathermen at the War Department Signal Service — the forerunner of the National Weather Service — plotted two storms. One contained cold air pouring over the Rocky Mountains. The second, filled with moisture from the Gulf of Mexico, was over Georgia.

Telegraphed out to Philadelphia and New York, the forecast for the Atlantic states on the brink of spring in 1888 seemed innocent enough. "Fresh to brisk easterly winds, with rain ... colder brisk westerly winds and fair weather for Monday."

The forecasters expected the western storm to head north, the gulf storm to move harmlessly out to sea. Late that Saturday afternoon, the local New York weather observatory made its forecast: "Cloudy weather followed by light rain and clearing, for Sunday, March 11, in the city and points within thirty miles." With that, the office closed as usual until Sunday.

The next day it did rain, but not the light rain of the forecast. It was the wind-driven rain associated with a classic northeaster. Roads and cellars from Virginia to New York began to fill with water. What no one knew was that the storm to the south had turned up the coast and was pulling in huge amounts of moisture from the ocean. Meanwhile, the cold air was beginning to make its presence felt.

Throughout the day, the temperature fell. By late afternoon, sleet mixed with rain; by midnight it was snow. At 3:00 A.M., it was twenty-nine degrees Fahrenheit; at 6:00, twenty-three degrees; at 9:00, eighteen degrees; and by noon, fourteen degrees. Winds were blowing at thirty-five miles an hour with gusts up to seventy-five.

New York lost contact with Washington and Philadelphia as, one by one, telegraph and telephone lines iced up and snapped under the weight of the snow. By Monday morning all four hundred lines to Washington were out.

At dawn, early risers looked out their windows to see a foot or more of wind-whipped snow. In New York City, most people could not see the buildings on the other side of the street. Those who could afford to rolled over and went back to sleep, but most people had to get to their jobs. "No work, no pay" was largely the rule of employers in 1888.

According to *The New York Times,* "Lots of respectable citizens, who had theretofore rather hugged the flattering delusion to their souls that it took a pretty good man to handle them, came to the conclusion before they had got many roads from their houses that home was a mighty comfortable place, and that Payne hit the nail on the head when he sang 'Home, Sweet Home.' Having come to that conclusion they turned round...."

A man tried to cross Ninety-sixth Street and was dug out the next day. A bored hotel guest went looking for a newspaper. His body was found in a snow bank two weeks later. In all, two hundred New Yorkers died, including three children poisoned by their mother because she couldn't stand to see them "cold and shivering."

By late afternoon, the drifts in famed Herald Square had reached thirty feet, and it was still snowing. Those who had made it to work in the morning had to return home. A clerk told of his seven-hour ordeal. "I do not know how I kept going. When I reached East 84th Street I was glazed in ice, nearly dead. The snow was up to the crosspiece of the lamppost. I had to crawl over that mound to get to my door."

On Tuesday it was still snowing, the temperature was five degrees, and there was a fifty-mile-an-hour wind. The city was completely paralyzed.

Fifty inches of snow fell on parts of Connecticut. In towns along the Hudson River, drifts of up to sixty feet were reported. In Livingston, New Jersey, a milkman named Xavier Zwinge chose to wait out the storm in a local tavern. His horse decided to make the trek home where Zwinge's alarmed wife reported him missing. "Alone [a local newsman surmised in print] he had gone to his reward in that blizzard-swept wasteland." A couple of days later, milkman Zwinge trudged home where neighbors were consoling his grieving "widow."

"I wasn't dead ... just drunk," he said.

In Ocean County, the people did battle with the elements. At the height of the storm on Tuesday, the temperature at Toms River was fourteen degrees with a gale-force wind. According to the *Ocean County Courier,* "The first blast of the storm, after the shift of wind, was terrific, and most of our residents were aroused by the rocking of their homes upon the foundations. With the wind came snow, flying, swirling, drifting before the blast, and by seven o'clock a full one foot of snow had fallen, which however, was piled up in drifts some of which attained the height of five or six feet.

"All through the day the storm continued, the snow falling and the wind blowing, until at night the ground was covered with a white mantle two feet deep on a level, piled up in spots to ten and even fifteen feet. Fences were obliterated, doors and windows shut in, and business was entirely suspended. It is probably safe to say that not $100 changed hands in this town during the day."

County residents were on their own, the newspaper said. "All communication with the outside world was cut off, no mails have arrived at the time of writing, and the telegraph wires beyond the station at Long Branch are down. Attempts were made on Monday to get two trains — one on the Pennsylvania Railroad and the other on the New Jersey Southern Railway — through, but neither succeeded. A train on the latter road, Frank S. Ellis conductor, left Barnegat at 6 a.m. and left [Toms River] at 7:03 a.m., on time, for New York, but at 1 o'clock p.m. had reached Farmingdale and was there stalled...."

Being cut off from the outside world was not the only problem for the county's coastal residents. On Long Beach Island, the monster northeaster produced high tides and flooding. Local papers later told, "The storm of last week was particularly severe at Beach Haven, where two new houses in course of erection were blown down, and a portion of Station Agent Baker's house was wrecked. The cottage owned by Charles Gibbons of Philadelphia was also damaged."

Other news accounts confirm the storm's severity: "The station building at North Beach Haven was blown down, and a portion of Dr. Tucker's new cottage was wrecked."

"The sloop yacht *Alice Ridgeway* went ashore on the beach meadows near Little Egg Harbor lighthouse. She is owned by William E. Cranmer."

"N. S. Cranmer's yacht *Sherwood* went ashore at Harvey Cedars and was badly stove."

"In some places at Beach Haven water washed over the railroad tracks, and the rails were coated with three inches of ice. The rails on the bridge across the bay were also covered with ice, which the section men had to knock off before the train could get across on Thursday noon."

Blizzard or not, the island's lifesaving stations were on alert. Lifesavers braved subzero temperatures, howling winds and a roaring surf. However, except for local accounts, their heroism went unnoticed.

"During the gale on Wednesday the schooner yacht *Whim*, bound from New York to Norfolk, Va., dragged her anchor at Barnegat Inlet and drifted out to sea, standing on Barnegat shoals," reported the *Courier.* "She was discovered on Thursday morning by the life-saving crew from the station at Barnegat Inlet and a line was shot to the vessel which enabled the crew to come ashore in the patent metallic life car. The yacht then drifted out to sea but drifted back to Barnegat on Friday and was boarded by the patrolmen, who turned her over to the crew. The vessel was found to be in comparatively good condition."

One final note: While New York and Philadelphia remained paralyzed for days after the blizzard, on Tuesday at the storm's height Stafford Township held a town meeting.

CHAPTER 10

Submarine Inventor Surfaces in Paterson

New Jersey was the home of one of the leading terrorist inventors of all times, Joseph P. Holland. Today he is honored with a major landmark named for him, but his terrorist inventions have killed thousands.

Born and raised in Ireland, Holland was a schoolteacher. His hatred for British rule in his homeland led him to daydream of an invention which would neutralize the symbol of Britain's might, her navy. He envisioned an underwater craft which would make the British fleet vulnerable to attack.

Not wanting the British to discover them, Holland kept most of his ideas secret. "I was an Irishman," he explained later. "I had never taken part in any political agitation, but my sympathies were with my own country, and I had no mind to do anything that would make John Bull [England] any stronger and more domineering than we had already found him." In 1873, he set sail for America.

Holland finally settled in Paterson where he also taught school. Operating in north Jersey was a clandestine Irish independence society known as the Finian Brotherhood, an organization of Irish exiles looking for ways to strike at Great Britain. Holland was soon introduced to one of its leaders.

"Dear Mr. Collins: I introduce to you a Mr. Holland of Paterson. He visited me in connection with a torpedo [boat] he has invented, and I wish you would have a few minutes' conversation with him."

A member of the society later recalled, "[Holland] was well informed of Irish affairs and was anti-English and with clear and definite ideas of the proper method of fighting England. He was cool, good-tempered, and talked to us as a schoolmaster would to his children."

Holland won the group's support to build a submarine. As the leader of the Finians wrote, "The salt water enterprise I fully endorse. We can do it and we mean to try.... It is a business must be handled, at least talked about very gingerly. No loose pavement nor barroom palaver will do for that work."

Irish immigrants donated money to fund Holland's "salt water enterprise." Finally, in 1878, he was able to test his prototype. He wrote triumphantly, "The longest time spent under water in this little boat was one hour."

But his first submarine wasn't a weapon. Soon, "my financial supporters, the Trustees of the Finian Skirmishing Fund, determined to build a larger boat," Holland wrote. Work now began in earnest on the *Finian Ram,* a true warship. She would be thirty-one feet long and carry a crew of three. She would also be equipped with a pneumatic gun which could fire a charge from underwater.

Holland described the *Ram:* "There is scarcely anything required of a good submarine boat that this one did not do well enough, or fairly well.... It could remain quite a long time submerged, probably three days; it could shoot a torpedo [projectile] containing a 100 pound charge to 50 or 60 yards in a straight line underwater and to some uncertain range, probably 300 yards over water."

Soon, on the Jersey side of the Hudson River, Holland was able to write of the *Ram,* "She lay at the Morris and Cummings Dredging Company's dock in Jersey City until July 3, 1883, during which time many experiments were made with her.... The first run on the surface was made in the Basin, or passage, east of the Lehigh Valley Railroad."

Over the next several months Holland continued to test his new submarine, but his backers were getting impatient; they wanted to sink British ships. On a dark night in November, militant members of the Brotherhood stole the *Ram* from Holland's dock and took her to Connecticut.

Holland wrote, "I received no notice of the contemplated move then, nor was I notified after.... I have no intention of advancing any excuses for the incident, as no official explanation was ever made to me concerning it. As a result, I never bothered again with my backers nor they with me."

Holland went on to sell the design of his terrorist weapon to the United States Navy.

The Finians, meanwhile, could never seem to master the art of piloting the boat. A year later a disgruntled Finian wrote, "I am so sick of the boat.... I should be inclined to let him take the thing and have it for a white elephant if I did not believe there is a prospect of selling it, if it was only put in decent condition."

The *Ram* ended up stored in a shed until 1916, when she was put on display at Madison Square Garden to raise money for the Irish uprising in Dublin. In 1927 the world's first terrorist weapon was placed in a park in Jersey City.

By that time Holland had won fame and respectability as an architect for the navy and eventually was honored with the tunnel to New York City — one that terrorists plotted to blow up in 1993.

CHAPTER 11

Jersey Socialist Grinds Up Meat Industry

In the fall of 1905, twenty-eight-year-old Upton Sinclair sat in the tiny shack which he had constructed just outside Princeton. He had just written a novel destined to change the life of every American, but he could not find a publisher.

Sinclair's novel, *The Jungle,* was an indictment of the capitalist system. It recounted the woeful tale of the immigrant family of Jurgis Rudkus, driven into endless poverty by a society where the rich live off the sweat of the poor. While Sinclair's book told a heart-wrenching story, it also described in graphic detail the real horrors of working in Chicago's meat-packing houses. It was because of these indictments of the industry that five publishers had turned down the book. They feared lawsuits or worse from the sons of Gustavus Swift and Philip Armour, the two giants of America's meat-packing industry.

Meanwhile, in Washington, D.C., a little-known bill known as the Pure Food and Drug Act was bottled up in committee. Swift and Armour had Congress convinced that they took all of the precautions needed to keep Americans healthy. Even the testimony of war hero Teddy Roosevelt on the subject of forty-year-old "embalmed beef" being sent to his troops in Cuba could not get the bill through Congress.

Sinclair, a graduate of City College of New York, was a Socialist. To research background for his book, Sinclair had dressed as a workman and, with lunch pail in hand, had wandered for seven weeks through Chicago's meat processing plants. This became the world of his novel's immigrants from Lithuania.

To keep himself fed during the writing, Sinclair sold excerpts to a Socialist weekly called *Appeal to Reason* and the more widely read *Colliers* magazine. While less than ten percent of the book would deal with meat packing, it was the articles that gave America a taste of what was to come in *The Jungle*.

In the introduction, Jurgis enters the visitors gallery for the first time to see modern meat packing in operation. "They don't waste anything here," said the guide. "They use everything about the hog except the squeal."

Of this fictitious factory Sinclair wrote, "No tiniest particle of organic matter was wasted in Durham's. Out of the horns of the cattle they made combs, buttons, hairpins, and imitation ivory; out of the shin bones and other big bones they cut knife and toothbrush handles, and mouthpieces for pipes; out of the hoofs they cut hairpins and buttons, before they made the rest into glue. From such things as feet, knuckles, hide clippings, and sinews came such strange and unlikely products as gelatin ... they made pepsin from the stomachs of pigs, and albumen from the blood, and violin strings from the ill-smelling entrails. When there was nothing else to be done with a thing, they first put it into a tank and got out of it all the tallow and grease, and then they made it into fertilizer."

All of these practices were good business and, however distasteful, necessary and legal. But this was only Sinclair's introduction into the world that prepared the nation's breakfasts.

The hog had "to pass a government inspector, who sat in the doorway and felt of the glands in the neck for tuberculosis.... He was apparently not haunted by a fear that the hog might get by him before he had finished his testing.... He was quite willing to enter into conversation with you, and to explain to you the deadly nature of the ptomaines which are found in tubercular pork; and while he was talking with you you could hardly be so ungrateful as to notice that a dozen carcasses were passing him untouched."

This laxity wasn't isolated to the meat inspectors. By 1900, aware of it or not, Americans were into the wonderful world of food additives. "They were regular alchemists at Durham's; they advertised a mushroom-catsup, and the men who made it did not know what a mushroom looked like. They advertised 'potted chicken' — and it was like the boarding house soup of the comic papers, through which a chicken had walked with rubbers on. Perhaps they had a secret process for making chickens chemically — who knows?... The things that went into the mixture were tripe, and the fat of pork, and beef suet, and hearts of beef, and finally the waste ends of veal, when they had any. They put these up in several grades and sold them at several prices; but the contents of the cans all came out of the same hopper." There were no unions, no government safety rules, no safeguards as the meat was cooked. Sinclair indicted a callous industry in graphic detail. Although Sinclair hoped to show how the evils of a capitalistic society were crushing the life out of working people, he later noted, "I aimed at America's heart but hit it in the stomach."

"There was never the least attention paid to what was cut up for sausage; there would come all the way back from Europe old sausage that had been rejected and that was mouldy and white — it would be dosed with borax and glycerine, and dumped into hoppers, and made over again for home consumption. There would be meat that had tumbled out on the floor, in the dirt and sawdust, where the workers had tramped and spit uncounted billions of consumption germs. There would be meat stored in great piles in rooms; and the water from leaky roofs would drip over it, and thousands of rats would race about on it. It was too dark in these storage places to see well, but a man could run his hand over these piles of meat and sweep off handfuls of the dried dung of rats....

"There was no place for the men to wash their hands before they ate their dinner, and so they made a practice of washing them in the water that was to be ladled into the sausage. There were the butt-ends of smoked meat, and the scraps of corned beef, and all the odds and ends of the waste of the plants, that would be dumped into old barrels in the cellar and left there. Under the system of rigid economy which the packers enforced, there were some jobs that it only paid to do once in a long time, and among these was the cleaning out of the waste barrels. Every spring they did it; and in the barrels would be dirt and rust and old nails and stale water — and cart load after load of it would be taken up and dumped into the hoppers with fresh meat, and sent out to the public's breakfast.... "

Finally, Doubleday, Page and Company sent editor Isaac Marcosson to talk with Sinclair and to do some independent investigating in Chicago. Marcosson documented the horrors of *The Jungle*. "I was able to get a Meat Inspector's badge, which gave me access to the secret confines of the meat empire," he wrote. "Day and night I prowled over its foul-smelling domain and I was able to see with my own eyes much that Sinclair had never even heard about.... "

This convinced Marcosson the book had to be published at any risk, and a release day was finally set for January 25, 1906. A special advance copy of the manuscript was prepared and sent to now president of the United States Theodore Roosevelt, who soon demanded to have Sinclair brought to the White House. Not totally sold on the story, Roosevelt sent his commissioner of labor and a veteran social worker to Chicago to investigate the meat-packing industry.

Within a few weeks Roosevelt had his report. It was beyond belief; *The Jungle* uncovered only the tip of the iceberg. Armed with the information, Roosevelt invited the heads of the industry to the White House and offered to suppress the gruesome report if the meat packers agreed to request government inspection of their plants. The packers and their lawyers refused, claiming it was unconstitutional and extortionate. The government could not force them to do anything.

A man of his word, Roosevelt released the report. The reaction was devastating to the meat industry. This time, the stories of horror in the morning papers, unlike Sinclair's fiction, were true. Orders for canned meat dropped by more than half. The meat packers demanded that the government come to their rescue. By June 30, less than six months after *The Jungle* went on sale, the Pure Food and Drug Act and the Meat Inspection Act were signed into law, and Americans had another inalienable right — the right to know what is going into their stomachs.

CHAPTER 1

Spies, Saboteurs and Black Tom

W hat were the causes of World War I? The sinking of the *Lusitania*? The Zimmerman telegram? Is it possible that several events in New Jersey also led the United States into a world war?

A look at the world in 1914 shows two armed camps, one led by Germany, the other by England and France. The spark which set off the great war in Europe was an assassin's bullet in Sarajevo aimed at the Archduke Francis Ferdinand, heir to the Austro-Hungarian throne.

In the United States, President Woodrow Wilson, former New Jersey governor and Princeton University president, proclaimed neutrality in the conflict.

"The effect of the war upon the United States will depend on what American citizens say or do," he said. "Every man who really loves America will act and speak in the true spirit of neutrality, which is the spirit of impartiality and fairness and friendliness to all concerned."

Wilson was having problems of his own. The nation was in a recession, his wife had just died and his attempts to overthrow an unfriendly Mexican government had failed. The war provided an answer for at least one of Wilson's problems. Desperate for supplies, the Allies — Great Britain, France and Russia — began to buy as much as U.S. factories could turn out. As a center for munitions factories, New Jersey was swept into an economic boom.

Lakehurst became a testing ground for Russian poison gas. DuPont opened a powder plant at Carney's Point on the Delaware River and at Pompton Lakes. By 1916, New Jersey was producing munitions by the hundreds of tons. Where Liberty State Park now overlooks New

York Harbor was "Black Tom," the major terminal through which these instruments of death were loaded on ships for transport to the Allies.

July 29 was a Saturday and a summer day like many others for the northern New Jersey area. The weather was clear with a high in the seventies. There was a strike against New York public transit. The Brooklyn Robins were in first place in the National League, Fanny Brice was starring in the "Ziegfeld Follies" on Broadway, and Mena Edwards, a part-time model, decided to leave the city and spend the weekend at the Jersey shore. She boarded a train for Atlantic Highlands to visit a friend.

Over in Jersey City at Black Tom, the workers closed down at five o'clock. Sunday was their only day off; the terminal would be quiet, with a few watchmen to keep an eye on the munitions. By midnight, most of the New York Harbor area was asleep. It was sixty-five degrees, a good night for sleeping.

Barton Scott, a private detective at Black Tom, was wide awake. "I was a short distance from the land end of the dock ... when I first caught a glimpse of a blaze.... The fire had started in the center of a string of cars on shore near the land end of the pier. The flames had gotten too good a start for us to do anything. I ran to a telephone and called for the yard engines to come and pull the other cars away, and within a few minutes after the discovery of the fire, shrapnel shells of the smaller calibers began to explode.

"These shells kept up the rattle continuously and the fire spread rapidly to other cars containing small explosives. I knew that a car in the center of the string was loaded with black powder and that once she was touched off the whole place was doomed.... Work of pulling the cars out began at once, but the fire was getting hot and the explosives were going off with increasing violence."

But the fire department was not called until 12:40, when an alarm went off in one of the buildings. By then it was too late.

"At eight minutes past two, the biggest explosion of all came," Scott later recalled. "The car of black powder had gone up. At the moment the big blast came, the ground seemed to reverberate from the concussion and the air displacement temporarily took away one's breath."

According to *The New York Times*, the blast was "like the discharge of a great cannon ... flaming rockets and screeching shells pierced the sky, like a great fireworks display, illuminating Miss Liberty from torch to base. Beyond her, the tip of Manhattan and much of the world's most spectacular skyline instantly were awash in light.

"From the large hotels women rushed out scantily clad, and men who wore pajamas covered with overcoats ... many women became hysterical ... police whistles were blown frantically, but the police themselves did not know what it was all about."

Switchboards in police stations as far away as Philadelphia lit up with calls. Windows of Manhattan skyscrapers blew out. Traffic stopped on the swaying Brooklyn Bridge. Ships in the harbor caught fire, and holes were blown through the Statue of Liberty. Where Black Tom had once stood was now a crater below sea level.

Frank Hague of the Jersey City Department of Public Safety investigated the blast and blamed the terminal owners for negligence. "On one point the various investigating bodies agree, and that is that the fire and subsequent explosions cannot be charged to the account of alien plotters against the neutrality of the United States, although it is admitted that the destruction of so large a quantity of allied war material must prove cheering news to Berlin and Vienna," he reported.

But that conclusion didn't make Mena Edwards feel any better. She was staying with a friend, Marie McDermott.

"I remember particularly how nervous I was that night ... because I could not tell Mrs. McDermott what I knew was probably going to happen.... The vibration of the house was terrible. Mrs. McDermott awakened with a great start and we both ran out in the yard. She thought at first it was a terrible thunderstorm and said, 'Let's get our bathing suits. They will get wet.' We ran out on the lawn in our kimonos. I remember that it was a clear night and we saw the light, and later watched the fire as it developed at Black Tom."

How had Mena Edwards known what to expect? The night before she had been at a party attended by many German officials, and she had seen and heard things that made her believe the fire was no accident.

Even before the outbreak of the war, the German government had anticipated the American claim of neutrality and had called its ambassador, Johann von Bernstorff, to Berlin. His instructions were, first, to keep the United States neutral as long as possible, and second, to set up a nationwide network of spies and saboteurs to destroy America's ability to supply arms to the Allies. When Bernstorff returned to his post, he brought $150 million in treasury notes to carry out the plan.

Within weeks of the outbreak of war, the network was launched. A "safe house" was set up on West Fifteenth Street in Manhattan. The location was selected as a good site to recruit German nationals and also Irish immigrants who were strongly anti-British. Besides, just across the river were the targets, sprouting like mushrooms. New Jersey was now the leading state in the production of war materials.

To destroy this industry, Bernstorff turned to a Hoboken chemist, Walter Scheele, who had been sent by the German government twenty years earlier to spy on America's chemical industry. Scheele produced a lead tube with two kinds of acid separated by a copper disc. The thicker the disc, the longer it would take the acid to eat through the metal. One of Scheele's men explained how it worked.

"We stood nearby: If the detonator worked, I could put my scheme into operation. I knew what use could be made of this 'diabolical' invention; and all that was necessary was that it should function. Heaven knows it did. The stream of flame which suddenly shot out of the confounded 'cigar' nearly blinded me. It was so strong and the lead melted into an almost invisible fragment."

158

Soon, men were recruited to place these "cigars" on outgoing ammunition ships. Many of the ships later reported as sunk by German U-boats really were destroyed by the Hoboken chemist. But as the war raged on, ships could not be sunk fast enough. The next step was to go after the factories.

On July 28, Mena Edwards had been entertaining several men at the safe house. She later remembered that they "had some explosives at the house and were talking to some men and giving them instructions as to how to handle them ... 'These are good for so long' ... or 'These will run for so long' ... referring probably to the fuses. There were to be three explosions planned in different places, one on the cars, and the others in sheds, or barges or enclosures. I remember something being said about boats being loaded to go to someplace.... This man, 'Mox,' whom I have mentioned before who was a printer in the daytime, was selected as one of the men to carry over the explosives to Jersey."

Afraid of what was happening, Edwards left the city for the Jersey shore the next morning. That night, three German agents went into action, landing in a small boat at Black Tom under cover of night. The three men put several devices in boxcars loaded with munitions, others on barges. The resulting explosion was heard as far away as Philadelphia.

Two nights later, Edwards returned to the safe house. "They were all talking about the success of the Black Tom explosion and dinner party followed in honor of that success.... I particularly remember that when the man named Mox came in — he came in late — he was greeted as a great hero because he had carried some of the explosives over to New Jersey.... I remember a number of questions being asked as to whether anyone knew if any people were killed in the explosion. They seemed to be concerned about that and apparently hoped that they had not killed many people."

Other mysterious fires hit New Jersey plants, and in June 1917 another fire destroyed nearly one million artillery shells bound for Russia. Successful sabotage led German agents to organize strikes in factories and on docks. Finally, a lab was set up to produce anthrax germs to be injected into horses as they waited in New Jersey stockyards for shipment to the western front.

As evidence of Germany's war on neutral America mounted, it had an effect on a moral Woodrow Wilson. Only three days before he asked for a declaration of war, a plot to blow up a rebuilt Black Tom was uncovered. Wilson later explained to the American people, "They filled our unsuspecting communities with vicious spies and conspirators and sought to corrupt the opinion of our people in their own behalf....

"Some of these agents were men connected with the official embassy of the German government itself here in our own capital. They sought by violence to destroy our industries and arrest our commerce."

These were harsh words from Wilson. The question, of course, was could the charges ever be proven and who would pay for the millions of dollars in damage that had been done? Thus began the bizarre, fourteen-year trial to prove that Germany blew up Black Tom.

For seven years American lawyers pieced together the puzzle. More than four hundred intercepted cables between Berlin and Washington were entered as evidence, appearing to show involvement of the German embassy. In 1925, Mena Edwards was finally enticed to tell all she knew of the German activities at the safe house.

Others testified about the manufacture of timing devices and payments from the German embassy. The defense attacked the credibility of the American witnesses, then placed the blame on New Jersey itself. In January 1929, just before the hearing, the Germans released a statement from a barge captain claiming that the infamous New Jersey mosquito had caused the explosion!

John Grudman reported, "There on the end of Pier Seven, right beside the watchman's shanty ... [was] a fire ... kind of burning rubbish, more gleaming than burning high, to produce smoke ... to drive away the mosquitoes."

In April, forty-five hours of arguments and seven hundred documents were presented to the commission hearing war claims. Finally, more than a year later, the commission ruled that Germany had authorized sabotage, but that the United States had not proven that any such act against Black Tom had taken place. The case was closed.

Newspapers had a field day at the expense of New Jersey. *The New York Times* explained, "The real story of the explosion ... is this: The watchmen employed to guard the millions of dollars' worth of war materials, sugar, salt, flour and explosives were bothered by the mosquitoes that infested the swampy land about Black Tom. They built themselves a smudge fire to drive them off. A spark from this fire ignited some excelsior which had been left carelessly under a box car on a siding less than a hundred feet from the watchmen's shanty."

A Virginia paper joked that the Black Tom explosion "was primarily due to native-born New Jersey mosquitoes."

The *Nation* wrote, "Mosquitoes as the indirect cause of the Black Tom explosion and fire in July, 1916, will seem altogether possible to residents of New Jersey who know their mosquitoes.... As it stands, [the decision] will serve to increase the friendly feeling of Germany toward an erstwhile enemy nation."

Stunned, the American lawyers vowed to continue the fight. To reopen the case they would now have to prove that the German defense had been based on fraud. A new lawyer, John J. McCloy, joined the American team and looked for a key to reopen the case.

More years passed. The Depression hit the world, Adolph Hitler became Fuehrer of Germany and, through the work of McCloy and others, evidence mounted that German eyewitnesses had lied.

James Larkin, an Irish labor leader, came forward telling of "specific plans ... for destroying the munitions at the Jersey City terminus by means of a loaded barge exploding alongside the pier or jetty. The barge, it was stated, already arranged for was a Lackawanna Railroad barge, it being explained that the detonation from these explosives would result in the explosion of the explosives stored in or about the vicinity."

In 1936 the case was reopened and the new evidence heard. By 1939 the tide of evidence against Germany had become a tidal wave. On the eve of World War II, Germany, fearing a reversal of the earlier decision, withdrew from the commission. The commission ruled anyway: Germany was guilty and must pay.

But the story doesn't end there. Just before the attack on Pearl Harbor, McCloy was appointed assistant secretary of war. After the attack, his experience with Black Tom led him to recommend to President Franklin D. Roosevelt placing Japanese-Americans and Japanese nationals living in the United States in concentration camps. In 1988 McCloy recalled a conversation with FDR.

"The Japanese had sunk our fleet at Pearl Harbor.... We knew they had planned subversion to be sure the United States wouldn't recover. The highest concentration of Japanese-Americans was on the West Coast. Roosevelt said, 'Move them.' We moved them to relocation camps to get them out of sensitive areas."

McCloy said that Roosevelt, who had been assistant secretary of the Navy under President Wilson, "knew all about Black Tom. He said to me, 'We don't want any more Black Toms.' "

Germany made the final payment on the Black Tom case in 1979. The U.S. government is still paying compensation to the Japanese-Americans who were placed in concentration camps. Decades later, the tremors of the Black Tom explosion continue.

CHAPTER 2

Death on Memorial Day

I t was the age of the great hotels at the Jersey shore. On Long Beach Island, the elegant Hotel Baldwin and the stately Engleside drew thousands of ladies and gentlemen. The Hotel DeCrab, a former lifesaving station, attracted sportsmen from Philadelphia and New York. Most came by train to the island, but the new wooden auto bridge across Manahawkin Bay had recently been completed. Now that the gravel roads of Manahawkin were directly linked to the island, change was in the air and many residents saw opportunities.

As George B. Somerville wrote, "Great preparations have been made in contemplation of the vital changes to be made upon Long Beach Island because of the solid roads and substantial bridge — a mending of nature's oversight — that are today, June 20, A.D. 1914, thrown open to the world."

Just eight days later, events in faraway Sarajevo, Serbia, would set off a chain reaction that would change Long Beach Island forever. World War I would bring death and destruction to Ocean County on a level not seen since the American Revolution.

As the war raged in Europe, America tried to stay neutral. Eventually, German attacks on U.S. ships, the sabotage of a New Jersey arms factory, and a German offer to return Texas and California to Mexico in exchange for that nation's collaboration led President Woodrow Wilson to ask for a declaration of war in 1917.

The wartime changes in New Jersey were tremendous. Part of rural Burlington County was transformed into Camp Dix, literally overnight. A two hundred-man barracks could be constructed in ten hours. Soon the camp boasted sixteen hundred buildings and handled seventy thousand recruits and seven thousand horses.

At Mays Landing, Bethlehem Steel built a shell-loading plant which employed more than six thousand workers, four times the population of the town. Near Cape May, the government built a town called Belcoville just to house the workers of a shell-testing range.

An Army base was constructed to protect Tuckerton from German attack and sabotage. Here the federal government operated a wireless station, originally built by the Germans in 1912. The 853-foot-high tower was second only to the Eiffel Tower as the world's tallest man-made object. (The station's tower anchors are still visible in Mystic Island.)

Along the shore, Coast Guard stations became lookouts run by the Navy, and patrols monitored coastal shipping. New Jersey also became the center for transporting troops. As the first troops left for France in June, a reporter covered the departure.

"Perhaps along the Staten Island shore commuters wondered as the big gray ships slipped through the Narrows to the seas. Perhaps next morning the off-shore fishing boats drew up their nets to watch the great convoy with attending destroyers come over the western rim of the sea.

"But back in the city none knew of their going. The six million in New York little guessed that the job of breaking the Kaiser's Army had begun in Hoboken."

Many of these servicemen were from New Jersey. By 1918 more than one hundred men from Tuckerton alone had served. Most Jerseyans were trained at Fort McClellan, Virginia. After visiting the troops, New Jersey Governor Walter Edge reported, "They have been rounded into magnificent soldiers. They had no complaints further than the desire to go abroad and get into the middle of it. I am sorry all New Jersey could not have seen their boys as we saw them — healthy, happy, ambitious, simply Americans."

That's the way most patriotic citizens felt as Memorial Day week approached. The war was to be fought "over there." But that weekend would change everything. The German high command had launched a spring offensive, planning to end the war before the full weight of America's might could reach the trenches of France.

In May, the Second Battle of the Marne raged only a few miles from Paris. The Allied lines began to falter, and the chances of a German victory were real. As part of this offensive to end the war, the German navy was determined to carry the war to the United States. Korvetten Kapitan von Nostitz was ordered to cross the Atlantic in the primitive submarine known as the *U-151* and wreak as much havoc as possible.

Von Nostitz arrived off Delaware Bay where he laid underwater mines. On May 25, he sighted three U.S. sailing vessels off Virginia. The *U-151* surfaced, and the unarmed ships surrendered. Twenty-six prisoners were taken aboard the U-boat, and the ships were destroyed with explosives.

Von Nostitz held the prisoners aboard the already-crowded sub to keep his presence secret. He had decided to turn north and look for the troop transports leaving Hoboken.

Memorial Day weekend arrived; the Long Beach Island Board of Trade looked at the numbers of visitors and was pleased. The more visitors who came by road and rail meant prosperity, even in wartime. What island merchants did not know was that by Sunday they would have an unwanted visitor. The *U-151* was planning to drop in, unannounced.

At dawn on June 2, the U-boat was off Barnegat Light in the heart of the sea lanes. As she prowled, *The Jersey Courier* reported, "Down at Beach Haven it is said that U-boats were seen several times last week but it was supposed they were our own vessels."

At 7:50 A.M., the *U-151* spotted the 160-foot, three-masted schooner *Isabel B. Wiley* heading south for Virginia. The *U-151* attacked on the surface with its six-inch gun. When the first shot landed within one hundred yards, Captain Thomas Thomason ordered his men to abandon ship in the motor launch.

As the U-boat prepared to make short work of the wooden-hulled *Wiley*, the *Winneconne*, out of Newport News, Virginia, steamed into view. The 220-foot freighter, commanded by Waldemar Knudson, was carrying 1,819 tons of coal. The *U-151* left the schooner and turned its attention on the *Winneconne*. A boarding party was sent to the freighter and the crew ordered into the three lifeboats.

The Germans placed charges inside the hulls of both ships. Von Nostitz then gathered all the lifeboats to the *U-151*. After dividing his POWs among the boats and making sure they had food and water, he set them adrift. The lifeboats' occupants watched as the bombs sent both ships to the bottom and the *U-151* sailed off.

The survivors decided the motor launch should try to reach shore to spread the alarm. The rest of the lifeboats began the long row toward Barnegat Lighthouse.

As the seamen rowed in the hot sun, the U-boat came upon the *Jacob Haskell*, a majestic four-masted schooner 116 feet long. The *U-151* fired two shots across her bow and ran up the international signal to abandon ship. Her captain, William H. Davis, quickly complied.

Davis and his eleven-man crew boarded the lifeboats after surrendering the ship's papers to the boarding party, who placed charges on the side of the wooden hull. As her crew watched, the explosives went off, and with all sails set, the *Haskell* silently slid beneath the waves.

Another lifeboat began to head for the coast of New Jersey. In less than six hours, the *U-151* had sunk three ships, and the day was only half over. Around midafternoon, Von Nostitz spotted the four-masted schooner *Edward H. Cole*, bound for Maine with a load of coal. Only hours before, the *U-151* had sent the *Cole's* sister ship, the *Jacob Haskell*, to the bottom.

Even under full sail, Captain Humphrey Newcomb could not outrun the U-boat. As Robert Lathigee, the 42-year-old mate, later told *The New York Times*, "It was just about ten minutes to 4 and the watch below had been called to be ready to come on deck at eight bells, when I saw a submarine come to the surface half a mile away on the port bow. A German officer was rowed over to the *Cole*. The officer, who wore gold shoulder straps and gilt buttons, and was the only one of the crew who was clean shaven, spoke courteously to Captain Newcomb and after listening to the statements as to the name, tonnage, cargo and ports of departure and destination, he made a brief inspection of the ship. Then he came to where we were standing and said, 'Now, Captain, get your crew together and tell them that they have ten minutes to leave the ship.' "

Some of the crew were still asleep. They were awakened and rushed to the ship's one boat.

The Germans put two bombs on each side of the *Cole* and, as the crew watched from the lifeboat, the charges went off. In minutes the schooner went down bow-first and under full sail. Then, as Lathigee remembered, "We saw a cloud of smoke on the horizon astern and the U-boat went off at full speed in that direction, presumably to attack the steamship if she proved to be unarmed."

The ship the *U-151* was chasing was the 331-foot SS *Texel*. She had been built in Denmark and was carrying a load of forty-two thousand tons of sugar from Puerto Rico to New York City.

Captain K. R. Lowery of the *Texel* reported, "Suddenly, without a moment's warning, a U-boat loomed up off the bow. It fired three rounds of shrapnel. The hail of exploding shells swept the deck like rain. The U-boat was about fifty feet away, so close that it almost crashed into the lifeboats that were later lowered.

"When the shrapnel struck us I stopped. The skipper of the U-boat, who came aboard, speaking clear English, cried, 'Let me see your papers.' I turned the ship's papers over to him. He looked at them for a moment curtly, then, turning on his heel, said, 'We will give you time to get off, then we shall sink your vessel.' "

The *U-151* made short work of the *Texel*, sending her to the bottom in only three minutes. Von Nostitz now looked for target number six and found it in the SS *Carolina*, returning from Puerto Rico and bound for New York City with 217 passengers and a crew of 113. The 380-foot ship was under the command of Captain T. R. D. Barbour and was unarmed. As most of the passengers sat down to dinner, the radio officer picked up a message about the sinking of the *Isabel B. Wiley* earlier in the day. Informed that the sinking had been only about twelve miles from his current position off Barnegat Light, Barbour ordered the *Carolina* to begin to zigzag in order to avoid torpedoes.

According to Trygue Wiley, the second deck officer of the *Carolina*, "We saw nothing of the submarine, until after we had heard three warning shots fired. We came to a stop and finally the submarine came in view about 200 yards away.

"The submarine appeared to be about 300 feet long and mounted two guns, which seemed to be of six-inch calibre. All of the fifty or sixty men on the large deck of the submarine were in German uniform and evidently there were no prisoners on board."

Captain Barbour ordered an SOS and the 19-year-old wireless operator, Edward Vogel, later recalled what happened.

" 'SOS, Steamship *Carolina* being gunned by German submarine,' was sent out a couple of times. Then I set my instrument for receiving. Within two minutes Cape May Coast Guard station had picked us up and queried for our location. But just then the German operator butted in and said, 'You don't use wireless — we don't shoot.' "

Barbour gave the order to abandon ship. One of the passengers remembered, "Ten boats were lowered and everybody got in. There was little or no confusion. All the time the submarine lay as close as possible, members of her crew standing on her deck watching us or busying themselves about the boat."

"Finally, when the submarine was very close to the ship, it trained one of its guns on the steamer near the beam and fired a shot which struck just below the waterline," Wiley would recall. "The gun was then aimed at a point a few feet distant at the waterline and fired a second time. Then the submarine moved around to the other side and fired two more shots. In a few minutes the *Carolina* was sinking and we saw her go out of sight. The submarine went on its way and disappeared in a few minutes."

A feeling of calm and unity prevailed among the passengers. Remembered one, "It was a beautiful Sunday evening, as we drifted, no one knew where. The sun began to set as the *Carolina* slowly went down. Then it got dark and a feeling of fear overcame many of us, but we hoped for the best. The sea was still smooth and there was no danger, apparently. We strained our eyes to see a light, but there was none. All the boats kept as close together as possible, everybody that was able taking a turn at the oars."

Of the ten lifeboats that had been launched, seven gathered around the boat of the ship's captain. One of the survivors in this group was Army Lt. Leslie Arthur from Massachusetts.

"Captain Barbour then called all the boats together and gave instructions to proceed west. Six men rowed in each boat.... By the time the last shot had been fired we were about 1,000 yards away from the *Carolina*. The submarine remained standing by until the vessel listed heavily to starboard and slowly sank....

"The Captain ordered the eight remaining boats lashed together and everybody seemed calm. About 10:30 Sunday night a thunderstorm came up very suddenly. It was accompanied by high winds and the sea grew so angry in a few minutes that the boats were unlashed to prevent their smashing against each other. Sea anchors were cast overboard to give the boats more steadiness and while the lightning flashed frequently some of the passengers prayed for help."

The eight boats made it through the storm intact with the survivors wet and hungry. Lt. Arthur continued.

"We kept rowing westward all night and in the morning rations of water and hard tack were served. The boats kept together well and at 10:30 A.M. there was a great cheer when the *Eva B. Douglas* appeared bearing directly down on the flotilla."

The schooner was bound for South America but immediately made for shore after rescuing the 150 passengers and ninety-four crew members.

166

The fate of those in the two missing boats was not as good. Lifeboat No. 5 had not been launched properly and overturned on hitting the water, dumping most of its twenty-nine passengers. They had to hold onto the sides until it was bailed out.

The other missing boat was the ship's motor launch which had returned to pick up a crewman left behind on the *Carolina*. Trygue Wiley was on the launch.

"We took one of the rowboats in tow. The boats soon scattered and we lost sight of the others. Shortly after the squall had started the towline between our launch and the rowboat snapped and in a few minutes we were driven in different directions, so that we lost sight of our boat. The squall became terrific and finally washed our boat completely over."

A passenger in the motor launch told of a night of terror.

"The storm came, quicker than we expected it. The wind blew a gale and kicked up a nasty sea. The boats pitched and soon became separated, and we, who were in a motor launch, seemed to be alone in the storm. Rougher and rougher became the water, and the boat rolled and pitched. Finally she capsized, and all of the thirty-five in her were thrown into the sea. The boat was righted and capsized again while we clung to her. This occurred several times. The storm passed, and the sea began to calm. It was pitch dark.

"Finally, we kept the launch righted, but she was full of water. We clung to her and bailed out the water with our hands. Some could not stand the strain, became exhausted, and let go their hold, and sank. It was terrible. We bailed out enough water to let one of us in, then he bailed furiously, and enough water was scooped out to permit a second to get into the launch. We kept on bailing until the launch was able to bear the weight of a third and a fourth."

By morning the last person was back in the boat. Seventeen were missing, as *The New York Times* reported.

"After a time an object was seen in the water. There was no way to reach it as the launch had lost her gasoline and oars. The launch, however, drifted close and the survivors were startled to discover a girl alive, clinging to the bodies of two drowned men. The bodies were incased in lifebelts, but the girl wore none. She appeared to be a good swimmer and clinging to the two bodies for support she managed to remain afloat. The launch got near enough to her to effect her rescue. She proved to be Elona Donato Virola, of Puerto Rico."

The motor launch was finally spotted by a British ship off Cape May.

On the last lifeboat was Lillian Dickinson of Massachusetts, another passenger recalled.

"I shall never forget the real heroine of the occasion. She was Miss Lillian Dickinson. Although we tried to dissuade her, that girl, who had just turned 18, insisted upon taking her regular turn at the oars. It was a case of one hour on and one hour off. Miss Dickinson inspired us by her conduct. In all we rowed between seventy and eighty miles. I know a lot of us would have given up had she not set the pace and the example. She was still taking her turn at the oars when we sighted Atlantic City."

At 2 P.M. on Monday the last lifeboat rowed to the beach at South Carolina Avenue in Atlantic City. The *Times* told of the bizarre scene that greeted the survivors.

"Throngs rushed to the beach at South Carolina Avenue, toward which the boat was heading. As it approached shore the crowds gave way to enthusiasm. Beach guards launched their boats and went out to meet the craft. Mystic Shriners, in full regalia, and hundreds of men, women, and boys fully clothed rushed waist deep into the tide to drag the boat to the beach. The band of Lu Lu Temple of Philadelphia, which was parading down the boardwalk from the Shriners Hall, joined the crowd and as the boat swept in it struck up 'The Star-Spangled Banner.' The crowds cheered and many women wept."

Black Sunday was over. That it has all but been forgotten is really simple to explain. Sharing the front pages of newspapers that June were stories from France: The first Americans were entering the Second Battle of the Marne at a place called Chateau-Thierry. The German gamble to thwart U.S. involvement had failed, and the U-boat war off New Jersey was suspended.

CHAPTER 3

Fight for Women's Rights Pays Off

The 20th century dawned with a vibrant progressive spirit. Teddy Roosevelt, the nation's youngest president, sat in the White House. He talked of reform, direct election of senators, fair taxes, control of the trusts, and suffrage for women. But even in an age of reform, just mentioning voting rights for women meant you had a fight on your hands.

By 1910, four Western states had granted women the vote. These victories gave people such as Senator Robert Owen of Colorado a stronger argument for nationwide suffrage.

"Women compose one-half of the human race," Owen stated. "In the last forty years, women in gradually increasing numbers have been compelled to leave the home and enter the factory and workshop. Over seven million women are so employed, and the remainder of the sex are employed largely in domestic services. Equal pay for equal work is the first great reason justifying this change of governmental policy....

"The woman ballot will not revolutionize the world. Its results in Colorado, for example, might have been anticipated. First, it did give women better wages for equal work; second, it led immediately to a number of laws the women wanted, and the first laws they demanded were laws for the protection of the children of the state, making it a misdemeanor to contribute to the delinquency of a child; laws for the improved care of defective children; also the Juvenile Court for the conservation of wayward boys and girls; the better care of the insane, the deaf, the dumb, the blind; the curfew bell to keep children off the streets at night; raising the age of consent for girls; improving the reformatories and prisons of the state; improving the hospital services of the state; improving the sanitary laws affecting the health of the homes of the state.... Above all, there resulted laws for improving the school system."

But not everyone agreed, not even all women. A Mrs. Gilbert E. Jones argued against women voting. "The anti-suffragists are not organizing or rushing into committees, societies, or associations, and their doings are not being cried out from the house tops.... Anti-suffragists deplore the fact that women are found in unsuitable occupations. But the suffragists glory in the fact that there are women blacksmiths, baggage masters, brakemen, undertakers, and women political 'bosses' in Colorado.

"The suffragists call this progress, independence, and emancipation of women. 'Anti's' ask for more discrimination and better selection of industrial occupations for wage-earning women."

Jones went on to look at women with the vote.

"The question of women suffrage should be summed up in this way: Has granting the ballot to women in the two suffrage states where they have had it for forty years brought about any great reforms or great results? No.... Have the saloons been abolished in any of the suffrage states? No.

"Do men still drink and gamble? Yes, without a doubt. Are the streets better cleaned in the states where women vote? No, they are quite as bad as in New York City and elsewhere. Have the slums been done away with? Indeed no. Have the red light districts been cleared away? Decidedly not, and they can be reckoned upon as a political factor, when they are really needed.

"Have women's wages been increased because women vote? No indeed. Have women equal pay for equal work? Not any more than in New York City. Are there laws on the statute books that would give women equal pay for equal work? No and never will be."

But the progressive spirit added five more states to the list granting the vote. In 1915 the battle shifted to New Jersey. Led by Alison Hopkins of Morristown, the suffrage movement had won the right for a statewide referendum on the matter. The voters of New Jersey would decide.

The two sides battled it out in newspapers. A satirical pro-suffrage ad began, "Because no man wants to settle any question otherwise than by fighting about it ... Because men will lose their charm if they step out of their natural sphere and interest themselves in other matters than feats of arms, uniforms and drums ... Because men are too emotional to vote. Their conduct at baseball games and political conventions shows this, while their innate tendency to appeal to force renders them particularly unfit for the task of government."

Led by James Nugent, Democratic political bosses battled back, fearing women voters would be hard to control. The day before the election, Nugent announced that women would destroy the state.

"New Jersey citizens through all history have stood for fidelity on contracts, the preservation of personal integrity of the courts, stability of government and above all the purity, privacy and loving unity of the home."

The vote was marred by fraud, with the open selling of votes. The final tally: 184,390 no votes and 133,282 yes.

Defeated in a key state, suffragists took a different tack. With World War I raging in Europe, more and more women began to work in industry. Alice Paul of Moorestown, a Quaker leader of the Women's Party, organized parades and picketed the White House. Arrested and imprisoned, she and others went on hunger strikes to dramatize their position.

When the United States entered the war, women were actively recruited to take jobs formerly held by men. The events of the war changed many minds. Some politicians felt that women had proven themselves in the armed forces. Others feared that working women might stop wartime production with strikes.

Finally, on June 4, 1919, the 19th Amendment to the Constitution was passed by Congress and sent to the states. New Jersey ratified it in a close vote on February 1, 1920. The amendment became part of the Constitution in August when Tennessee became the thirty-sixth state to ratify.

It had been seventy-one years since the Declaration of Rights at Seneca Falls, New York, when women had first demanded the right to vote. Finally in the fall of 1920 women across the country flocked to the polls for the first time to vote for the president. Along with their experienced brothers, they carried into office a new president, Warren G. Harding.

Oh well!

CHAPTER 4

Stickin' to the Union: Paterson Silk Strike

Just what are the rights of picketers? Is there a constitutional right to strike? Do unions even have a legal right to exist?

To answer these and other questions, follow one of New Jersey's first industries as its workers attempted to organize. That industry was the silk industry and the place was Paterson.

In 1791 Alexander Hamilton, the first secretary of the treasury, proposed building an industrial city at the great falls of the Passaic River. Thus was built America's first planned industrial community; it was named after the state's governor and signer of the U.S. Constitution, William Paterson.

The prospect of water power lured manufacturers. Most popular were weaving mills. Powered by water, huge looms could turn out finished cloth. The most profitable was silk. Soon the Paterson mills were producing some of the finest silk in the world, and rural New Jersey was dotted with factories which needed large numbers of unskilled laborers.

Factory owners tapped any source they could find. The major source was children, and the factory owners took advantage of them. A mill owner in 1794 wrote that important men and women shouldn't be allowed to see working conditions inside the mills because "It will be impossible to keep the children to their work whilst this is suffered, and the Society [owners of the mill] cannot afford to keep up such an establishment as a Show Shop."

By 1835 it was not unusual for an eight-year-old mill worker to toil more than thirteen hours a day, six days a week for a few cents an hour. During this time, social reformers also began the drive for free public education. But what to do about the children of Paterson?

The mill owners proposed that the children attend night school. A parent outlined a child's typical work day in Paterson.

"A night school would not benefit the mill hands inasmuch as they could not stand it. It is a well known fact that the children have to rise ere dawn of day, consume their morning meal by candlelight, and trudge to the mill to commence their labor ere the rising of the sun.

"At noon a very short time is allowed them for dinner, and their labor terminates at what is called 8 o'clock at night, but which is really [by the time they have their frames cleaned] much nearer 9 o'clock.

"They then take supper and immediately retire to bed in order that they may arise early in the morning — this being the mode of labor pursued in this and other manufacturing towns."

Throughout New Jersey and other growing industrial states, early attempts at labor organization were begun. The first unions were formed, but there was a particular problem in these. Until 1883 New Jersey employers invoked an ancient English common-law interpretation of conspiracy, saying if workers assembled "for the purpose of changing conditions of employment," they had committed a crime. Hundreds were arrested just for joining a union.

As the strikes became more violent, the state finally gave workers the right to organize, saying they now had the basic right to "enter into any combination for organizing, leaving, or entering into the employment of others."

But, as workers in Paterson won this small victory, mill owners turned to a new tactic. They would import thousands of immigrants to work cheaper and longer. Since most immigrants were unable to speak English, it would be harder to organize the workers, a bonus for the factory owners.

Labor organizer Terence V. Powderly summed up the situation in New Jersey in 1892: "Corporate greed is alone responsible for the sweeping tide of immigration now flowing in upon us.... The corporation reaps the benefits of the immigrants' presence by having its labor performed for half nothing; the poor immigrant lives but twenty-four hours ahead of the poor house, the man he replaces becomes a tramp."

In cities and towns, the reaction of the now out-of-work native-born citizens drove the immigrants into areas such as Little Italy or Little Poland, as described in 1910.

"The immigrant sees less of America than we think. He comes over with Slovaks, goes to a Slovak boarding house, a Slovak store, a Slovak saloon, and a Slovak bank. His boss is likely a Slovak. He deals with Americans only as the streetcar conductor shouts, 'What do you want, John?' or when boys stone his children and call them 'Hunkies.' "

The tide of immigration following World War I and the Communist revolution in Russia gave the owners yet another union-busting tactic: These foreigners had brought with them communistic ideas. These unions were un-American. The owners were the true heroes, standing up for the rights of the individual against the masses of workers. The scene was now set for the crucial confrontation of labor versus management.

The roots of the 1924 Paterson silk strike also go back to World War I. A by-product of the war was a new synthetic material called rayon. By the 1920s, less expensive rayon was the rage, and the silk market began to slip. To combat this, owners increased the workload in the silk mills, the number of looms to be tended by a worker going from three to four.

The Associated Silk Workers union objected; on August 8, union officials proclaimed, "The manufacturers have taken advantage of a severe slump in the Silk industry to force this evil system [three and four looms] on the workers," and called for a general meeting to be held at Paterson's Turn Hall on the corner of Ellison and Cross streets.

Unfortunately, this time unions came under attack: World War I had brought on the Communist revolution in Russia, and workers' unions were felt to be part of a worldwide Communist movement. Both the federal government and the state of New Jersey had shown they would act swiftly against any such group. As recently as 1920, roundups of suspected communist aliens had taken place, and they had been deported without benefit of lawyers or trials.

Despite this, the silk workers went on strike on August 12. As the strike continued into its second week, tempers wore thin. Several small mills settled, but the large mills were determined break the union. The companies went to court to get an injunction to stop picketing. The head of a statewide union described the injunction as being used to "make an act unlawful during a strike that would be perfectly lawful at another time."

On September 6, a New Jersey court gave the owners all they wanted and more, placing an injunction on picketing or even meeting in numbers of more than three. Arrests began the next day. Desperate, the union telegraphed the four-year-old American Civil Liberties Union for help: "Police terrorism launched here today.... Request your organization take a hand in the situation and help protect our rights."

Once in the battle, the ACLU notified Paterson's mayor the arrests were "an unwarranted invasion of the established right of peaceful picketing."

The ACLU was ignored and more injunctions followed, limiting speech, picketing and even public meetings by union membership "with a view to persuading them to refrain from ... employment ... acts or conduct; picketing; and aiding or abetting, in any manner whatever, the aforesaid acts."

By the end of September the police closed Turn Hall so union workers could not meet and hear what the police called "outside agitations." The ACLU planned a meeting to protest the closing of the hall. Roger Baldwin of the ACLU tried in vain to find a site for the meeting. Finally, he decided on a public place — City Hall Plaza. The object of his meeting was to test if there was freedom of speech in New Jersey.

At the meeting, Baldwin held an American flag while John C. Butterworth read the United States Bill of Rights to the crowd. Then the police arrived, swinging nightsticks and splitting scalps. Baldwin later testified he had "never seen so flagrant an exhibition of unprovoked and unnecessary police lawlessness."

Baldwin and Butterworth were arrested under an English common law definition of conspiracy, but the ACLU wouldn't give up; it scheduled another meeting and invited many prominent speakers, saying, "If the chief of police chooses to lock up a bishop of the Episcopal church together with other distinguished citizens, he will have the opportunity."

This meeting was held without any incident and Butterworth, out on bail, finished reading the Bill of Rights. But for the strikers it was a hollow victory. By the end of October most had gone back to work. The following April, Baldwin and Butterworth were found guilty of an illegal assembly under the common law definition and sentenced to six months in jail for meeting to read the Bill of Rights.

Based on the Paterson case, arrests in other parts of the state were made. The ACLU appealed, eventually reaching the New Jersey Supreme Court. The ACLU's case argued the immense importance of "the question of where the line is to be drawn between unlawful assemblage and the constitutional right of freedom of speech and assemblage ... and pointed out that these liberties could be as effectively nullified by sedulously seizing upon trivial or isolated circumstances ... as by denying them outright."

So what was the outcome of the case?

Several important issues were settled. It was established that workers in New Jersey do have the right of peaceful assembly, and since that time unions have used this right to voice their other constitutional right of free speech. Without assembly in New Jersey, all other rights would be moot.

And oh, yes: Roger Baldwin and John Butterworth were acquitted.

CHAPTER 5

Airships:

Flights of Fantasy at Lakehurst

In the 1930s Cape Canaveral was just sand dunes and alligators, worthless land sold as part of some Florida real estate swindle. America's space programs focused on aerospace, not outer space, and the world's attention was not on Florida but on New Jersey. More specifically, it was on a little clearing in the famed Jersey Pine Barrens: Naval Air Station Lakehurst.

Dignitaries from presidents to millionaires bounced along Pine Barrens roads in Ocean County just to get a glimpse of the latest marvels on display. Fishermen hauling in their nets off Long Beach Island could look up almost regularly and see something three football fields long flying over their heads. Ocean County was the center of the aviation world.

At the dawn of aviation, the science quickly broke into two distinct branches. One was made up of heavier-than-air objects which fly because air moving over a wing causes lift. These became the airplanes of today. However, airplanes initially took a back seat to craft in the other branch which developed lighter-than-air flying. These airships weighed less than the air around them and floated on air, just as a piece of wood floats on water.

By the end of the American Revolution, the French had launched balloons carrying men by heating the air inside to make it expand and become lighter than the air outside. The problem, as statesman and inventor Ben Franklin pointed out, was making a hot air balloon move sideways, not just up and down. Over the next one hundred years, many attempts were made to improve these flying machines.

In August 1927 the 670-foot Los Angeles *rises by the tail due to a divergence in temperature. Standing on her nose on the 172-foot-high mooring tower, she later returned as if nothing had happened.*

By 1900, Ferdinand von Zeppelin, a wealthy German, had become the leading proponent of lighter-than-air ships. Von Zeppelin had served in the Union army during the Civil War, then returned home to his favorite pastime, flying. He designed a cigar-shaped frame of lightweight metal and put balloons, called cells, inside the frame. Each cell was filled with highly explosive hydrogen gas. Gondolas attached under the body housed the newly invented gasoline engines which turned propellers and pushed the craft through the air.

Three years before the Wright brothers entered the scene, von Zeppelin unveiled his ship. Because of the rigid framework, he dubbed his 400-foot-long flying ship a dirigible. People were amazed that something that big could fly.

By the outbreak of World War I, zeppelin fever had swept Europe and England. During the war, the value of the dirigibles was shown in their ability to scout and to drop bombs on cities. Hundreds of zeppelins bombed England, and by war's end a long-range dirigible was being readied to cross the Atlantic, bomb New York City and return to Germany.

The United States had stayed out of the dirigible race, but during the war the U.S. military had seen them in operation in Europe. At home, the Americans had flown some smaller, not rigid ships called blimps for coastal patrol, but at the end of the war, the Navy argued for the need for long-range dirigibles.

The Navy ordered two. The *ZR-1* was to be built in Philadelphia, and the *ZR-II* was purchased from the English. Each dirigible was to be more than six hundred feet long. As the Navy awaited its first battleship of the air, a search began for a suitable home.

Just west of the sleepy fishing village of Toms River lay the "Jersey Desert," the Pine Barrens. Here, in 1915, the Eddystone Ammunition Corporation had bought a tract of land to test shells being sold to Czarist Russia. When the United States entered World War I, the Army bought the land and called it Camp Kendrick, using the out-of-the-way spot to test poison gas.

At the end of the war, Camp Kendrick was put up for sale until Acting Secretary of the Navy Franklin D. Roosevelt decided the area met the Navy's requirements: It was near the coast close to New York City and Philadelphia and had a railroad and water. The price was right — seventeen hundred acres of Pine Barrens for $13,088. FDR signed the papers, and Naval Air Station Lakehurst was born.

The first order of business was to construct a barn or hangar for the two ships. Hangar Number 1 was one of the world's largest buildings. On the outside, it measured 943 feet long and 350 feet wide. Inside floor space measured 804 feet long by 264 feet wide. The clearance at the peak was 193 feet. Barnegat Lighthouse could have stood inside the hangar with twenty-one feet to spare. Three sets of railroad tracks ran through the hangar to pull the great ships so one could be centered or two placed side-by-side. Two doors on railroad tracks closed the ends. Each door had four twenty-horsepower electric motors and took thirteen minutes to open and close. They were 177 feet high, 136 feet wide, free standing and kept upright by 350 tons of concrete ballast.

By June 28, 1921, the base officially opened and the humongous hangar was the center of attraction. In the years to come, planes were flown through the hangar and stories told of clouds entering the building and raining inside. Lakehurst was home base for America's flying dreadnoughts.

Of all the dirigibles to prowl the skies over New Jersey, the *ZR-III,* the *Los Angeles,* is the one most pleasantly remembered. Originally built in Friedrichshafen, Germany, she was part of war reparations to the United States. Measuring 670 feet in length, with a top speed of 79 miles an hour, she left Germany on October 12, 1924. Seventy-five hours of nonstop flying later, the ship appeared over New York City, then turned south toward Lakehurst.

178

The East Coast went wild: Remember, this was three years before Charles Lindbergh would make his trans-Atlantic flight.

At Lakehurst, the ship was moored in the big hangar. The explosive hydrogen was vented off and soon non-combustible helium filled her cells. For the next year, the *Los Angeles* shared the headlines and the hangar, but never the skies, with the *Shenandoah*; the Navy could afford enough helium to fly only one dirigible at a time. The precious gas was passed from one ship to the other.

Following the crash of the *Shenandoah*, one of its survivors, Lt. Comdr. Charles E. Rosendahl, took charge of the *Los Angeles*. Rosendahl would spend the next forty years of his life in Ocean County and become the nation's authority on lighter-than-air flying.

With Rosendahl at the helm, the *Los Angeles* lived up to its nickname, "The Pride of the Navy." He landed the airship on the deck of the aircraft carrier *Saratoga*, and later the airship herself became an aircraft carrier. By means of a trapeze arrangement, the dirigible launched and recovered fighter planes over Barnegat Bay, a docking procedure later used by NASA.

While the *Los Angeles* was always considered a lucky ship, her two closest brushes with disaster came in the skies over Ocean County. The first took place in August 1927. The ship had been placed on the 172-foot-high mooring mast so its helium could expand in the warm sun, when suddenly a cold ocean breeze moved in. With hot air at the nose and cold air two football fields away at the tail, the tail began to rise. At first the twenty-five men on board paid little attention. Neither did the two men heading up the mooring tower. But within minutes, the tail was up forty-five degrees. In the control car, orders were given to try to keep the ship level but it was no use.

To try to level the airship, the crew ran to the tail, but the angle became steeper. At seventy-five degrees, the men grabbed girders and held on as anything not fastened down hurtled toward the nose. The outer skin of the *Los Angeles* was just fabric over aluminum girders, so falling meant certain death. Tools and instruments ripped out of the fabric and rained down on the ground as the airship stood on its nose. Inside, the crew waited for the ship to impale itself on the mooring mast.

Meanwhile, water ballast and tools smashed into the roof of the mooring mast's elevator, terrifying the men inside. For a moment the tail towered 842 feet above the Pine Barrens; then, just as gracefully, the ship rolled on her nose and settled peacefully and perfectly on the other side of the mast. The ship was largely undamaged, but the crew could not even get a nerve-calming drink as it was Prohibition.

The *Los Angeles'* second near-disaster took place the following year. A Navy plane was missing from the carrier *Lexington,* and the airship was taking part in the search. Late on the night of March 2, Rosendahl decided to refuel at Lakehurst and resume the search the next morning.

As the airship tried to reach its mooring mast, winds were blowing from thirty-five to fifty miles a hour. She dropped her mooring cable, which was attached to winches, and the ground crew started to pull her to the mast when a gust caught the ship and snapped the half-inch cable like a kite string. Rosendahl decided a mast landing was too dangerous and signaled for a ground landing. This meant lines would be dropped from her nose and tail and hundreds of ground crew would actually pull the ship down as Rosendahl released valuable helium.

Everything was going well. The wind had dropped, and the crew got the ship to the ground as men were hanging onto rails outside the gondola and engines under the giant hull. As the ship was walked into the hangar, a snow squall hit, dropping the air temperature by ten degrees. Lighter than the cold air surrounding it, the airship shot up like a cork in water. Rosendahl ordered the ground crew to "let go everything."

Most of the ground crew heard the order as "let go." But some men on the engine railing held on too long and fell off at fifteen to twenty feet above the ground; they were little more than shaken up. By the time the *Los Angeles* was at five hundred feet, one of the officers looked outside the control car window and shouted to Rosendahl, "My God, Captain, we've carried a bunch of men up on the hand rails. We've got to get them in at once, sir."

In the icy darkness, eight men held on for dear life as snow and wind tried to knock them off to certain death. Windows were kicked out of the control car and two of the men were able to climb in by themselves. Four more men were reached by leaning out and pulling them up by their arms. The last two were so weakened by the cold that a volunteer had to climb outside as the ship hovered five hundred feet over the field.

Rosendahl radioed the ground to see how many men were missing and could have dropped off the railing before being noticed. After a few minutes, Lakehurst radioed back, "Eight missing." The dirigible had saved them all and would remain a lucky ship.

The *Los Angeles* continued to fly until 1932 when she was retired to seven years of testing and training on the ground at Lakehurst. Finally, the ship with a perfect record was sold for scrap in 1939.

CHAPTER 6

Flying Aircraft Carrier Falters Off Coast

The morning of April 3, 1933, was cloudy with occasional rain, but inside the big hangar at Lakehurst there was an air of excitement. The USS *Akron*, the Navy's 780-foot-long flying aircraft carrier, was about to take off. The dirigible's mission was to fly up the East Coast to New England to calibrate the Navy's new radio direction finders, but most of the trip's excitement was caused by an important passenger, Admiral William A. Moffett, head of Naval Aeronautics.

With Moffett on board, the 75-man crew knew that weather would never delay the flight. Moffett had publicly declared the *Akron* to be safe in all weather and as a show of confidence even ordered her not to carry life jackets.

Throughout the day, there were reports of severe weather, but at 7:28 that evening, Captain Frank McCord, the aircraft's new skipper, gave orders to cast off, and the *Akron* rose into the fog. McCord immediately realized that the fog was worse than reported and radioed Lakehurst not to launch the airplanes which were supposed to rendezvous with and be hoisted on board the airship.

McCord decided to fly inland toward Philadelphia where the weather was better, then turn back as it improved along the coast. By the time the *Akron* reached Philadelphia, the city's lights

Over the Jersey Shore, the flying aircraft carrier USS Akron *catches a scout plane on its trapeze.*

were visible, but to the south, flashes of lightning could be seen. In the control car, McCord and his second in command, Herbert V. Wiley, disagreed on the flight plan. McCord wanted to head northeast to outrun the storm over the ocean; Wiley wanted to head west and let the storm pass, then follow it.

McCord overruled Wiley and headed the ship northeast. Five of the crew were survivors of the 1925 *Shenandoah* crash, and they knew firsthand the power of a thunderstorm. As the *Akron* continued toward the coast she again ran into fog. McCord ordered her up to sixteen hundred feet and, at that altitude, lost contact with the ground. At about ten o'clock the ship passed over what McCord thought was Asbury Park. Here he planned to ride out the storm over open water.

After an hour, the storm caught up with the ship. Lightning surrounded the *Akron* and lit up the control car. Next, rain pelted the giant hull while the air remained relatively calm. McCord again ordered a change in direction, to the west toward shore. Around midnight, the *Akron* reached the coast. McCord thought he was near Asbury Park, but the crew of Barnegat Light Coast Guard Station could hear and occasionally see the giant airship.

In the air over Long Beach Island McCord began to realize he had a problem. Earlier, a crewman had misunderstood a fifteen-degree change in the ship's course for fifty degrees. Now McCord had no idea where he was. For all he knew, the ship could even be heading for New York City and its skyscrapers. Immediately, the captain ordered the *Akron* to head back for open sea; below, island residents could hear her head out the inlet.

The *Akron* was now engulfed by the storm, and the thunder shook the ship. While the sky exploded with lightning, Moffett came into the control car to ride out the storm, and Wiley moved forward, looking for a break in the clouds. Shortly after midnight, the ship encountered severe turbulence and heavy lightning.

The elevator wheel tore from the control man's hands and he shouted to Wiley, "We're falling!" The crew dropped emergency ballast as Wiley and others frantically grabbed at the wheel. The plunge stopped at what appeared on the instruments to be eight hundred feet, but the altimeter in a storm could be off by more than a hundred feet, and the *Akron* was 785 feet long.

To everyone's relief the ship started to rise. "Now bring her up to 1600 feet gradually and then level off," Wiley ordered, but as the turbulence continued, Wiley sent "all hands to landing stations." The entire crew was on alert.

Again the big ship began to drop. McCord ordered, "Full speed," and all eight engines responded. "Up ship," the captain continued. The propellers were turned to lift the nose twenty-five degrees. With the tail lower than the nose and the control car altimeter reading three hundred feet, the *Akron* continued to fall.

The crew heard a popping noise, the sound of the lower rudder hitting the water and breaking away. "Stand by to crash!" Wiley ordered. On shore, a radio operator in Wildwood picked up a message from the ship in distress. "Control broken ... ship bad condition ... heavy storm ... strong wind ... nose up breaking center ... run into something ... crashing."

On board the German oil tanker *Phoebus*, Captain Karl Dolldorf was on watch. He saw lights in the air and knew they weren't the Barnegat Inlet lights which he had just passed. He watched the lights descend and realized an aircraft was in trouble. He ordered the *Phoebus* to the rescue.

The control car of the *Akron* began to settle toward the ocean. Wiley later remembered "perfect" discipline in the car as the crew prepared to meet the icy water. "I asked the altitude and the answer was 'Three hundred feet.' I gave the order, 'Stand by to crash,' and that signal was run up to the engine cars. Almost immediately we hit the water. We had, as I remember, a list to starboard, that is, to my side of the car, and the water rushed in my window and carried me out the other window. I tried to swim as rapidly as I could to get from under the ship and finally came to the surface.

"I could see the ship drifting away from me when the lightning flashed. The bow was pointed up in the air and the whole structure was a general wreck. I saw two lights on what I thought was the stern and, looking to one side of them, I saw the lights of a ship. I also thought I could see the glare of Barnegat Lighthouse."

Meanwhile, men inside the giant hull were trying to escape. Seaman Moody Irwin and Chief Dick "Lucky" Deal — a nickname earned because he had survived the *Shenandoah* crash — knew the ship was finished. As the *Akron* fell, they tried to work their way to the nose and reached a group of sailors holding onto girders, waiting for the end to come. In the dark of the storm the men couldn't tell if they were over land or water; as they waited, they discussed which would increase their chances for survival.

At the impact, Irwin jumped from the girder through the fabric which formed the *Akron's* outer skin. Deal chose to cling to a girder. Seconds later, Deal felt something at his feet, near-freezing water. His biggest fear, however, was not the water temperature, but getting tangled in the maze of wires and girders which shaped the *Akron*.

When the ship crashed, Deal's right leg caught in some wires. As he was being driven under, he frantically tried to free himself. Living up to his nickname, Deal had been asleep when the *Akron* got in trouble and, still groggy, had forgotten to put on his heavy flying boots. Without them, he slipped the wire off his right foot and swam to the surface.

Nearby, Irwin had a different problem. He had landed in the water but as he began to swim, the giant hull settled down on top of him. He braced his feet against a supported part of the hull, then pushed off and dove as deep as he could, swimming until he thought his lungs would burst. When he surfaced, Irwin had just cleared the hull. He removed his heavy flying coat and swam from the ship, fearful of being caught in the suction as the dirigible sank.

As Deal and Irwin swam, each realized the *Akron* carried no life jackets. Deal wasn't a good swimmer and knew he would not last long. Irwin, on the other hand, believed he could easily reach Long Beach Island but he was afraid of sharks and flailed his arms wildly to keep them away. Just then, to his surprise, he saw a 120-gallon fuel tank floating by with two men hanging on. He swam over and grabbed hold.

Deal knew that if he didn't find some debris to buoy himself, he would soon drown. By lightning flash, Deal spotted the tank and the three men and started for it. A few feet short, he ran out of strength and slipped beneath the surface. Suddenly, he felt a hand pulling at him; the next thing he knew, he was holding on to the tank.

"Who's here?" Deal gasped. Irwin answered, and Deal felt safe until he heard the cries for help from his shipmates.

From what Deal could hear, most of the men had survived the crash and were in the water. Wiley was about two hundred yards from the ship, clutching a three-foot-square of plywood. He tried to share it with another survivor who kept losing hold in the rough water.

Several miles away, Dolldorf ordered his crew to the lifeboats and turned on all searchlights.

Meanwhile, the men on the tank could not hear any more cries for help. Irwin began to feel pleasantly warm and realized that meant he was freezing to death. Deal reached over the tank and grabbed Irwin's arms and the two men held onto each other. The other two men kept getting knocked off and had to continually swim back to the tank. Finally as they reached the top of a wave, Deal shouted, "There's a ship!" As the *Phoebus* got closer, Irwin cried, "I can't hold on any longer!" Deal urged him to hang on saying, "We'll be all right in five minutes."

One of the other crewmen slipped from the tank for the last time. Just as the three men were losing consciousness, a life ring was thrown from the *Phoebus*. Deal and Irwin lived; the third man died on board.

With his plywood, Wiley kicked toward the ship and also was pulled on board. Meanwhile, lifeboats from the *Phoebus* searched for more survivors. At 1:50 A.M. the *Phoebus* radioed, "Airship *Akron* afloat off Barnegat Lighthouse with 77 men. Picked up some. Can't get all. Chief officer, three men saved."

In Toms River and Lakewood, early morning phone calls informed wives and families of the crash. Most chose to go to the Lakehurst air station, center for the rescue operations. By dawn, the station's welfare building was crowded with relatives hoping to get information. Outside, gale-force winds and occasional showers kept rescue aircraft on the ground.

The base's acting commander, Jesse Kenworthy — the base commander was on the *Akron* — had refused the offers of airplane and blimp pilots to search for survivors. Around midmorning, hopes were raised when a message was picked up at Lakehurst: The British ship *Panther* had just reported seeing forty men drifting on wreckage off Barnegat Light.

When the message came in, David E. Cummins, commander of the twin-engine, 196-foot blimp *J-3*, volunteered to take life jackets aloft to drop to the survivors. As he was preparing to take off, Cummins noted a problem with the port engine, but he and his six-man crew volunteered to give it a try.

As Cummins left, Kenworthy told him, "Don't lose any more men; the ship is nothing." The *J-3* cruised the coast from the lighthouse to Atlantic City as low as two hundred feet but with no success. Then Cummins turned the blimp north and into the wind. To make any headway, full speed was needed and the port engine was beginning to vibrate, tearing itself loose from its mounting. Cummins reduced speed and headed for shore and safety.

As the *J-3* struggled to reach shore, a crowd gathered on the Beach Haven boardwalk. One of the men was R. E. P. Elmer, a retired naval officer from Princeton. Elmer realized that the blimp was in trouble and might try to make an emergency landing on the beach.

The Navy blimp J-3 took off in a gale to attempt to drop life jackets to the survivors of the Akron *in the waters off of Barnegat Light.*

Quickly, Elmer organized fifty people into a landing crew. As Cummins reached the board-walk, he saw the makeshift landing crew and dropped the *J-3's* landing lines. Some of the lines hit high tension wires, but since the ship was filled with helium and not explosive hydrogen, there wasn't any fire, only a lot of sparks.

Elmer and his impromptu ground crew grabbed the lines and started to pull down the blimp. As the *J-3* descended, the copilot pulled the rip cord, a zipper which releases helium quickly in emergencies. Just as the rip cord was pulled, a strong gust pushed the blimp which hit the ground and bounced back into the air.

The wind took the *J-3* toward the ocean like a kite. The islanders' ground crew couldn't hold onto the landing lines and the ship drifted a thousand feet off the boardwalk and into the rough seas. The crash knocked Cummins unconscious, and the crew tried to hold up his head as they struggled with their heavy flying suits and boots in the icy water.

Just south of the crash, a New York City Savoy amphibious police airplane was refueling at Bond's Coast Guard Station on the island. When Sergeant Joseph Forsyth and Patrolman Otto Kafka saw the sparks from the high tension wires, they knew the *J-3* was in trouble. After takeoff, Forsyth decided to risk everything and land his plane in the heavy seas to save the crew.

186

Once on the water, the plane taxied to the wreckage where Kafka pulled two men onto the plane's floats. With the added weight, the plane couldn't take off, so Forsyth taxied to the surf where some of Elmer's ground crew took them ashore. The plane taxied back to the blimp, and three more men and the unconscious skipper were pulled to shore.

Beach Haven's only doctor was out of town so Cummins was rushed to the Atlantic City Hospital, where he was pronounced dead on arrival from drowning. Forsyth and Kafka searched in vain for the final member of the crew of the *J-3*. The body of machinist mate Pasquale Bettio washed ashore later.

The Coast Guard had ordered every cutter from New York to Cape May to race to the *Akron* crash site and save the crew. However, the report of forty survivors hanging onto wreckage was false. Of the seventy-six men on the ship, only three survived. Added to the deaths of Cummins and Bettio in the waters off Long Beach Island, seventy-five airmen died, the worst airship disaster in history: More than twice as many people perished compared to the better-known *Hindenburg* disaster.

The crash soured the American public on the giant airships and spelled the beginning of the end for the Navy's dirigible program. Back at Lakehurst, cars were still parked, waiting for their owners' return, and five or six dogs sat patiently, including "Rummy," William Moffett's dog. Moffett's order not to carry life jackets would be rescinded; never again would any naval aircraft take off without life preservers.

On Memorial Day 1933, six thousand people crowded the boardwalk at Centre Street in Beach Haven to pay tribute to the airships' crews. Coast Guard cutters and the *Akron's* own airplanes dropped flowers on the sites of the two crashes.

CHAPTER 7

The *Hindenburg*

Although the German airship *LZ-129* had been built for a peaceful purpose, political decisions made in both Washington and Berlin would eventually doom innocents on board.

Early in the 1930s, thanks mainly to the visits of the airship *Graf Zeppelin* to Lakehurst, German-American relations were on a firm footing. American investors looked forward to regular transatlantic passenger service. Meanwhile, the investors were using their influence to convince the United States government to lift its ban on selling nonflammable helium to Germany.

But in 1935 Hugo Eckener, pilot of the *Graf Zeppelin*, was called into the office of Doctor Joseph Goebbels, head of the Nazi propaganda department. Goebbels wanted the *Graf* and the *LZ-129* to have huge swastikas on their tails to show the world Nazi power. Eckener argued against the idea, but Goebbels finally made it an order, and the swastikas were applied.

The reaction in the United States was mixed. Even though President Franklin Roosevelt supported the sale of helium to Germany, a civil service employee in the Department of the Interior kept the paperwork so backed up that Eckener finally gave up, and the new ship was filled instead with hydrogen gas.

On March 4, Eckener took the *LZ-129* aloft for its first trials. Later, as the ship flew over Munich, he announced to the world the airship would be called the *Hindenburg*, although it would never be called that in Germany. The Nazis had planned to call it the "Adolph Hitler."

The *Hindenburg* was 803 feet long, almost the length of three football fields. Its lifting capacity was about twenty tons, and it could cruise at a speed of eighty miles an hour with an effective range of about ten thousand miles.

Inside the ship, passengers found luxurious accommodations. Two decks with twenty-three staterooms formed the passenger area. Each room contained foldaway beds, a sitting area, a toilet, and hot and cold running water. On board were men's and women's showers, a bar with an aluminum piano, and a restaurant which stocked everything from fresh turkey to live lobsters. On each side of the ship were glass promenade decks, one hundred thirty feet in length and lined with benches so passengers could enjoy the view.

The *Hindenburg* blended safety and comfort. Although all matches and lighters were confiscated from passengers, the ship had a special room for smokers who entered it through an air lock; the room was pressurized to keep out the hydrogen. The Germans announced that the *Hindenburg* was perfectly safe.

On the airship's first trip to America in the spring of 1936, she flew over New York and Boston, where wild, screaming crowds and car horns almost drowned out the hum of the dirigible's four Mercedes diesel engines. Finally, the craft arrived at Lakehurst, where a crowd of more than one hundred thousand had braved the traffic to see the spectacle. On landing, Eckener was taken to see President Roosevelt.

The *Hindenburg* made nine more visits to Lakehurst in 1936, bringing the rich and famous. Actor Douglas Fairbanks, boxer Max Schmeling and financier Nelson Rockefeller crossed the Atlantic in the ship. American Airlines announced that its new twin-engine DC-3 would link Lakehurst with all other United States airports. The little air station was about to become the "Gateway to the World."

During the winter, some modifications were made to the *Hindenburg* and more staterooms were added. Early in the morning of May 3, 1937, the dirigible lifted off from Germany for the first flight of the year. On board were ninety-seven people, thirty-six passengers and a large crew including trainees. In command were Captain Max Pruss, on his first trip, and the ship's former captain, Ernst Lehmann. Eckener had been forced out of command because of his dislike for Hitler and the Nazis.

By this time, the flight across the Atlantic was almost routine. The previous year, the *Hindenburg* had even ridden out a hurricane off New Jersey. The only problem on this flight, however, seemed to be a persistent headwind which delayed the estimated time of arrival at Lakehurst.

Late on the afternoon of the sixth, the *Hindenburg* arrived over New York City. The ship circled Ebbets Field as the Dodgers beat the Pirates, then turned toward the Statue of Liberty and New Jersey.

Already eight hours late, the *Hindenburg*, held aloft by seven million cubic feet of hydrogen gas, finally arrived at Lakehurst at 4 P.M. The base commander, Charles E. Rosendahl, "Rosie" to his men, informed Captain Pruss of an approaching thunderstorm and recommended a delayed

The HINDENBURG. D-LZ 129   Naval Air Station, Lakehurst, New Jersey.

Kevin Pace / Official U.S. Navy photograph; Navy Lakehurst Historical Society

Along with the Nazi flag on the tail, the Olympic symbols are displayed (front, midsection) on a 1936 happy landing of the luxury ship of the air, the Hindenburg, at Lakehurst, New Jersey.

landing. Pruss agreed and headed toward the Jersey shore for some sightseeing. By 4:25 the *Hindenburg* was over Barnegat Light where passengers snapped pictures of the lighthouse.

Ten minutes later the few people on the beach at Ship Bottom waved as the 803-foot monster blotted out the sun. Passengers were taking a last look at the famed Beach Haven boardwalk when Pruss received word that the weather was improving. The captain turned the dirigible west. By 6:44 Pruss radioed that he was over Forked River and coming in.

At Lakehurst station, Rosendahl made preparations for the landing. A ground crew of two hundred, including boys from Lakewood and Toms River high schools, were paid one dollar each to help pull the airship down. Reporters from New York and Philadelphia papers were on hand to cover the landing and its passengers.

All day there had been occasional showers, and the ground crew on the field were getting tired. Rains persisted, postponing the landing until after seven when the skies finally cleared and the *Hindenburg* made her final approach. On the ground, Jack Snyder of the *Philadelphia Record* put a new plate in his camera. It was number thirteen. "Something's bound to go wrong with this picture," he muttered.

Near the radio building, announcer Herbert Morrison from WLS-Chicago prepared to make an audio recording of the landing for the next day's "Dinner Bell" program on NBC. There was no live broadcast from Lakehurst that day. Inside the ship, passengers were packing and placing luggage in the halls. Many stood on the promenade deck looking for friends in the Lakehurst crowd.

Morrison reported, "It's hanging there like a giant feather. The vast motors are just holding it, just enough to keep it from … " He stopped for an instant. There was dead air. What Morrison saw at exactly 7:25 P.M. changed everything.

Just forward of where the *Hindenburg's* tail fin met the body, a flash of light lit the sky, and flames burst from the ship. Morrison was just about to complete his recording when he paused and, a second later in a frantic, cracking voice, said, "It's burst into flames … Get out of the way, please!… It's burning, bursting into flames and it's falling … Oh, this is one of the worst … Oh … It's a terrible sight for all humanity."

To the ground crew there was a flash and, when they looked up, they saw the *Hindenburg* bearing down on their heads. Rosendahl shouted, "My God, it's on the ground crew!" It was run or die. Each man and boy spent the next few seconds running in the wet sand of the pines, thinking his life was over.

Rosendahl, an airshipman to the last, ran into the wind, a choice which saved him. One civilian, Charley Hamaman of Lakehurst, tripped on the railroad tracks and died as the hull fell on him.

Inside the control car, Pruss felt a quick shock and then heard the noise of the explosion. Looking down, he saw the ground crew start to run and heard the screams of the crowd.

"The ship's on fire!" shouted the radio officer as the *Hindenburg* began to settle tail first.

Pruss' first thought was to drop water ballast to keep the ship level, but he decided to let the tail settle. For the passengers and crew, the next thirty-four seconds determined everything.

As the nose shot up to five hundred feet, people and furniture inside were dumped and careened toward the tail. Flames sucked the air from the passenger space and turned the aluminum furniture white-hot. Passengers and crew had to make a choice: burn or jump.

Passengers punched out windows on the promenade deck and began to jump. Joseph Spah, an acrobat, had been taking pictures and had seen his family waiting below. Then he saw the flames. He broke the glass with his camera and, with two other men, prepared to jump. Each realized it was too far and tried hanging from the window. The first man fell several hundred feet to his death. The second slipped, grabbed Spah's coat and held on for an instant; then the coat ripped. Spah clutched the window frame as the ship settled down. At about forty feet, he dropped to the ground, got up and ran to safety. The fourteen-year-old cabin boy was spared when a thousand gallon tank of water burst over his head and drenched him.

The four crewmen in the nose were farthest from the fire when it started, but as the nose rose upward, each had to hold on. The towering nose became a chimney as the flames shot up.

Each man held on to the metal girders as they turned red hot; one by one they dropped into the inferno. One man managed to wrap his legs around a girder and held on until the nose finally settled down.

The men in the control car jumped, but the burning hull fell on their heads. Pruss escaped unhurt. An emergency call went out and doctors from as far away as Tuckerton raced to Lakehurst and the Paul Kimball Hospital. There was little they could do for the serious burn victims.

Twelve passengers, twenty-three crew and Hamaman died. The commercial airship business never recovered, and regular transatlantic flight would have to wait for the airplane. Plans for Ocean County to become a world-class airport and playground for the rich would have to wait for better land transportation.

CHAPTER 8

Asbury Park's Dream Turns Deadly

Sometimes events are so complicated that it takes years for them to come into focus. Since the *Morro Castle* burned off the Jersey coast, new evidence and later events have filled in gaps in that most horrifying of all disasters, a fire at sea.

The story, oddly enough, began as the summer of 1884 was drawing to a close and the wealthy began to leave their shore cottages for the winter. In Asbury Park, the *Daily Spray*, a local paper, made a lighthearted request to extend the season.

"We want a first-class shipwreck," the paper stated. "Why? To make Asbury Park a famous winter resort. There is a very comfortable berth for a big ship between the fishing pier and the Asbury Avenue Pavilion. She should strike head-on, so that her nose would ram the Baby Parade grandstand, and her tail might hop around even with the end of the pier. We could accommodate her all winter. Pontoon or suspension bridges could be built from the pier and the pavilion, so that the ship could be used as a casino. We need a spectacular ship."

For fifty years that wish went unfilled. Then, in 1934, a strange set of events started a chain reaction that would fulfill it almost to the very street.

On September 1, when Captain Robert Wilmont gave orders for the SS *Morro Castle* to cast off from her New York pier, she was a troubled ship. For four years she had been the pride of America's merchant marine. She was also a beautiful ship, 528 feet in length and designed to serve people who could afford the good life. She carried the rich on vacation to Cuba, where they indulged in the famed Havana nightlife.

The Morro Castle *beached at Asbury Park almost at the exact spot where, 50 years earlier, a local newspaper had said, "We want a first-class ship-wreck."*

According to the brochure, the one-week cruise was a giant party, a way to escape the Depression and the realities on life on shore. The 318 passengers paid from $65 to $160 and the ship's operators gave them their money's worth.

But beneath the surface gloss, the *Morro Castle* had serious problems. The crew was under-paid, with most of the 230 men making only about $1 per day. Food and living conditions were also poor. Assistant radioman George Alagna tried to form a union, but his attempts failed because most crewmen feared that they would lose their jobs if they joined. His activities singled him out to Captain Wilmont as a man who should be watched.

Wilmont was uneasy because the ship carried other things besides passengers. Each time she cleared New York Harbor, the *Morro Castle* carried explosives, guns and ammunition deep inside her sealed hold. These arms were for the right wing dictatorship running Cuba. For several years the Communists had been trying to overthrow that government, and the Ward Line, owners of the *Morro Castle*, had been smuggling arms since her launching. Communists in New York and Havana had vowed to stop these shipments.

On the previous trip there had been a fire in the hold containing the explosives. The automatic fire fighting system extinguished it, but an investigation showed it had been deliberately set.

Wilmont had one other problem: He was sure someone was trying to kill him. On July 29, after taking a mouthful of fish, he had become violently ill, and this convinced him that some-one on the ship wanted him dead.

As the *Morro Castle* headed down the East Coast, Wilmont stayed in his cabin as much as possible. While this caused gossip and speculation among the passengers, he felt it was a wise move. He had done all in his power to give the passengers the party atmosphere they wanted. He had suspended all lifeboat drills as "upsetting to the passengers" and, when a passenger slipped on a wet deck caused by a leaking hose, he ordered all fire hydrants capped and all fire hoses stored away. He also ordered no more fire drills.

While the passengers enjoyed Havana, the arms were unloaded and a return cargo of salted hides was put on board. At once the stench spread throughout the ship. Wilmont ordered the ventilation system shut down to keep the smell in the hold. But enforcing that order also shut down the smoke and fire detection system which had saved the ship only days before.

Just before leaving for New York, Wilmont received two tips. The first said the Communists were going to try something, and the second said radioman Alagna had brought two bottles of a strange liquid aboard. Wilmont believed that the two events were linked and that Alagna was his problem. He ordered First Officer William Warms and George Rogers, chief radio officer, to keep a close eye on Alagna.

By noon on September 7, the *Morro Castle* was heading north. Off the coast of Virginia the weather worsened, and by nightfall the ship was in a major storm. Many of the passengers would never make the captain's farewell dinner because they were seasick.

Neither would Captain Wilmont.

At 7:30, First Officer Warms had been with the captain who had just been brought a tray of scrambled eggs and melon. Fifteen minutes later Captain Wilmont was found lying face down in his bathtub. The ship's doctor blamed the death on acute indigestion and heart failure, but several officers noticed that Wilmont's skin had turned a strange blue color.

William Warms was now captain. As the *Morro Castle* continued through the storm, passengers were informed about the captain's death, and all official parties were canceled. Warms knew that if all went well he would be in New York the next day. What he did not know was that he had a maniac on board, a man who had been in and out of jail since he was thirteen and who had the interesting hobby of making timing devices for explosives.

The man was not Alagna but Chief Radio Officer George Rogers. He had been informed by the Ward Line that this would be his last trip since his criminal record had recently been made known to them.

As the ship pushed its way through storm-driven waves, most of the passengers retired to their quarters. At 2:50 A.M. as the stewards were cleaning the first-class lounge, they smelled smoke. One minute later, a night watchman reported to the bridge that he had seen and smelled smoke coming from one of the ventilator shafts.

Warms rushed to the ventilator to check, then ran back to the bridge and called his first officer. About this same time, two crewmen entered the writing room where they found the floor covered with smoke, apparently coming from a locker.

This was the same locker where the Lyle gun (a line-throwing gun for emergencies) and its twenty-five pounds of gunpowder were stored in the false ceiling. As one of the crewmen went to investigate, he made the mistake of opening the door to check inside. Once the door was opened, the fire had all the oxygen it needed and roared to life.

The crewman tried to close the door and ran. By the time someone arrived at the blaze with an extinguisher, it was a major fire. Engulfed in a storm, the *Morro Castle* was in a real crisis with a fire on board and with passengers who had not practiced lifeboat or fire drills.

The crewmen knew they needed water to fight the fire and one of the officers, Clarence Hackney, called the bridge to inform the captain. As he left the area, he made a mistake: The ship had been equipped with fire doors designed to isolate any fire. In his excitement, Hackney did not close the doors.

The captain called the engine room and asked for all possible water pressure to fight the fire. He learned that one of the boilers was down and that pressure was going to be low. He told the engine room to have Chief Engineer Eban Abbot call as soon as he arrived at his post.

Meanwhile, the fire was spreading. Ten minutes after the fire was discovered, Warms ordered the general fire alarm sounded. "Get all the passengers out!" he yelled. By then it was too late.

As some of the crew uncapped fire hydrants and tried to find hoses, others went up and down hallways banging on doors and pans to wake passengers from a sound, and in some cases, a drunken, sleep. But the fire spread with amazing speed, so quickly in fact that the hydrant closest to the writing room was never used.

Besides the failure to close the fire doors, there were two more reasons for the fire's rapid spread. First, the ship's lavish interior consisted of wooden paneling covered with layers of varnish. The paneling was held to the metal bulkheads by six-inch wooden studs, creating an air space to feed the flames. The other reason was Warms' orders to keep the ship at full speed. The gale-force wind made the ship a floating blowtorch, sweeping the flames toward the stern.

When the alarm sounded, Chief Engineer Abbot put on his dress white uniform and headed for the bridge instead of the engine room, which was his fire station. He could see the fire spreading and by the time he reached the bridge, he was visibly shaken.

The ship was rocked by a thunderous explosion as the fire set off the gunpowder for the Lyle gun. In the radio room, George Rogers and George Alagna waited for orders to send an SOS. When he heard nothing from the bridge, Rogers sent Alagna for permission to send out a call. When Alagna returned he told Rogers, "I couldn't get Warms to pay any attention to me. He was saying, 'Is it real or am I dreaming?' "

Rogers had a wet towel over his face, and the radio was on emergency power. He sent Alagna back to the bridge. At 3:10, Alagna returned saying, "They've all gone crazy up there on the bridge. I can't get any cooperation." At 3:13 Rogers picked up a ship, the *Andrea Lucken-back*. It was calling the Tuckerton Coast Guard Station, asking if there had been any distress signals received because a ship north of Barnegat Light was burning.

At 3:15, Rogers sent out a CQ, a call to "stand by for an important message." Tuckerton ordered the ship to be quiet, because ships were supposed to listen for distress signals at quarter after and quarter to the hour. Alagna made another trip to the bridge where he found Abbot sitting in a corner wringing his hands and saying, "A hundred hoses won't hold this fire."

Alagna screamed in Warms' face, "Rogers is dying in there!" The captain answered, "I can't do anything." The radioman hollered, "How about some orders?"

At 3:24, Rogers went on the air to Tuckerton. "SOS ... SOS ... SS *Morro Castle* afire twenty miles ...." It had been twenty-four minutes since the general alarm had sounded.

Panicked, some passengers and crew jumped into the ocean, but the majority coughed and choked their way toward the stern. Warms ordered the whistle to sound, the signal to abandon ship. Abbot left the bridge and got into lifeboat number 3, shouting, "Lower away!" but a cable fouled. He jumped into boat number 1 and ordered, "Lower away!" The first boat to hit the water had a capacity of seventy, but there were only eight people on board, six of them crew.

Of the first eighty people to leave the ship, seventy-three were crew members. Warms ordered the engines cut and the anchor dropped to prevent the ship from hitting the beach. By the light of the fire, the passengers were driven toward the stern where they faced their own hellish choice, either jumping into a gale-whipped ocean or burning.

The only ship's officer in the stern was Bob Smith, the cruise director. He did his best to quell the panic by telling the passengers not to jump because help was on the way. The few remaining crewmen threw deck chairs and anything that would float over the side. They tied ropes to the rails so people could slide down.

Smith had good reason to tell the passengers to hold on because until Warms ordered the anchor dropped, the ship's two giant propellers were still turning. Those who ignored Smith and jumped were sucked under the water and into the propellers.

When the engines finally stopped, the decks started blistering under the passengers' feet. Someone shouted, "The ship is going to blow up!" An elderly woman grabbed Smith's arms and said, "Mr. Smith, please save me!" Without a word he took off his life preserver and gave it to her.

Newlyweds held hands and stepped off the ship together. Others tried to slide down the ropes. Having never practiced a lifeboat drill, many passengers did not know how to jump. The heavy, cork-filled life jackets became a nightmare. If their arms were loose when they hit the water, passengers slid right out of the jackets. For those who held tightly, the cork was driven upward on impact and knocked the wearer unconscious. Others jumped without life jackets, and some held onto bodies to stay afloat.

Those who were good swimmers set off for shore. Most, however, chose to ride the ten- to fifteen-foot waves up and down and waited for help they were sure was on the way.

The *Morro Castle* had been slow in sending out a distress call, waiting more than thirty minutes after the fire started. However, nearby ships responded. The *Andrea Luckenback* was seven miles away and coming at full speed. The ocean liner *Monarch of Bermuda* was just entering Sandy Hook and reversed course. After some confusion, two Coast Guard cutters, the *Tampa* and *Cahoone*, ordered full speed to the *Morro Castle.*

Coast Guard stations from Beach Haven to Sandy Hook responded as well. From Barnegat Light, a motorized whaleboat was launched and sent out of the inlet into the teeth of a northeast gale. The Manasquan packet boat was underway by 3:30 A.M., and some stations even launched their eight-oared surf boats and began the backbreaking job of battling the headwinds.

Others would also be willing to take a risk. Brielle's John Bogan, captain of the sixty-foot fishing boat *Paramount*, first learned the *Morro Castle* was afire off the beach from the radio. When he arrived at the dock, he found a group of captains and mates from other fishing boats already there. The consensus among these experienced seamen was to take out the *Paramount* and see if their help was needed. As the boat cleared the inlet they could see the glow of the *Morro Castle* and the Coast Guard boats bobbing in the waves. As they neared the ship they saw the first of the sixty-seven passengers they would save, Mrs. James F. Kennedy.

To the rescuers' surprise, she was in a bathing suit. She was a poor swimmer and had jumped wearing a life jacket. Her husband, a strong swimmer, did not have one. After a while he said to her, "I can't go on. Save yourself." When the *Paramount* tried to pick her up, she refused, saying, "Where's my Jimmy?" She swam to a corpse to check. A crewman from the fishing boat yelled that someone would get him. "No, I know Jim's drowned," she answered. Finally, she was pulled on board.

For the next several hours the *Paramount* circled, picking up most people as they were nearing the end of their physical endurance. Ironically, one pulled on board was a newlywed, Mrs. Paul Lemprecht, who had fished many times from the deck of the *Paramount.* One woman was found holding her husband's body. "We couldn't waste time with the dead but it took 10 minutes to convince her," a crewman said.

On the bow of the *Morro Castle* there were still fourteen people alive: Captain Warms, his two radiomen, and eleven crewmen. The wind had kept the fire from them, but their feet blistered as the deck grew hotter and hotter.

At about 5:45 A.M. Madelaine Clancy, head of the Spring Lake unit of the Red Cross, was awakened by a telephone call from the police. "Something has happened with a ship offshore," they told her. "People are in the water, swimming this way. Some haven't any clothes at all and some are in their nightclothes."

Clancy grabbed what extra clothing she had stored and sent someone to a local store. When she arrived at the beach, she found local lifeguards plunging through the raging surf to bring in exhausted survivors who had been in the water for more than three hours. Volunteer ambulance crews from nearby communities took those in the worst condition to hospitals.

Oceanfront residents offered armloads of blankets and clothes and took those who could walk into their homes. Two hotels delivered sandwiches and coffee, and a summer resident, Walter McManus, appeared at the first aid building with a dozen cases of whiskey.

As the first lifeboats came ashore, most of the spectators became aware that there was something terribly wrong. Said Clancy, "Those crew members saved their own skins." The first boat ashore had only twenty-nine people: three passengers and twenty-six crewmen including the chief engineer, the second ranking officer on the ship.

As the lifeboat neared shore, Abbot tore the gold braid and the marks of rank from his uniform, muttering that he would go to jail for coming ashore with so few passengers. The first to jump ashore, Abbot turned and yelled at the crew, "Remember, none of you should talk to the newspapermen. They would never understand."

On the *Morro Castle*, Warms and the handful of crew huddled in the bow. By midmorning most of the rescue ships had departed to rush survivors to hospitals and the tug *New York* had offered Warms a tow. Then the Coast Guard cutter *Tampa* arrived and also offered a tow which Warms accepted.

A chief bosun's mate climbed up a line from the bow of the *Morro Castle*. Around his waist was a light line which was tied to a twelve-inch hawser. Warms and his crew now began the backbreaking job of hauling up and securing the giant rope that would span six hundred feet from the *Tampa* to the *Morro Castle*.

Warms sent George Rogers below for a hacksaw to cut the anchor chain. The *Morro Castle* was now under the control of the *Tampa*, whose captain ordered the crew off. One by one, they slid down a line into the *Tampa's* lifeboat. The two-hundred-fifty-pound Rogers fell the last few feet into the boat and landed on several bodies picked up earlier.

Now there wasn't a living person on board the *Morro Castle*. At noon, Earle G. Rose, captain of the *Tampa*, ordered his cutter underway. Slowly, the hawser pulled from the water grew taut and the *Morro Castle* inched forward. Rose had planned to get the ship inside Sandy Hook where fireboats could extinguish the blaze, but almost at once, he knew there were going to be problems. As the *Tampa* pulled the *Morro Castle* north against a northeast gale, the ship was being pushed slowly but surely toward the Jersey shore.

Rose increased the *Tampa's* power to stay away from the beach which only put more stress on the tow line and the smaller line to the tug. At 3:20 P.M. Rose radioed, "It appears the tow line is going." At 4:15, the battleship *Arizona* (later sunk at Pearl Harbor) offered assistance. Rose refused because by now they were too close to the beach.

By six o'clock they were only a few hundred yards off Asbury Park's Convention Hall. Rose ordered the cutter's engines speed increased and radioed, "*Morro Castle* in danger of grounding." At 6:12, there was a loud crack and the *Tampa* shivered. The hawser had broken and the line had wrapped itself around the cutter's propellers. Rose dropped anchor and quickly sent men over the side to cut the line free. At 6:23, the propellers were clear and Rose ordered slow ahead.

The *Tampa* was undamaged but the *Morro Castle* was adrift on its own. In Convention Hall, WCAP radio announcer Tom Burley was reading the news. He had just said, "The *Morro Castle* is adrift and heading for the shore," when he looked out the window and saw the burning liner heading straight for him. Over the air he blurted out, "My God, she's coming in right here!"

Crowds gathered on the beach to see the sorry hulk. Boardwalk shops reopened even as New Jersey's governor asked the curious to stay away. Everyone had to see the shipwreck.

As the rescue ships docked in New York City, throngs of onlookers, family members, and, of course, press and radio reporters crowded in. Early reports raised questions about the lack of fire and lifeboat drills. What killed Captain Wilmont and what started the fire?

Warms was met at the docks by a swarm of lawyers from the Ward Line. It would be a full day before he would talk to anyone. The press had a field day during the hearing and grand jury inquiry that followed. The officers, almost to a man, believed the fire had been deliberately set.

Next came the handling of the fire itself. Why had ninety-four passengers died while only thirty of the crew perished? Why were 75 percent of the people in the lifeboats crew?

The hearing pointed out that Abbot had left the ship in the first lifeboat, and there had been a delay in sending an SOS. The wood paneling was not fire resistant, and no one would ever find out what killed the captain because the body had been incinerated. Had Wilmont committed suicide knowing what was about to happen to his ship?

But the press also found an unlikely hero in George Rogers. He recounted his ordeal in the radio room awaiting orders to send an SOS, keeping his feet off the floor to prevent them from being burned. Rogers said he thought he was going to die but stayed at his radio until his assistant dragged him from his post. Rogers became an instant hero and eventually went on the vaudeville circuit to tell his story.

The burning ship was a boon for an off-season shore town. The story played itself out. Asbury Park eventually was happy about having the wreck and even charged admission for people to look at it from Convention Hall. But as the months passed, the wreck started to emit strange odors. By the spring, few people were upset when two tugs pulled the ship off the beach to be sold for scrap.

Warms, Abbot and the Ward Line were charged with misconduct and found guilty, but the verdict was reversed on appeal and all were exonerated. Abbot would never return to the sea, but Warms was given command of a Ward Line freighter which he ran aground off Mexico within a year.

The Ward Line received $4,186,000 in insurance payments for the *Morro Castle* from which they paid the heirs of those killed an average of $900. No one was accused of setting the fire, and the company was not found to be at fault: The disaster was considered an act of God. The Ward Line turned a profit of $263,000 in the midst of the Depression when few could afford cruises.

In the years since the fire, a strange series of events indicates a possible arsonist. Rogers, the unlikely hero of the disaster, may also have been the cause.

As his fame began to fade, Rogers opened a radio repair shop in Bayonne. Business was not good, and in February 1935 there was a mysterious fire in the shop. Although not enough evidence was found, police suspected arson. Ironically, Rogers was later appointed as a patrolman with the city's police department. He was assigned to assist Vincent J. Doyle in running the radio system.

Rogers wanted Doyle's job and disliked him for openly doubting his story of the *Morro Castle* fire. Doyle started to investigate Rogers' background and discovered that Rogers had been born with a pituitary disorder which made his body balloon to an enormous size by age thirteen. He grew rebellious and was arrested for stealing and placed in a state school. He had been kicked out of the Navy. Once this was discovered aboard the *Morro Castle*, Rogers had been told he would be fired as soon as the ship reached New York.

Doyle learned for himself about Rogers' "hobby" of making explosive devices. Rogers bragged to Doyle how he had started the fire aboard the ship by putting an explosive pen in a jacket in the writing room.

Soon after, Rogers told Doyle a package was waiting for him at the police station. When Doyle opened the package, he found an unsigned, typed note explaining that the box contained a fish tank heater that needed repairs. As Doyle moved to test the heater, Rogers left the room saying, "I am going to mail a letter."

As Doyle plugged in the heater, there was a tremendous explosion which crippled his leg, blew off three fingers and ruptured an eardrum. An investigation showed that the note was typed on Rogers' police typewriter and that parts of the bomb matched items in his garage.

Rogers was sentenced for twelve to twenty years for the attack but was released after less than four to join the service during World War II. After a short time at sea, he was discharged and got a job at a defense plant where he was questioned after someone poisoned a water cooler in the factory. In 1954, Rogers was found guilty of the bludgeoning murder of an elderly couple to whom he owed money. In 1958 he died in Trenton State Prison where he had also been accused of setting several fires.

Can it ever be proven Rogers started the fire that roared to life on the *Morro Castle*? Probably not. But on a lighter note, the ship has affected each and every one of our lives in a strange way. As thousands poured into Asbury Park to see the wreck, Police Chief Alfred N. Giles faced a traffic nightmare. Then he came up with an idea: Use the whole street for one-way traffic. With some paint and posterboard, the *Morro Castle's* legacy remains as the one-way street.

CHAPTER 9

Martians Invade New Jersey

The year was 1938, and the United States was on the edge of despair. In early fall, the world had been brought to the brink of war over Hitler's demands for part of Czechoslovakia.

In the Pacific, the war was real as Japan invaded China. At home, Americans watched helplessly as the nation slid into another depression, and all the hope generated by Franklin Roosevelt's early economic success turned into dread. Meanwhile, in a New York office, Howard Koch was in charge of modifying an existing plan of attack, used forty years before against England, to bring New Jersey to its knees. Koch had spent long hours working on the plan. He had even left his office and driven unnoticed into the Jersey countryside looking for a likely site for an initial airborne attack.

On that visit he picked up a road map. Later, after his role in the plot had been exposed, Koch told of choosing the landing site.

"I just closed my eyes ... jabbed the point of my pencil straight down onto the map, then looked at the name of the place it had hit. Grovers Mill. A crossroads near Princeton, New Jersey. It had a good sound...."

Over the next few days, John Houseman and Orson Welles, two little-known radio actors, helped work out the final strategy and tactics to be used. The time set for the surprise invasion was shortly after eight o'clock on Sunday evening, October 30.

New Jersey residents had no warning that they were in danger. As the sun set, many turned to the radio for some escape from world crises and a worsening economy. At eight, most tuned in Edgar Bergen's "Chase & Sanborn Hour" to hear the comedy of the wisecracking Charlie McCarthy. Only a few tuned in the Columbia Broadcasting System to hear the Mercury Theater presentation of a forty-year-old novel by English author H. G. Wells.

The first inkling that this was not a typical Sunday night came when a CBS announcer interrupted regular programming with a government weather bureau report stating that unusual activity on the planet Mars had been observed. Few listeners paid close attention as CBS quickly returned to "Ramon Raquello and his orchestra in the Meridian Room at the Hotel Park Plaza in downtown New York City."

After two minutes of "Stardust," another bulletin from Intercontinental Radio News was read: "Professor Farrel of the Mount Jennings Observatory near Chicago had reported observing several explosions of incandescent gas occurring at regular intervals on the planet Mars.... The spectroscope indicates the gas to be hydrogen and moving towards the earth with tremendous velocity."

A few minutes later, the music was interrupted again, this time closer to home with a CBS remote pickup of reporter Carl Phillips interviewing astronomer Richard Pierson at Princeton University. In the middle of the interview, Phillips announced, "The Natural History Museum in New York had registered a shock of almost earthquake intensity occurring within a radius of twenty miles of Princeton. Pierson played down any possible connection with the disturbances on Mars: 'This is probably a meteorite of unusual size and its arrival at this particular time is merely a coincidence.' "

Seconds later came another bulletin. "Now nearer home comes a special announcement from Trenton, New Jersey. It is reported that at 8:50 P.M. a huge, flaming object, believed to be a meteorite, fell on a farm in the neighborhood of Grovers Mill, New Jersey, twenty-two miles from Trenton. The flash in the sky was visible within a radius of several hundred miles, and the noise of impact was heard as far north as Elizabeth."

At this point the vast majority of New Jerseyans and the nation knew nothing of what was going on in Grovers Mill, but just then Charlie McCarthy introduced a mediocre female singer, and hundreds of thousands of listeners fiddled with their radio dials in search of better entertainment. Many tuned in to CBS just as Phillips and Pierson arrived at Grovers Mill from Princeton in world-record time.

"I wish I could convey the atmosphere ... the background of this ... fantastic scene," reported Phillips. "Hundreds of cars are parked in a field back of us.... Their headlights throw an enormous spot on the pit where the object is half buried. Some of the more daring souls are venturing near the edge. Their silhouettes stand out against the metal sheen."

Professor Pierson described the object as "definitely extraterrestrial ... not found on this earth.... This thing is smooth and, as you can see, of cylindrical shape."

Phillips interrupted him. "Just a minute! Something's happening! Ladies and gentlemen, this is terrific! This end of the thing is beginning to flake off! The top is beginning to rotate like a screw! The thing must be hollow! Ladies and gentlemen, this is the most terrifying thing I have ever witnessed.... Wait a minute! Someone's crawling out of the hollow top. Someone or ... something. I can see peering out of that black hole two luminous disks — are they eyes? Good heavens, something's wriggling out of the shadow like a grey snake ... I can see the thing's body. It's large as a bear and it glistens like wet leather. But that face. It ... it's indescribable. I can hardly force myself to keep looking at it. The eyes are black and gleam like a serpent. The mouth is V-shaped with saliva dripping from its rimless lips that seem to quiver and pulsate...."

Listeners were told that the New Jersey State Police quickly held back the crowds while three troopers advanced with a white flag.

"Wait a minute," Phillips said. "Something's happening.... A humped shape is rising out of the pit. I can make out a small beam of light against a mirror.... What's that? There's a jet of flame springing from the mirror, and it leaps right at the advancing men! It strikes them head on! Good Lord, they're turning into flame! Now the whole field by the woods has caught fire! The gas tanks, the tanks of automobiles ... it's spreading everywhere! It's coming this way now! About twenty yards to my right." There was a moment of dead air as Phillips was cut off.

CBS returned to more music, but within a minute a report from a Trenton hospital told that at least forty people were dead, "their bodies burned and distorted beyond all possible recognition. And in a Trenton hospital, the charred body of Carl Phillips had been identified."

As the New Jersey State Militia rushed from the Grovers Mill site to defend its beloved homeland, people across the country began to panic.

"In Newark, people wrapped their faces in wet towels and took to the streets in flight. A hospital there treated more than twenty people for shock. At a college campus in North Carolina, students fought over the few available telephones. The editor of the *Memphis Press-Scimitar* called his staff back to work for an extra edition on the bombing of Chicago. A woman in Pittsburgh attempting to swallow poison was saved by her husband. A power shortage in a small Midwestern town at the height of the show sent people screaming into the streets. In Boston, families gathered on rooftops and ... could see the glow of red against the night sky as New York burned."

Back at the front, the militia struck. According to CBS, "Those strange beings who landed in the Jersey farmlands tonight are the vanguard of an invading army from the planet Mars. The battle which took place tonight at Grovers Mill has ended on one of the most startling defeats ever suffered by an army in modern times; seven thousand men armed with rifles and machine guns pitted against a single fighting machine of the invaders from Mars. One hundred and twenty known survivors. The rest strewn over the battle area from Grovers Mill to Plainsboro crushed and trampled to death under the metal feet of the monster, or burned to cinders by its heat ray...."

Valiantly, New Jerseyans fought back without success. "The monster is now in control of the middle section of New Jersey.... Communication lines are down from Pennsylvania to the Atlantic Ocean. Railroad tracks are torn and service from New York to Philadelphia discontinued.... Highways to the north, south, and west are clogged with frantic human traffic. Police and army reserves are unable to control the mad flight."

By 8:40, *The New York Times* had received almost nine hundred phone calls, and the Associated Press had put out a special bulletin explaining the invasion. During its regular station break, CBS reassured the world that New Jersey was safe and that this broadcast was only H. G. Wells' play "War of the Worlds." Police hurried to CBS headquarters to protect Welles and Houseman from any angry counterattack.

Finally at 8:59, Welles came on the air and said the show was his way of dressing up and saying Boo!

"So goodbye, everybody, and remember ... the terrible lesson you learned tonight ... and if your doorbell rings and nobody's there, that was no Martian ... it's Hallowe'en."

CHAPTER 10

Goose-Stepping in Andover

Many times people gloss over history's low points in the mistaken belief that "it can't happen here!" However, if there is a lesson to history it is to always study the good with the bad.

One of these low points in New Jersey history took place in the little north Jersey town of Andover. The time was the early 1930s when the Great Depression was at its worst. Millions were out of work, and the industrialized sections of the country, such as those in north Jersey, were hard hit.

People were desperate and looked for someone to blame. Radio evangelist Father Charles Coughlin had a listening audience of millions as he blamed the Depression on the "international Jewish money lenders."

Immigrant groups were especially affected by the Depression, and some organized to help themselves. One group that felt particularly threatened in the post-World War I atmosphere was the Germans.

German immigrants formed a group called Friends of New Germany to bring aid and comfort to its members. But outside events were to shape the Friends into something much more.

In Germany, where there had been economic chaos since 1919, a new party had taken control, the Nationalist Socialist German Workers' Party, better known as the Nazis. The leader of the party was a charismatic speaker, Adolph Hitler. His theme was simple and repeated a thousand different ways: The German race was destined to rule. The party line blamed the defeat in World War I and the Depression that followed on the Communists and the Jews. Hitler promised to make Germany great again.

During the early thirties the world watched in amazement as Hitler brought Germany out of the Depression and put her on the road to recovery. Meanwhile, the German-American self-help group had been taken over by Nazi sympathizers, and in 1936, the Friends changed its name to the German American Bund (League).

The Bund chose as its new leader a thirty-nine-year-old, German-born, unemployed Detroit auto worker, Fritz Kuhn. Speaking in English with a heavy German accent, Kuhn inspired admiration and trust in his followers. He at once began to revamp the Bund. First he changed his title as leader of the group from president to bundesfuehrer.

Next, he introduced jackboots and swastikas to Bund meetings and uniforms. He reorganized the group from the national level all the way down to the local neighborhood. That same year the organization purchased a two hundred-fifty-acre site at Andover in Sussex County. Here the youth of the new order would go to camp.

"Activities in the youth camps were highly regimented, and much time was devoted to the study of *Mein Kampf* and National Socialism in general. A typical day at Camp Norland began with reveille at 6 A.M., followed by swimming and exercising. After breakfast the boys practiced marching while the girls attended lectures on National Socialism. Afternoon activities included public speaking, music, gymnastics and a variety of sports."

As part of the reorganization, Kuhn initiated a new arm of the Bund which was officially called "Ordnungs-Dierst," or OD. This paramilitary group wore uniforms and was open to "male members 18 years of age or older with proof of Aryan origin." They carried no weapons but looked remarkably like Germany's infamous storm troopers. The OD became the most visible arm of the Bund, marching in parades in uniforms and acting as ushers at meetings.

The raised right arm salute of the Nazis was also adopted by the Bund with some interesting twists. It was required when the "The Star-Spangled Banner" or "America the Beautiful" was played. When it was used as a greeting, instead of saying "Heil Hitler," the Bund proclaimed "Free America."

In June 1936, Kuhn made a trip to Germany where he had a very brief visit with Hitler, a meeting Kuhn portrayed as support from the fuehrer. By 1937 as many as ten thousand supporters at a time crowded Camp Norland, as Andover was now called, to hear Hitler praised and the Depression blamed on "Communists, Jews and Roman Catholics." The followers goose-stepped in review and each time FDR's name was mentioned, jeers and catcalls could be heard.

By February 1939, as the world was on the brink of World War II, the Bund was at its peak. Madison Square Garden was rented for a Washington's Birthday Rally. American flags and swastikas flanked a giant portrait of the general and uniformed OD members ringed the stage to hear Kuhn.

"My fellow countrymen! We German-Americans are unequivocally committed to the defense of the flag, Constitution, and sovereignty of our United States. We stand before you, loyal and law-abiding ... resolved to restore America to the true Americans ... Free America!"

As Kuhn went on to attack blacks, Jews and Catholics as the poison in a white America, a young Jewish man, Isadore Greenbaum, broke out onto the stage and rushed Kuhn. He was jumped by the OD, knocked down and badly beaten. For many who later saw newsreels of the incident, the beating exposed the true purpose of the Bund.

The Bund had grown in numbers, and the U.S. government was becoming uneasy. It was to investigate the Bund that the House Un-American Activities Committee was formed, and Kuhn's treatment by the committee when he was called to testify was so prejudiced that he looked more like the victim of a dictator rather than the supporter of one. Kuhn called the committee the "Un-American Committee for the Persecution of German-Blooded Americans."

When the committee was unable to discredit the Bund, Kuhn's personal financial dealings were scrutinized by the city of New York. Some mismanagement of Bund funds was discovered, and in May 1939, he was indicted. After a quick trial and sentencing, Kuhn entered prison in December 1939. He would remain in prison until 1943. When paroled, he was held as an enemy alien until 1945, then deported to Germany and finally held as a war criminal.

The Bund never recovered from the arrest of Kuhn. It became less vocal and in 1942 ceased to be a public organization. It is ironic that after World War II broke out, approximately 120,000 Japanese-Americans were interned as security threats to the United States, while Americans of German descent remained unaffected, even though the sounds of jack-booted, goose-stepping Bund members still echoed through the quiet hillsides of New Jersey.

CHAPTER 11

U-boat Terror at the Jersey Shore

W hen Jersey beaches are crowded with tanned vacationers and colorful umbrellas, it is hard to envision them covered with death and destruction. There was a time, however, when the United States and the Jersey shore were under enemy attack, a time when the waters off our beaches were a battleground in a world struggle. The Revolution? The War of 1812? No, not so long ago. It was the spring of 1942.

Prior to the attack on Pearl Harbor, Adolph Hitler avoided war with the United States and had kept his U-boat force away from the East Coast. But four days after the Japanese attack on December 7, 1941, Germany declared war on the United States, and the eastern seaboard became an open hunting ground for the U-boats.

Fortunately for the United States, as the country staggered from the shock and humiliation of the defeats in the Pacific, it took several weeks for the six German U-boats dispatched by Hitler to arrive off the coast.

This gave the U.S. Navy a short grace period to prepare. Immediately, mine fields were laid and antisubmarine nets and booms placed outside of harbors like New York. The area from the coast of Maine to Florida was designated the Eastern Sea Frontier and placed under the command of Adm. Adolphus Andrews, who made his headquarters in New York City.

Andrews would be responsible for protecting the hundreds of ships which daily plied the coastal waters. To accomplish this, he basically had a meager fleet of outdated Coast Guard boats and only two destroyers.

As the weeks of December passed into January, all eyes were on the Pacific and a growing list of defeats. Sentiment on the West Coast was growing against Japanese-Americans with each setback. What would happen if the war came to the East Coast?

The first sinking took place off Cape Cod on January 12, and slowly newspapers began to take notice. There were few attacks at first, but starting on February 27, New Jerseyans discovered that they were at war and death could be swift.

Just northeast of Barnegat Light the Esso tanker *R.P. Resor* was making for New York Harbor and safety when at about 9 P.M. she was struck by a torpedo and exploded as her cargo of oil ignited. One of only two survivors related the story of seeing a ship loom out of the blackness two points off the starboard bow as he stood watch.

"All of a sudden," the survivor recalled, "he flashed on his running lights and I thought he was a fisherman.... I gave the engine room two bells to slow up when the torpedo hit us on the port side right about amidships.

"I was thrown to the deck and then got a raft and threw it overboard. I jumped in after it and found 'Sparks' — the radio operator — on the raft."

Out from Barnegat and Manasquan came the Coast Guard and private craft to the rescue. The first boat on the scene was piloted by John D. Daisey of Point Pleasant. As he approached the hulk, "The oil on the sea was so thick it looked like tar.... It was so greasy and so thick that we barely had steerage way. Every time we got a chance we pushed closer to the ship because we figured there might be somebody near her."

As they approached a survivor, "We tried to get him into the boat but he was so heavy we couldn't get him over the side.... So then we put a line around his feet and another under his arms and pulled again. He must have weighed nearly 600 pounds with all that oil on him. In the end we had to just cut the clothes off him while he was in the water. Then we rolled him aboard like he was a sack of wheat."

An *Asbury Park Press* photographer described the scene the next day.

"Two more oil-caked bodies drifted by. The oil slicks on the water became more frequent and larger. Other things floated by — two empty life rafts, bits of wreckage, a metal box which somehow floated high on the water....

"Up until now the ship itself was not discernible. But now we could see red tongues of flame licking the front of the tanker.

"The close-up view was a sickening and awful sight — a phantasmagoria of bright red spurts of fire eating the long black hulk. I felt as though I was watching a newsreel. The stern was up with the propellers showing and amidships, where the torpedo struck, was close to water level. The dense screen of black smoke prevented us from seeing where she had been hit on the port side. Besides, we couldn't go nearer on that side because the water was afire with blazing oil."

As soon as the attack on the *Resor* was reported, Andrews ordered the destroyer *Jacob Jones* to investigate and aid in rescuing the survivors. The *Jones* was a World War I leftover, a four-stack ship armed with four-inch guns and depth charges.

The *Jones'* captain was familiar with the waters. Lt. Comdr. H. D. Black of Oradell, a 1926 graduate of the U.S. Naval Academy, circled the burning wreck for two hours without finding any survivors. Giving up hope, Black ordered his ship to head south along Long Beach Island to try to find the sub.

At first light of dawn on February 28, the *U-578* saw the *Jacob Jones* steaming south off Atlantic City. The U-boat fired one torpedo.

The Navy reported, "All but 11 officers and men, including LCDR Black, were killed. The survivors, including a badly wounded signal officer, went for the lifeboats. Oily decks, fouled lines and rigging, and the clutter of the ship's strewn, twisted wreckage hampered their efforts to launch the boats.

"The *Jacob Jones* remained afloat for about 45 minutes, allowing her survivors to clear the stricken ship in four or five rafts. Within an hour of the initial explosion, the *Jones* plunged bow-first into the cold Atlantic. As her shattered stern disappeared, her depth charges exploded, killing several survivors on a nearby raft.

"The first torpedo blew up the bow and apparently killed all the personnel on the bridge, as well as the men sleeping in the forward living compartments. The second torpedo, which was fired after the submarine circled ahead of the *Jacob Jones*, blew up the stern and all the depth charges. The only survivors, except one man from the after engine room, were in the amidship section when the stern was blown up."

More than one hundred thirty sailors had gone down with the *Jacob Jones*. Another thirty-eight had perished on the *Resor*.

By early March, on the West Coast, hysteria and racial prejudice prompted Franklin D. Roosevelt to order all Japanese and Americans of Japanese descent rounded up and placed in concentration camps.

In New Jersey meanwhile, the FBI started making raids in Monmouth, then in Ocean and Atlantic counties. On March 3, nineteen enemy aliens were arrested in Monmouth. The FBI uncovered "nine pairs of binoculars, three bayonets, one sword, one dagger, five revolvers, five still cameras, two motion picture cameras, several 16mm projectors, several swastika jewels, three shortwave radio receivers and sending sets, several maps of the coastal area." A few days later, seventeen aliens were arrested in Ocean and Atlantic counties.

Spying from shore was simple since one of the few protective measures authorized by Admiral Andrews was to have coastal shipping stay as close to the beach as possible. Just how close can be indicated by the reopening of Barnegat Lighthouse, not as a navigation aid, but as a lookout tower for enemy submarines.

Late on the night of March 8, a Gulf Oil Company tanker was within sight of the beach at Ship Bottom. Seas were running high as the *Gulftrade* battled a typical March northeaster. The tanker had been built in 1920 and operated out of Philadelphia; on this trip from Port Arthur, Texas, she was loaded with oil.

The crew breathed a little easier since New York and safety were only a few hours away. Fifty-six-year-old Capt. Torger Olsen had the ship blacked out, but as he approached Barnegat Inlet at eleven o'clock there was a report of a Coast Guard cutter and several larger ships ahead. Olsen ordered his navigation lights turned on.

According to Olsen, "A little while later the third mate came down to my cabin for further orders. I told him to leave the lights on. I saw we were up to Barnegat and I thought they shouldn't be able to get us now anymore. I made a mistake."

At 12:40 A.M. Olsen was in his cabin studying charts of the mine fields at New York Harbor. The *Gulftrade* was making ten knots when suddenly the ship shook from stem to stern. Olsen ran to the bridge, looked out and saw flames shooting up to the top of the mast. A storm wave swept over the *Gulftrade* and put out the fire. The captain found that the ship had been broken in two by the blast of a torpedo, and that he was on the stern section with fifteen others.

On Long Beach Island, windows rattled and the fireball lit the sky. At once, Barnegat, Ship Bottom and Bond's Coast Guard stations launched rescue boats. On board the tanker, Olsen surveyed the situation. His ship was broken in two and his radio had been destroyed along with one of his four lifeboats. He could see Barnegat Lighthouse, but the seas were running like mountains, and there was only one lifeboat on his half of the ship.

Olsen ordered the crew to launch the lifeboat, but Guy Chadwick, the chief engineer, and eight other seamen refused to go, saying that no lifeboat could survive the storm.

Olsen and the six crew members who joined him were picked up in about a half hour by a Coast Guard cutter. But for Chadwick and the others, it was not so easy. They watched as other shipmates on the bow launched a lifeboat and drifted in the darkness. Then to their horror, the sub surfaced. They hid on deck, fearing that they would be machine-gunned.

"One young seaman, Leonard Smith of Port Arthur, became so nervous that he wanted to jump into the water," Chadwick recalled later. Smith was fearful that the stern would sink and carry them down with it.

"I argued with him. I said, 'Let's stick with the ship as long as she'll stick with us.' I reminded him that the water was pretty cold. That worked. He is a game kid, and so were all the other men with me.

"We could see the bow section drifting off, but we knew there were no men on it. Nobody said much at all. We all just sat around on the deck and smoked. When the rescue boat showed, I never saw anything that looked so good in my life. I hollered as much as the kids."

The bow section eventually settled on a sand bar off the island; the next morning islanders could see World War II a stone's throw from the beach. For the next two days Navy blimps and the few warships available searched for the rest of the survivors and the submarine.

One survivor was found, but he was not from the *Gulftrade*. He was the captain from a Chilean cargo ship, the SS *Tolten*, which had been torpedoed only hours after the *Gulftrade* and couldn't even get off an SOS. The captain was the only survivor of a crew of twenty-one.

The attack on the *Gulftrade* finally prompted action. On March 12, the government announced the partial dim-out of shorefront lights. To prevent panic, government officials from FDR on down assured the people the shore area was safe. Such assurances rang hollow with island residents, especially when the *Beach Haven Times* ran a banner headline, "Long Beach Island Safety Assured for Summer." Underneath the headline was a large photo of the bow of the *Gulftrade* just outside the breakers of Barnegat Light.

In the summers during the war, even resorts were expected to dim their lights. According to the *Asbury Park Press*, "Concentration of light in beach front areas casts a brilliant glow skyward against which ships, passing along the coast, are sharply outlined, making them easy prey for the underseas craft. It is this condition that Navy officials seek to correct....

"Under the order, every other light on the boardwalk was extinguished and those remaining were shielded on the ocean side; neon signs were extinguished and hotels notified guests occupying rooms with eastern exposure to keep shades drawn."

Resort areas were not happy. Samuel Elliot Morrison, official naval historian, later wrote, "One of the most reprehensible failures on our part was the neglect of local communities to dim their waterfront lights, or of military to require them to do so, until three months after the submarine offensive started. When this obvious defense measure was first proposed, squawks went all the way from Atlantic City to southern Florida that the 'tourist season would be ruined.' Miami and its luxurious suburbs threw up six miles of neon-light glow, against which was silhouetted southbound shipping that hugged the shore to avoid the Gulf Stream. Ships were sunk and seamen drowned in order that the citizenry might enjoy pleasure as usual."

Still the sinkings went on at the astounding rate of a ship a day, faster than U.S. shipbuilders could turn them out. Things got worse as German agents were landed by submarines on Long Island, New York, and in Florida.

One Sunday in early May, the Civil Defense and the Army and Navy held a massive drill to prepare for a possible enemy attack. The reaction to the drill from the business-as-usual shore community was swift and, in retrospect, hard to believe.

Franklin Holmes, director of the state's Board of Commerce and Navigation, announced that state defense officials were "carrying things too far" with a practice sea invasion along the Monmouth-Ocean county coast on a Sunday, "the seashore's best day for business."

"There's no need for spending thousands of dollars of state money to publicize the shore and offset these rumors when another state body is doing [measures] to drive people away."

Holmes went on to demand no more alerts or blackouts until after Labor Day because this was the height of the tourist season. As the debate raged, world events moved forward.

As everyone knows, the Jersey shore's tourist season opens with Memorial Day which was always observed on May 30. In 1942, the thirtieth fell on a Saturday, so for business, things were looking up. It would be a Memorial Day weekend, and thousands could travel to the shore.

During World War II within sight of New Jersey beaches, the crew of the SS Persephone *are still in their life boats, on May 30, 1942, as a Navy blimp searches for the U-boat that sank the ship.*

Things were quiet on Long Beach Island the Monday before the big weekend. At Barnegat Light, there were a few people on the beach, most of them avoiding the still-chilly water. The war was far away, even though the wreckage of the *Gulftrade* could be seen. Few noticed as the SS *Persephone*, a merchant ship flying the Panamanian flag, came into view at about midafternoon from the direction of Ship Bottom.

The ship was directly off the beach. Fishing boats were in the inlet, and all appeared normal. Less than two miles from the lighthouse, however, a German sub watched the bathers and the ship. At 3 P.M. the sub fired the first torpedo; thirty seconds later came a second.

The attack came without warning. The thud of a torpedo plowing into the ship's starboard side, near the propeller, was the captain's first intimation of the submarine's presence.

According to an account of the attack, the second torpedo crashed into the engine room and set it ablaze.

The report went on, "As the freighter began settling by the stern at a sharp angle, two lifeboats were launched, the first by the second mate and members of the crew from the starboard side; the second forward on the port side, by the captain single-handed 20 minutes later."

The ship's mascot, a puppy, made it to a lifeboat, but one crewman remembered that his life savings were in the pocket of a pair of pants. He rushed belowdecks and reappeared holding the pants, but all the boats were gone. As the ship sank into the shallow, he climbed the smokestack, going higher and higher as the *Persephone* settled. Eventually, he was saved from his lonely perch.

Within minutes of the explosion, tourists watched as Coast Guard cutters and fishing boats rescued twenty-eight of the crew of thirty-five. Next a blimp appeared and bombed the area around the sub. Two Coast Guard cutters carried on the attack until dark. The war was here, and no one questioned the fact again.

The news of the attack, however, was slow to get out. Due to government censorship, the story was not published until Friday, and the ship was not identified by name. Finally, the *Ocean County Courier* carried a government story which was totally false. It read in part:

"The German submarine which sunk the tanker, which was of Panamanian registry, was captured by the Coast Guard and the Navy, survivors said as the U-boat was trapped and forced to surrender.

"According to eyewitnesses, the submersible was caught between the burning tanker and a Coast Guard cutter and a Navy blimp was flying over. Water at that point is about 40 feet deep and the German craft could neither run forward or backward and was unable to dive deeply enough to avoid bombing by the blimp because of the shallow water."

If truth is the first casualty of war, then World War II began for the Jersey shore in May 1942.

CHAPTER 12

Bad Year for the Blimp

The summer of 1960 at the Jersey shore was not much different from those today. Sure, the beaches were free and less crowded, but things seemed secure. The Hurricane of 1944 was a memory, and everyone agreed a storm like that could never happen again. On the beaches, talk centered around the California cool of the Beach Boys, Fidel Castro taking over Cuba and Francis Gary Powers' ill-fated flight over the Soviet Union.

And, of course, there was the missile race. Americans worried about ICBMs because Russia had them while ours still seemed to be on the drawing board. Early warning of a Russian attack became more and more important since an intercontinental ballistic missile would take only fifteen minutes to reach New York City.

As the summer started, beachgoers got a firsthand look at their nation's attempts to improve early warning. Along the coast, giant blimps cruised up and down the beaches, interrupting the tanning of zealous sun-worshippers.

These blimps, stationed at Naval Air Station Lakehurst, were the world's largest. The ZPG class was four hundred three feet long, more than double the length of today's "Goodyear" blimps. The gondola was as long as three buses parked end to end and housed equipment and quarters for a twenty-one-man crew. Atop the airship's bag was a large fin which made the blimp resemble a giant shark.

Inside the bag was the reason for the monster blimp's existence: a forty-foot-high radar dish. In reality, the blimps were flying radar stations. The twin 1,525-horsepower engines gave them a cruising speed of seventy-five miles per hour, and they could stay aloft for days on end.

For every additional mile off the coast the blimps cruised, it meant more warning time in the event of a missile attack, time that the Strategic Air Command needed to get bombers off the ground. That June, the blimps were a familiar sight over Jersey beaches.

Nineteen-sixty was a presidential election year; as the month drew to a close, the nation prepared for the Democratic National Convention in Los Angeles. John F. Kennedy was the frontrunner, but there was strong opposition. The latest announcement was that the New Jersey delegation would nominate Governor Robert Meyner.

Buried in the back of the sports pages and noticed by few on June 27 were reports that the annual Bermuda to Newport, Rhode Island, yacht race had started on schedule.

The Fourth of July came and went, and the drama of Los Angeles grew in peoples' minds. Who would be the Democratic candidate? On the fifth, the Coast Guard announced that two of the yachts in the race were overdue and started a 20,000-square-mile search from Virginia to Massachusetts.

The thirty-five-foot ketch *Carastee* and the forty-foot sloop *Vat 69* were missing. The wife of the skipper of the *Vat 69* calmly told reporters, "It is not unusual for sailing boats to be overdue. There have not been any distress signals in the area, and I have no reason to believe that there is anything wrong."

On the seventh, the weather report for Barnegat Light was clear skies and a light wind. It would be a great day for fishing.

At the docks, Capt. Charles Eble and his mate, Frank Mikuletzky, prepared the party boat *Doris Mae III* for a busy day. Farther north, Edward Gardner boarded the *Miss Belmar* for a pleasant day of fishing off Barnegat Light.

At Lakehurst, Lt. Joseph Saniuk from Omaha, Nebraska, had received new orders to take the *Reliance*, a PG-3W blimp, and join the search for the yachts. If they were located, the blimp was to continue on to a training mission for the craft's radar detection equipment.

The flight was scheduled to last thirteen hours. At about 9 A.M., Saniuk gave the traditional "Up ship" command and the *Reliance* circled Lakehurst before heading in the direction of Barnegat Light.

At the air station the day was a normal one. The wives of the blimp's crewmen paid little attention to the flight. The weather was good, and Saniuk was a good skipper.

Elsie May Saumier, whose husband, Donald, was a crewman, planned to visit Nancy Turner, whose husband, Edward, was also on board.

As the *Reliance* headed east, the blimp assumed its flying routine. Since its mission lasted much longer than an airplane flight, a blimp would have men rotate duties.

A radio message was picked up from the *Carastee*. She was about two hundred miles southeast of New York, running late because of a storm. Now only the *Vat 69* was missing.

At noon, shifts were relieved on the blimp, and off-duty men turned in to get a little rest. Twenty-year-old Joseph G. Culligan of Middletown Township climbed the ladder to the upper deck of the gondola and the crew's quarters. Culligan stretched out on his bunk and, along with about ten other crewmen, went to sleep.

Around two o'clock, a Navy submarine positively identified the *Vat 69* and relayed word to the other air-sea searchers.

At 2:29 P.M., the *Reliance* was cruising three hundred feet over Barnegat Inlet and dozens of local fishing boats.

Eble looked up from the *Doris Mae* and saw the airship. "It looked like a banana with both ends sticking up in the air and sagging in the middle.... It seemed to settle very slowly, and, as it settled, the middle section seemed to split in two, and it fell like a wet dishrag.... Black smoke belched from the aircraft for a few moments, then everything was quiet." Without hesitation, Eble turned his fishing boat in the direction of the stricken blimp and began to broadcast a Mayday.

In the blimp, Donald Saumier was at his radar console. "Suddenly there was a loud crack and in the wall all kinds of jerking ... we started down to the water, jerking and cracking.

"I knew that the bag was torn from the way we were falling. I saw the water coming up on me and I braced my back against some equipment on the compartment wall. We hit. There was a lot of noise. It sounded like the end of the world to me — just a great, big bang. It had been jerking all the way down and groaning and snapping about. I thought the whole thing had disintegrated, but apparently it didn't. We filled up with water as soon as we hit.

"The plexiglass front must have given way. We hit the water nose down and it rushed in. I didn't lose consciousness. All kinds of equipment was floating around the compartment. I was trying all the time to get out, beating my head all around against the equipment.

"I had just about given up. I just decided I was going to drown when suddenly I saw a patch of light. I had somehow gotten out of the compartment. Luckily, the gondola didn't break loose from the bag or we would all have been killed. The bag acted as a sort of parachute. The front and back ends went up because of the gondola weight in the middle. That slowed us down."

Above Saumier in the crew's quarters, Culligan was awakened by a sudden jolt. "I stood up ... water was in the compartment. I picked up a jagged piece of metal, cut a hole in the bag of the blimp and dove into the water.

"We saw a fishing boat about 300 yards away coming toward us."

As the *Doris Mae* closed in, Eble could see survivors. "Two of them climbed up on the collapsed bag and the others remained in the water. They were all bloody.

"We threw life preservers to them, but they were unable to get to them ... they were apparently too badly hurt or shocked to help themselves."

Eble's first mate grabbed a life preserver and jumped into the water. All four crewmen were hauled on board the *Doris Mae*, but Mikuletzky could not get into the gondola.

"It was impossible to go in there.... All the windows were broken and it was all a twisted mass of wire and metal."

Mikuletzky tried to cut holes in the bag to enable anyone trapped underneath to escape. By now other boats had joined the rescue efforts and Charles Price, a passenger from the *Doris Mae*, was also in the water.

The *Miss Belmar* came alongside and hooked a line on the gondola in a vain effort to keep it afloat. The Barnegat Light Coast Guard cutter was on hand and a helicopter from the carrier *Essex* was on the way, but no more survivors would be found.

Of the four men picked up by the *Doris Mae*, Saumier and Culligan, along with Antonio Contreras, suffered minor injuries. The fourth, Edward Turner, whose wife had been visited by Saumier's that day, was transferred to a fishing boat but died on his way to Barnegat Light.

Eighteen of twenty-one men died in almost the exact spot where the giant dirigible *Akron* had crashed in 1933.

There was one more fatality in the *Reliance* tragedy. The Navy grounded the three sister ships during an investigation of the crash and subsequently phased out the lighter-than-air program.

CHAPTER 13

The Texas Tower Disaster

J ersey shore vacationers find it hard to believe that the soothing, refreshing ocean has been the battleground in two world wars which brought life-and-death struggles close to the coast. But what about the Cold War? Did young Americans die to prevent the spread of Communism when there was no all-out war raging? The answer, of course, is yes.

The year was 1957. Dwight D. Eisenhower was in the White House and Nikita Kruschev was in the Kremlin. Russian scientists were preparing to launch Sputnik, and the main offensive weapon of the USSR was the bomber.

America's defense to an attack was interceptor planes and guided missiles. The key to the defense plan was early warning, but since the range of radar in the presatellite world was limited, a line of radar bases was set up. The distant early warning or "DEW" line stretched from the Arctic to the coast of New Jersey. To gain another few minutes' warning, some radar stations were placed off the East Coast on platforms similar to oil drilling rigs in the Gulf of Mexico. Thus their nickname, Texas Towers.

Four towers were to be located from Cape Cod south to site No. 4, seventy-five miles due east of Barnegat Light. One was never completed, but the other three became sentinels listening for the sounds of Soviet bombers.

Tower No. 4 was different. The other two towers rested on solid bedrock while No. 4 sat on clay and soft sand. Also, the water in which No. 4 stood was almost twice as deep, but government engineers did not seem to be concerned. The tower was designed to stand on three giant legs, each twelve feet in diameter and the length of a football field. Once the legs were in place, a triangular platform, 185 feet long on each side, would be fastened on top.

During the early summer, the parts were towed from Portland, Maine. Once the material was off New Jersey, fate played tricks on the project. High winds and seas delayed the righting of the legs, forcing the construction fleet to ride it out. Finally on July 9, the first two legs were towed out, then the third, and sunk about fifty feet into the sand. Finally, the platform was hoisted sixty feet into the air and placed on the legs. Construction began at once on the covering of three large radar antennas which gave the tower the distinctive look of three golf balls on a table.

The tower, in effect, was a self-contained outpost. Seventy airmen were assigned to the platform which had a gym, a dining hall and recreation facilities, even television.

In the enlisted men's quarters, there were four bunks to a room. Because of the type of equipment it held, the tower was air-conditioned. In the summer, off-duty airmen sunned themselves on the helicopter pad. Three desalinization units provided twenty-five hundred gallons of fresh water a day. Equipment was repaired on board. Woodworking and ceramic shops improved morale, and from the deck, cod fishing was good. Two cranes could reach over the side and down into the holds of cargo ships.

Life on No. 4 was good. A tour of duty was fifteen months divided into sixty-day blocks, forty-five days on the tower and fifteen days off. Few Long Beach Island residents were reminded of the tower's existence. Occasionally on marine radio islanders heard the fishing was good off the tower, but for the most part, they never gave it a thought.

But on the tower there were problems. The soft bottom was causing settling, and high winds produced vibrations which proved unnerving. Within a few months, the tower was nicknamed "Old Shakey." In 1958 the crew had its first big scare when Hurricane Daisy hit the tower full force. Waves beat against it, throwing spray above the flight deck. In all, there was $500,000 in damage to the structure.

To compensate for the rocking, the Air Force had giant crossbraces attached to the three legs. On September 12, 1960, Hurricane Donna hit the tower. Designed to withstand forty-foot waves, Old Shakey was battered by sixty-foot monsters. After the hurricane passed, engineers discovered underwater damage to the braces. In November as John F. Kennedy was being elected president, the Air Force decided to cut back the tower's work force to a skeleton crew for safety.

Engineers believed that concrete in the legs would improve the tower's stability, so over the winter fourteen construction workers were brought on board to make repairs while fourteen airmen manned the radar screens.

As the gales of winter began, the tower's commander, Capt. Gordon Phelan, battled with the Air Force, repeatedly telling the brass that the tower was unsafe. One of the construction workers wrote, "Every time there was a strange noise or a screeching of metal, the Air Force men would rush over and say, 'What's that? What's that?' And then they would kneel and pray and shake and shiver."

Part of the Cold War-era defense shield known as the "DEW" (distant early warning) line, the Texas Tower stood precariously on soft sand and clay 185 feet above the ocean floor 75 miles east of Barnegat Light for only three years.

Staff Sgt. Elmer Green of Elmira, New York, wrote home saying, "I hope it [the tower] lasts long enough to get home and see you and the kids again."

Finally, the Air Force gave in. The tower would be abandoned for the winter, but not until February. On January 15, however, a northeaster began to build. On shore the only concern was whether the storm would interfere with the inaugural parade and ceremonies for JFK and his lovely wife.

Off Barnegat Light, Phelan called his wife twice during the afternoon to tell her he was all right.

At 7:25 P.M., however, Phelan sent out an SOS as eighty-five-mile-an-hour winds drove thirty-foot waves into the tower. He was told to ride out the night; a helicopter would be sent at dawn. Meanwhile, ships, including the aircraft carrier USS *Wasp*, began to converge on the tower.

Seamen on the ships could see the tower on radar, but in the driving snow, visibility was down to five hundred feet. At 7:35, a Navy radar tender twelve miles away from No. 4 saw the tower on its radar screen. Soon afterward, both radar and radio contact were lost.

From New London, Connecticut, the USS *Sunbird*, an undersea rescue ship, was dispatched in the hope men might be trapped in air pockets in the collapsed tower. As the flotilla searched, UPI reported that "the only trace ... of the 28 men aboard was a clutter of debris nine miles downwind and one floating body."

Destroyers searched the ocean bottom with sonar. Their hopes soared when, according to an AP report, "Fourteen hours after the tragedy, crewmen aboard the destroyer *McCaffery* heard tapping signals coming from the wreckage. The sailors hammered on the destroyer's hull in reply.

"The responses received were man-made and had intelligent characteristics.... It's possible that some men could have gathered in an airtight pocket."

It was midmorning on the seventeenth before divers from the *Sunbird* could descend to attempt a rescue. Once they found the huge wreck in the murky waters, the divers tapped the wreckage, searching for signs of life. Nothing answered them.

The *Sunbird* remained on station to recover bodies and gather information. The ship's captain, Allan Crabtree, reported on the triangular-shaped tower's condition. Two legs had broken off at the top and one at the base. The platform was resting at an angle. "All external hatches and doors ... blown away. Most windows blown out. Minimum depth over main structure is 65 feet, one radio mast intact and straight, top 25 feet below surface.... No lifeboats sighted. All handrails missing and inflatable life raft rack distorted."

Three-man dive teams explored the living spaces. One diver stayed outside to guide electric lines while "the other two men swam to their designated search area, through doors and passageways, down stairwells and corridors through the eerie gloom of the structure, expecting at any moment to be confronted by dead men. They pulled over mattresses, chairs, tables, and other debris as much as possible to make sure they were not missing anything."

Finally, a dive team cut its way into Phelan's cabin. He had been hastily packing for the rescue that never came. A diver brought back his suitcase.

"Among other things, the suitcase was found to contain a small clock which was stopped at 7:28. Since it was also found to be wound and presumably running up until the instant that the tower collapsed, the exact time of the disaster was pinpointed for us."

After spending one month over the tower, the *Sunbird* left, having found only one body of the twenty-eight men who had been on board. Twenty-five were never found; neither were the two lifeboats. On March 15, the men were officially declared dead. Had they abandoned ship in the lifeboats or had the tower collapsed while they were on deck? The mystery still remains. Today it is sport divers who explore the wreck and one thing is sure: Texas Tower No. 4 is an unofficial monument to the Cold War and to the twenty-eight men who died there to give the United States ninety seconds of extra warning in an attack that never came.

BIBLIOGRAPHY

BOOKS:

Bailey, Thomas. *American Spirit.* 2 vols. Boston: D. C. Heath, 1963.

Carrington, Henry B. *Battles of the American Revolution.* New York: Promontory Press, 1877.

Clarke, James W. *American Assassins.* Princeton: Princeton University Press, 1982.

Commager, Henry Steele, ed. *The Spirit of '76.* New York: Bonanza Book, 1983.

Cunningham, John T. *New Jersey: A Mirror on America.* Andover, N.J.: Afton Publishers, 1988.

Dann, John C., ed. *The Reverend Remembered.* Chicago: University of Chicago Press, 1980.

Farrand, Max, ed. *Records of the Federal Convention.* 4 vols. New Haven: Yale University Press, 1957.

Fleming, Thomas, ed. *Founding Fathers.* 12 vols. New York: Newsweek, 1975.

Gerlach, Larry R., ed. *New Jersey in the American Revolution.* Trenton: New Jersey Historical Commission, 1975.

Hawke, David. *Paine.* New York: Harper & Rowe, 1974.

Hood, Joseph. *When Monsters Roamed the Skies.* New York: Grosset & Dunlap Publishers, 1968.

Horgan, Thomas. *Old Ironsides.* Dublin, N.H.: Yankee Publishing Inc., 1963.

Hunt, John, ed. *The Dissenters.* New York: Library of Freedom/ Grammacy Books Press, 1993.

Hutchinson, William T., ed. *Papers of James Madison.* Chicago: University of Chicago Press, 1971.

Juet, Robert. *Juet's Journal.* Newark: New Jersey Historical Society, 1959.

Kavenagh, W. Keith, ed. *Foundations of Colonial America: A Documentary History.* 8 vols. New York: Chelsea House, 1983.

Malone, Dumas. *Jefferson.* 6 vols. New York: Little, Brown and Co., 1951.

Martin, Joseph. *Private Yankee Doodle.* Boston: Acorn Press, 1979.

Mayo, Katherine. *General Washington's Dilemma.* Chapel Hill: Harcourt, Brace and Co., 1938.

Moulton, Phillips, ed. *Journal of John Woolman.* Richmond, Ind.: Friends United Press, 1989.

O'Connor, John F. *William Paterson.* New Brunswick: Rutgers University Press, 1979.

Pancake, John S. *1777: Year of the Hangman.* Tuscaloosa: University of Alabama Press, 1977.

Pyne, Henry R. *Ride to War.* New Brunswick: Rutgers University Press, 1961.

Rakove, Jack. *Beginning of National Politics.* New York: Alfred A. Knopf, 1979.

Salter, Edwin. *A History of Monmouth and Ocean Counties.* Bayonne: E. Gardner & Son, 1890.

Schachner, Nathan. *Alexander Hamilton.* New York: A. S. Barnes, 1961.

Siegal, Alan A. *For the Glory of the Union.* Madison, N.J.: Fairleigh Dickinson University Press, 1984.

Sinclair, Upton. *The Jungle.* New York: Doubleday, 1906.

Skemp, Sheila. *William Franklin.* New York: Oxford University Press, 1990.

Witcover, Jules. *Sabotage at Black Tom.* Chapel Hill: Algonquin Books, 1989.

MAGAZINES and PERIODICALS:

American Heritage
American Historical Review
American History Illustrated
New Jersey History
Prologue: Journal of the National Archives
William and Mary Quarterly

NEWSPAPERS — 1750 to 1960

Asbury Park Press
Beach Haven Times
Gazette of the United States
National Gazette
Newark Daily Journal
New Brunswick Fredonian
New Jersey Gazette
New York Times
New York Tribune
Ocean County Emblem
Ocean County Journal
Pennsylvania Gazette
Philadelphia Bulletin
Richmond Dispatch
Tuckerton Beacon

LIBRARIES:

Colonial Williamsburg Foundation
James Madison Collections
Library of Congress
Maryland Historical Society
Monmouth County Historical Association
Mystic Seaport Library
National Archives
National Park Library at Morristown
Newark Public Library
New Jersey Historical Society
Ocean County Historical Society
Ocean County Library
Philadelphia Free Library
Princeton University Library
Smithsonian Institution Air and Space Museum
Trenton State Library
University of Virginia

A lifelong New Jersey resident, Tom Farner was born in Mount Holly, moving to Long Beach Island in 1958. He received a bachelor's degree in history from then-Mansfield State College in Pennsylvania. He served in the U.S. Naval Reserves and began teaching at Pemberton Township High School in 1970. He has been recognized twice in *Who's Who Among American Teachers*.

His newspaper column, *200 Plus*, was first published in 1974 as part of the celebration of the bicentennial of the American Revolution. The articles focused on major historical events with a unique perspective on New Jersey's participants. This focus has continued through the years in his current writing.

Mr. Farner's work on constitutional issues has won recognition for him as a national judge in competitions sponsored by the Congress on the Constitution and the Bill of Rights. He has been an invited speaker at a Smithsonian Institution forum on the implications of a Supreme Court decision involving the internment of Japanese-Americans during World War II.

Mr. Farner lives in Manahawkin with his wife, Carol, and their very large Newfoundland, appropriately named Theodore Roosevelt Bear.

Down The Shore Publishing offers
many other book and calendar titles
(with a special emphasis on
New Jersey shore history).
For a free catalog, or
to be added to the mailing list,
just send us a request:
Down The Shore Publishing
Box 3100, Harvey Cedars, NJ 08008.